Insomnia

Insomnia

A Cultural History

Eluned Summers-Bremner

REAKTION BOOKS

Published by Reaktion Books Ltd
33 Great Sutton Street
London EC1V 0DX

www.reaktionbooks.co.uk

First published 2008
Printed and bound in Great Britain by Biddles Ltd, King's Lynn

British Library Cataloguing in Publication Data
Summers-Bremner, Eluned
   Insomnia : a cultural history
   1. Insomnia   2. Insomnia - Social aspects   3. Wakefulness in literature
   4. Sleep - Folklore
   I. Title
   306.4′61

ISBN: 978 1 86189 317 8

Contents

Introduction

What is insomnia? Medical practitioners describe it as the habitual inability to fall asleep or remain asleep when one wishes or needs to do so. As such, it would seem to be an individual complaint. And yet, sleep specialists also maintain that the contemporary world continually reproduces the conditions for insomnia. Many of us work longer hours than our parents did, leaving less time to switch off into leisure mode, and globalization has made our jobs increasingly re-configurable, giving rise to worry as well as to the presence of work in the home space. We are accustomed to communicating all the time, by technological means when others are unavailable, and have largely abandoned the resource of the free and available-for-musing moment in which sleep is likely to catch us. Bright lights make night into daytime, and 24-hour licensing laws make night a potentially endless, noisy party. It seems that the contemporary Western world's tendency to erase all borders from which it cannot profit – indeed, it has profited from erasing and redrawing several of those – meets its match on the border between sleep and waking. We long for the restorative oblivion that sustains continuous work and enjoyment, and are at a loss when oblivion does not come.

Our understanding of sleep may be partly to blame for our world's generation of an environment unfavourable to it, however. We tend to assume that night and sleep go together because of what they lack – light and activity – and that it is their natural task to subsidize the labours of the day. It was not always thus. In recent decades, scientists have reached greater understanding of the way in which our circadian (biological) clocks evolved gradually to enable us to adapt to changing physical and social environments. These clocks are the equivalent of hunger pains that tell us when to eat. They would have been particularly important in the ancient world when sleep was by no means an event to which individuals felt they were entitled, or, like hunting for food, one that was always easily achieved. To begin to grasp the history of insomnia, we moderns need to think of sleep in terms similar to those in which we think of going forth in battle and finding or subduing a food source. For our ancestors, sleep was, like these activities, something to be striven for, a quiet state that needed to be gained.

While we, like our ancestors, do battle in and with the dark hours, we also relentlessly calculate and recalculate their value, often cutting sleep time in favour of other obligations. And we tend to be surprised when sleep researchers reveal the variety and extent of the lives we are unknowingly living while we sleep. Our ancestors would not have been surprised by this. To them, sleep was an active part of life whose only distinction from waking activity was that it usually took place in darkness. The gods might visit a sleeper with prophetic dreams, or an enemy take advantage of a hasty slumber, but for early humans the rewards of oblivion were in active relation to everything else worth living for. We are far more likely to see sleep as the necessary evil required for a productive and happy life.

The chief difference between ourselves and our forebears with regard to insomnia is the devaluation of sleep that modernity has brought us. When sleep is described in the language of awakeness (as in the psychiatrist William Dement's well-intended catchphrase 'The brain never sleeps!', intended to indicate that sleep is highly active[1]), its darkest qualities – its enigma, dreamscapes and mortal connotations – become invisible, hidden by the light. Consequently, for us, although we do not always know it, insomnia means much more than loss of sleep. But what it means is hard to access, because, as well as undervaluing absence – and what is insomnia but the absence of the oblivion one longs for? – we have difficulty attributing agency to dark states. Nocturnal literacy, a term I have coined to describe awareness of the complex interactions of different kinds of darkness in their own right, is something globalized modernity does not value, so we lack a lexicon for nocturnal aptitude. And when Westerners do recognize dark activity, it is often in a limited and fearful – if ironically archaic – fashion. While darkness is increasingly crowded out by neon and by 24-hour work-and-play lives, it is still being invoked to cast opprobrium on others. The globalized West has a centuries-long history of deploying *dark* as a term of abuse.

Where and when did this change in world view begin? And how did it become so commonplace? This book attempts to answer such questions, albeit in an exploratory manner rather than definitively. It does not consider insomnia primarily as a medical symptom, however, for going unintentionally without sleep has not always been seen as a problem, or primarily as an individual matter. And because we are largely in the debt of the European Enlightenment for today's faith in medical advances, it is worth looking beyond the purview of such claims, for they are heir to the equation of light with reason and thus not automatically attuned to the interrelations of an unconscious, opaque state – sleep – with the environment in which we usually seek it: darkness. At least one scholar has gone so far as to claim that the European eighteenth century, the period of the Enlightenment, gave rise to modern insomnia,[2] which is to say that the change from understanding sleep as an active state with its own requirements to understanding it as a passive state that simply occurs, and is not always to be desired even then, took place at this point in Western history.

Prior to that moment, and indeed later in some non-Western cultures, relations between dark operators such as sleep and night were not seen as non-existent, and the absence of sleep could indicate the presence of other important states of being. In medieval India, the love of the divine Krishna for the cowherd Radha was thought to produce sleeplessness when the lovers were separated – a cause of insomnia also prevalent in the literature and art of the medieval West – night additionally being the time in which those working the land heard the story told. In a world governed by unseen forces such as the annual cycle of the monsoon rains – which separated lovers away on business when the storms broke – and with the darkened sky giving way to nights pining for one's absent lover, sleeplessness was less a disruption to life than an expression of the absences that gave it meaning. When medieval

9

lovers in European contexts experienced insomnia while apart, it was also reliably interpreted as a sign of their love. Insomnia is the absence of the necessary oblivion that sleep is, while love is the exchange between two people of another absence: the absence of certainty about the future against which lovers assert their love, but which they also share with each other.

Even so, there is a history of regarding insomniacs as guilty or morally suspect that appears to accompany the increase in importance of the individual in society, bringing with it a sense of individual relations to time. Insomnia has always had a relation to time because our circadian body clocks are our built-in timers providing signals that we need to sleep. Wasting time first became sinful in the West in the fourteenth century, and in the newly mercantile economy that followed several different kinds of time were in contestable operation. Religious opposition to merchants was based on the fact that lending and borrowing money changed the value of time, to which only God, having created it, should grant meaning. The new mercantile time produced anxiety – usually about one's fate in the afterlife, the end of time – and anxious awareness of time is a significant aspect of insomnia.

The Devil is one example of a sleepless being bent on evil, but the morally uncertain sleepless were also to be found, as capitalism gained pace, among the godly. Seventeenth-century Dutch Calvinists were vexed by the way in which proof of their happy status after the final sleep, the sleep of death, had to be evidenced by non-attachment to wealth, while the hard work and releasing of capital back into the economy that were equally signs of devoutness increasingly re-posed the problem. A cycle not unlike insomnia itself was set in train, where anxious thoughts about the final sleep's outcome produced more anxious thoughts as care with wealth produced more money. This circular scenario is one of a number of ways in which the monetary economy, the workings of which are always partly invisible to us and which tends towards increase, seems to exacerbate insomnia in Western modernity. Certainly, idleness, a state that needs to be partly cultivated for good sleep habits to take hold, was much maligned as modernity wore on, particularly in America, where the Evangelical movement known as the Great Awakening produced an active alliance between godliness, business and busy-ness. The work of saving souls was often described in market terms, while nineteenth-century Puritans made even the day of rest into a time of tireless devotion.

However, while insomnia may be called forth by the reigning conditions of a given culture, it cannot be said to be entirely caused by cultural arrangements either. Insomnia's doubling of a crucial absence – the absence of unconsciousness, of sleep – indicates where society loses its purchase on the individual, because it doubles the place where the individual loses purchase on his- or herself. As such, insomnia often highlights areas where societies are already making complex – and, often, contested – uses of absence they cannot fully control, as in the Protestant Reformation's espousing of radically new versions of the afterlife – a state no living person has ever returned to speak of and thus an absence for those still living – or in the growing taste in England for the consumer products of coffee, tea and sugar (products linked, as we now know, with wakefulness) produced by unseen African and Caribbean slaves. In both scenarios, sleep was rendered difficult due to new mobilizations of desire, the material contradictions of which fell upon individuals.

And because insomnia is the kind of state in which causes may mask themselves – for waking life does not automatically attune us to the requirements of unconsciousness – it continues to take on larger social meanings, even while awareness of them, in a world increasingly privileging the individual, may decrease. Insomnia's increase in the eighteenth-century West, for instance, was not only due to an overt devaluation of sleep but also to the complex meanings of darkness being generated in the period, meanings which, importantly, gained part of their power from the fact that they were not immediately accessible to consciousness. The traffic in slaves produced the first large-scale venture capitalists, who were obsessed with the future value of their investments. Slaving business was often done in England's eighteenth-century coffee houses, which, as well as keeping people up at night with coffee, fostered gossip and political debate, assisted by the newspapers they made available to patrons. Debt, and the coffee and financial speculation that followed, brought excitement, peril and systemic rush not only to newspaper-reading individuals in London coffee houses, but to the larger system of global trade. Borrowing and lending and the drug foods of sugar and coffee appeared to drive the newly inter-connected economy, at an increasingly hectic pace, into the future, along with the hopes of those who had invested in it. Yet, like insomnia, the slave trade was an actively dark state – dark because unseen, often distant from the site of investment and dealing – as well as a lack: the inability to see how to run an econ-omy without it.

Of course, insomnia can also result from the simple pursuit of pleasure. The oldest human hero, Gilgamesh, who experiences significant insomnia, first goes without sleep because he has so much energy for work and celebration. By the nineteenth century, European cities were making the most of gaslight's ability to show-case the night itself as a zone of spectacle, shadows and wonder. Even today, in countries like India where lighting is not always reliably centralized, city trading and leisure-related activities may continue long into the night. And yet, when we consider insomnia as the absence of sleep in the face of sleep's being intentionally *sought*, we meet an impasse in historical or, at least, historicist explanations. Insomnia gives the lie to the idea that each historical period contains all its own meanings – '[Boredom] is both cause and effect of modernity'[3] – because it is not only made by the world it then reproduces, but also hovers at the unacknowledged produc-tion point of that claim. To wake from sleep is to be found in the world and to have been remade by it, and to experience insomnia is to be kept from seeing, most often by means of excessive thoughts, how the productions of consciousness forestall the arrival of an unconscious state. An impasse to consciousness is significantly functional in insomnia, which teaches that entry into sleep is both materially necessary and ungraspable as such.

Shall we call insomnia, then, the insistence of our material relation to the world at its most basic? The need for sleep is a human universal, which means that it is embodied singularly by each human being, but also unconsciously, for our own way of being in the world is something we ourselves can never see. The often sleepless poet Charles Simic conveys the mockery that insomnia makes of arguments for positivist production and the peculiarly theatrical way in which it displays our singularity in 'The Congress of the Insomniacs', where a hotel ballroom 'with mirrors on every side' yields to an unseen speaker:

> There's a stage, a lecturn,
> An usher with a flashlight.
> Someone will address this gathering yet
> From his bed of nails.[4]

The single '[s]omeone' opens the floor to all insomnia's sufferers, however, the 'bed of nails' the only condition of belonging. Pierced flesh is the entry point of sharing in a strange temporality: that of 'yet', where insomnia's end is the one thing that cannot be counted on while being the one thing for which each member of the sleepless community must continue to hope. Lying on a 'bed of nails' is a continuing experience of pain, perhaps a figure for the continuity of nocturnal suffering in history. But it is also an apt figure for each person's location within that history, which, like pain, cannot be taken on by another and is thus a mark of isolation, as is insomnia today. Even so, at the point at which the nails pierce flesh, the sleepless sufferer is bound to others who also inhabit a singularly unreckonable time, the time of waiting. A strange suffering, insomnia, marking one's exception from the human community by emphasizing a need all human beings share. In today's world of mass-produced enjoyments and enhancements, we could do worse than consider insomnia's history, not only because of what our world cannot know of us, alone and sleepless in the night-time, but because of what we might not know about ourselves.

Chapter One
Sleeplessness in the Ancient World

Insomnia as we know it today was not to be found in the ancient world. The ancients did not have our sense of individual ownership of and beholden-ness to time. Time as a commodity is a modern invention. Yet the contradictions embodied in contemporary insomnia – our time is ours yet not ours, because time is money – *are* to be found in the sleeplessness of the ancients. Although ancient sleeplessness was not primarily the property of afflicted individuals, it does indicate where important divisions, physical and social, were operating. Day and night, madness and sanity, divine and human were significant distinctions in many ancient societies, and, as in modernity, sleeplessness can indicate where they were being crossed. But these crossings seldom privilege the will or well-being of the individual human sufferer as much as they reaffirm – or unsettle – his or her place in the larger scheme of things.

Like us, ancient people were kept from sleep by noise, hunger, anxiety, war, love, lust and moonlight, but in ancient texts gods, too, sleep, wake and are themselves kept – as well as keeping human beings – from sleeping. The Babylonian *Atrahasis* epic, composed in the first half of the second millennium BCE, opens with a war among gods in which the older gods kill the lead troublemaker and make of his remains the first human beings, whom they set to work at manual labour. But the humans reproduce so rapidly that their noise keeps Enlil, an important god, from sleeping. Punishing plagues and other torments follow. In the creation story *Enuma Elish*, the clamour of the younger gods keeps the older ones similarly sleepless and resentful, as does the noise of the energetic

Gilgamesh, himself characterized by wakefulness in at least one reading of the eponymous epic.[1]

This complex continuity between divine and human means that in ancient times what we moderns would name external causes were not purely external, for both mortal feelings and divine messages permeated normal consciousness and were not always readily sorted out. In a world of religious immanence, 'divinity appears whenever life calls out with a peculiar intensity', as the name Zeus, for instance, 'began as a cry – "it lightens" – and only later became god of light'. Or, as Ruth Padel explains of fifth-century-BCE Athens, the scene of Greek tragedy, '[y]ou experience feelings as you experience the nonhuman outside world: gods, animals, the weather coming at you, random and aggressive'.[2] Although the ancients would not have recognized our medical diagnosis of insomnia – for early physicians, sleeplessness was always a by-product of something else – they were conversant with its environment in ways we have lost. In the ancient imagination, darkness, blackness and night had multifarious meanings. They explained as much, or more, than light and day did. They were to be respected and feared, and to fail to yield to them may have had moral and ethical implications. Sleep and sleeplessness, in this context, indicate a habitation of, and by, the perilous energies of night.

In the earliest human societies, the night sky was the domed roof under which people slept. Full moonlight would naturally have precluded or threatened sleep, but since the same would be the case for animals, this extended period of light may well have been used for hunting and gathering, just as the dark of the moon was more suitable for mating and sleep. But a sky roof means no walls, either: one estimate claims that even in the nineteenth century in India, when villagers had weapons and organizing means, 'tigers ate some 300,000 Indians as well as several million animals on farms'. In ancient times, the threat of attack from large wild animals was greater, quite possibly requiring lighter sleep, even if only to tend the fire to keep beasts at bay. In ancient Athens, religious ceremonies were held by moonlight, and 'important military and naval engagements' might be influenced by foreknowledge of the moon's brightness on a given night.[3] Sleeplessness, then, could vary according to strategy or season. But while moonlight, battle or beasts precluding sleep makes sense to modern people, there were more significant ways in which night, particularly the behaviour of the moon, affected ancient peoples' sleep relations.

Because the actions of the night sky are more visible – and were even more so to the ancients, who lacked artificial light – than those of the day, and seem closer at hand, it is thought that most of the globe's peoples originally counted the days from the nights. The early Polynesians called night '*po* and tomorrow *apopo*, the "night's night", while yesterday was *poi-i-nehe-mei*, the "night that is past"', as was fitting for a people who navigated by the course of the stars. In Sanskrit 'the word for "daily" was "night by night", *nicanicam*, and the Saxon word *den* (day) – as in . . . "Good day" – really meant "night", or literally "Good Moon-day"'.[4] Whereas for us, day is the realm of public activity and presence with the night as its private support, for the ancients night was presence and the unknown world's fullness, with the day as night's absence, respite.

The relation of people to the behaviour of the moon and the night sky was concrete and practical. When a strange occurrence such as a falling star was visible, 'the night sky was . . . speaking'. In the East Indies, the eleventh and twelfth days of the moon's cycle were in the past known as 'little pig moon' and 'big pig moon', respectively, because on these dates the moon, well into her gibbous phase when light outweighs dark, would excite pigs to escape their pens and run around the fields, presumably requiring their owners to go and catch them. Aboriginal peoples in the vast outback of Australia lit fires at night to communicate with each other. But the moon was also thought to be the originator of abstract thought and so, eventually, of our own system of temporal management. This arose from the work of observation. Noting that the moon had four phases of activity, only three of which were visible, early humans had to posit the dark phase to account for the renewal of the waxing and waning cycle. Thus the moon became 'an idea, not [only] an immediate object of sense'.[5]

Thought as the result of the moon's absence in darkness is not insomnia, but there is a connection. The mind works harder when faced with something it cannot see yet fears. It needs to supplement or interpret the darkness. Counting days from night made sense in early societies because it is the moon, not the sun, that has different phases in a recurring cycle, or a succession of variant parts to one (recurring) whole. Thought is involved here (as it is not with the passage of the sun), for the phases of the moon's cycle are the parts to the whole, and the whole is visible only in the phases, leading the mind 'beyond the frame of the senses' to a larger hope and supposition. The moon's cycle, while invisible in itself, 'yet contains the visible phases, as though the visible comes out of and falls back into the invisible – like being born and dying and being born again'.[6] If darkness and lack of moonlight equal death, rebirth must be imagined. Thinking and darkness and life go together in a form of cyclical, regenerative relation.

In one ancient version of the moon's cycle read as a heroic (masculine) succession myth, the visible moon vanquishes 'the devil of darkness' as the moon waxes to maturity: so the moon's face 'blazes forth triumphantly at the peak of his career – the full moon. But then the devil begins to eat away at him, and he starts to wane, lose power and wither away in his old age.'[7] Understanding the night to be full of powerful forces in this way makes sleep something night may or may not allow, rather than a natural right for humans, as we tend to regard it. And this in turn makes ancient insomnia difficult to conceptualize, because mysterious awakeness is the condition of the vast unknown world, at its most unknowable at night. Yahweh could not have had insomnia when, in the Hebrew creation myth, he brooded in darkness on the face of the waters (Genesis 1 : 1–2), for he had not yet made night, but the dark deep is night-like, as in Hesiod's version, where the nine Muses appear 'in a cloak of Night' portending enlightenment. And for the Greek Hesiod, Chaos came first, 'before broad-bosomed Earth', so a prior, intractable activity or sleeplessness preceded us.[8]

The challenge of thinking ourselves back into this lost world view is figured by the etymology of our term *insomnia*, which suggests the impossibility of understanding the deepest darkness – death – by hiding it. The second-century-CE founder of dream interpretation, Artemidorus of Daldis, distinguished between two kinds of dreams: those that are mortal, relate to the dreamer's desire and are inspired by his or her past (*enhupnia* or, in Latin, *insomnia*) and those that are divinely sent and prophetic (*oneiroi* or *visa*). Whereas we make a clear distinction between dream-troubled sleep – the original meaning of the term – and the inability to sleep, and use the word *insomnia* to describe the latter, both Artemidorus and the later Macrobius regard it as a sign and product of our 'irrational desire' and fallen nature.[9] What we retain in English is the sense of inconstancy, of wavering on a border – for us, between waking and sleep. What we have lost is the sense of a functional operation within experience that both eludes us and shows that we are mortal.

Human functions that elude us, including mortality in some instances, are now most often presented in the futuristic language of scientific progress, our own version of prophetic dreaming. Insomnia's passage into English is in keeping with this trend, for it has lost the association of something inscrutable and substantial that thickens and troubles human sleep (Artemidorus, in keeping with ancient views, says that *enhupnia* (*insomnia*) may be the result of surfeit or lack of food[10]), and has come to figure a relatively simple lack: sleep's absence. Sleep is now described in the language of quantifiable function and activity, but it also continues to be regarded – and it is significant that this aspect is more often assumed than stated, for assumption works darkly, unnoticed – as that which supports other human functions and activities. Without our being aware of it, our term *insomnia* contains invisibly in its history the meaning of something about a would-be sleeper's past that is unclear. Recall that *insomnia* for the ancients carried a desiring message from the past that had to do with the sleeper's mortal, fallen nature. We have emptied the term of the inscrutable darkness of mortality, but in doing so we have unwittingly been true to the ancient meaning. For it is this deep darkness of death that is incompatible with post-Enlightenment science and from which we have turned away through a long process of historical change in world view. Sleep's death-likeness sleeps in contemporary history. A further darkness works here, that of our not knowing that we have lost the mortal associations of insomnia. For the ancients, *insomnia* are dark, desirous dreams within other dark states: sleep, night and death, the deepest. The imbrication of light with agency in the contemporary West makes it difficult to conceive and speak clearly of kinds of darkness that interact with each other in this way. We moderns are missing a language for that interaction, and, like

Gilgamesh, as we shall see, the problem is that we seldom know it. Powerful nocturnal forces of the Hesiodic kind as well as keen contemporary insights abound in the epic of *Gilgamesh*, the oldest human story and the first to feature a hero suffering from insomnia. The sleeplessness Gilgamesh endures is closely bound to his relations with the natural world: destruction of the environment is central. And the fact that the epic has not ceased producing contemporary versions suggests that insomnia is still imbricated with primal distinctions – darkness and light, death and life – in ways that are not immediately evident.[11] *Gilgamesh* dramatizes at the outset of history how human aspiration itself carries costs, and how the gains of civilization make them dark to us. The invisible realm of sleep becomes the region in which these dark costs manifest, and the hero must learn to value what he has lost in order to read them.

The real Gilgamesh ruled the city of Uruk – in present-day Iraq – in Sumeria around 2700 BCE (the location making the epic's tracking of ravages yet more prescient for contemporary readers). While the most complete version of his adventures, dubbed the 'Standard Version' because of the uniformity of its copies, did not appear until the seventh century BCE, there are several previous, more fragmentary versions, and it is likely that stories about the ruler's deeds circulated in his own time as well. Gilgamesh's fame is connected with the medium of his story, and with his insomnia, which both makes possible, and marks the limits of, movement between worlds. As a ruler in the region of the first known human civilization, Gilgamesh was famed as the 'Builder of Walls'. In the case of the ancient Mesopotamians, the connection between walls and writing was not superficial, for they wrote by carving signs on clay tablets: in effect, on building materials. Together, writing and walls mark the point from which historians begin to speak of civilization, a life carved out of and distinct from the land. In fact, the narrator of *Gilgamesh* begins his tale by taking us on a journey around the walls of Uruk, telling us to find and unlock from within the wall the 'tablet box' in which Gilgamesh himself wrote, on a tablet of lapus lazuli, his story of enduring 'every hardship' (I).[12]

We begin, thus, with marks on stone that, secreted in the wall of Gilgamesh's achievement, tell the story of a journey beyond. The story and the walls are of the same substance, just as the journey Gilgamesh makes gives the shape to his tale. And while his journey and story are full of adventures, their end is the wall that is imaginary or physical but never both: the wall of death that for humans has only one side. The epic's first half tells of Gilgamesh and his companion Enkidu's heroic exploits, while the second depicts the grief-stricken journey the hero undertakes once his great friend has died.[13] Two-thirds god, one-third human, Gilgamesh is initially a strong protector of his people, but he is caught between worlds. His involvement with Enkidu – and Enkidu himself embodies the conflict of culture with nature, of walls with land – brings the mortal part to light as it emerges in fear of death and mourning. From this point the hero's insomnia changes meaning, becoming more recognizably human. It is no longer the sign of his disruptive, driven energy, but of what such ambition cannot hold.

Gilgamesh is initially described as ever wakeful – literally, 'not sleeping (*la salilu*) day and night' – and this is a source of his strength (I). He is notable for not undertaking the traditional means of ensuring one's earthly memory: 'establishing a household and having descendants'. In some way – perhaps as a result of this singular focus, or because his wakefulness needs tempering – he oppresses the citizens of Uruk, and the gods create a companion for him. Enkidu is Gilgamesh's foil. Raised by beasts, he is primal man, and the sub- and superhuman powers at work in his creation are condensed when a hunter, angered that Enkidu has been releasing animals from traps, has a harlot from Uruk ensnare him and deplete him of his powers.[14] Thus estranged from nature, he goes to meet Gilgamesh in the place of civilization. If Gilgamesh's fate is signalled by the walls of Uruk, his relationship with Enkidu is figured by doors. Enkidu, walking down the street, 'block[s] the way through Uruk', and his first encounter with Gilgamesh is a fight in a doorway. After the struggle the two become friends. It is the first experience of true companionship for each (II).[15]

Walls create the illusion that everything can be kept out- or inside, but they also raise the question of human limits. Enkidu has shifted worlds, but Gilgamesh's love for Enkidu is the doorway through which he enters into a mortal knowledge that the walls prevented. Enkidu is also described as wakeful and as the new focus for Gilgamesh's restlessness. Both men lose their 'vitality and wakefulness', Enkidu through death and Gilgamesh, as a result of this death, through a transition from wakefulness to sleeplessness to knowledge.[16] The narrative features a number of reversals and changes of orientation that together indicate Gilgamesh's suffering as the result of civilization, associated with walls and wakefulness. The hero achieves insight into his sufferings only at the end of the narrative journey, because, until then, his success stops him seeing that his suffering has been caused by his success.

In an independently circulating fragment, Gilgamesh peers over the walls of Uruk and sees dead bodies floating down the river, part of ancient Sumerian funeral rites, whence his awareness of mortality begins. Cedar logs were also transported this way from the east, since Mesopotamia at this time was devoid of forests. As nearby forests were depleted, longer and more challenging journeys were required. Written records show that a leader could 'derive considerable fame from a successful expedition' of this kind.[17] In the Standard Version, too, it is clear that Gilgamesh sees such a journey as the antidote to death: he and Enkidu will go to the cedar forest to slay the forest demon Humbaba, the severing of whose head represents dominion over the forest. Gilgamesh will be remembered for this heroic act.

The journey is the last positive expression of what Gilgamesh's mother calls his 'restless [unsleeping] heart' in Book III. From this point on, the hero's travels are generated not by action, but by emotion. The shift to an inward register is presaged by ominous dreams that visit Gilgamesh during the journey to the forest, of the kind that in Latin are called *insomnia*, dreams that trouble sleep and make us fear it. This is the first time the night has not brought pleasure to Gilgamesh, 'not sex or celebration or progress', but real wakefulness, 'visions of destruction'.[18] The turning point of the narrative is also marked by Enkidu's insisting, in Book IV, that the two men make a huge door from the wood of the 'towering Cedar' they have destroyed after killing Humbaba and transport it by raft back to Uruk. It becomes the sign of the threshold Gilgamesh has crossed.

Now it is Enkidu's turn to have a nightmare that foretells his death (VII). He curses the cedar door, like him a working liminality, culture's walls opening to a lost primal past.[19] Further back, he curses the trapper who led the harlot to trick him across the human threshold, before he crosses that threshold a final time and dies. For Gilgamesh the loss of Enkidu is devastating. His greatest friend has entered the doorway to the House of Dust and Darkness, in punishment, as some versions have it, for his own restless crime. While personal guilt as we understand it is too interiorized a concept to be in play here, Enkidu's death spells the end of the hero's belief in his own power. Jack Sasson notes that the epic's second half reverses the trajectory of the first, and from this point 'the voyages take on a surrealistic dimension paralleling the distraught mind of the hero'. It is even conceivable, he suggests, 'that the epic's remaining travels . . . are but one night's [sleepless] hallucinations'.[20]

Gilgamesh's sleeplessness now is tortuous and fearful. '[W]hat is this sleep which has seized you?' is the question that brings Enkidu's death home to him in Book VIII. He flees and takes on the role of Enkidu, growing beast-like in appearance, covered in furs. Regressing from his previous drive to fame and honour, he enacts the near-oblivion he fears. As a last resort he makes a journey through the night, again without sleeping, to find Utnapishtim, the only man known to have found eternal life. To him Gilgamesh insists on his insomnia – 'through sleepless striving I am strained'; 'sweet sleep has not mellowed my face' – but Utnapishtim says, '[y]ou have toiled without cease, and what have you got?' (x).

The alignment of sleep with death and a lack of spiritual awareness in Near Eastern traditions makes staying awake a suitable test of Gilgamesh's potential for immortality.[21] It is the test Utnapishtim proposes. But immediately the hero is commanded not to sleep 'for six days and seven nights'; sleep blows over him in his exhaustion and he sleeps for the same amount of time. His insomnia has become what it is for every human being: a sign of suffering that must end if he is to go on living. The fall into sleep effects the reversal in Gilgamesh foreshadowed by the bodies in the river, the foreboding dreams and the dark sleep of Enkidu, a journey back to earth from the heights of civilization. Gilgamesh now knows that his fate is to be Enkidu's, and also, in a new sense, that every man's fate is the same.

Benjamin Foster reads the hero's final lesson as the stripping away of layers. First, Utnapishtim cannot be fought, but instead offers wisdom. The second layer is the more recent acquisition of a self in mourning, the mimicry of Enkidu. Finally, the sleep fall returns us to the opening scenes of all-night partying and disturbance of the gods, a thoughtless awakeness to match mortal sleep. Gilgamesh learns two lessons on waking: first, that he is mortal, and second, that insomnia is neither a sign of divinity nor of death, but of the life that makes its way between them. In the last lines, he describes the walls of Uruk as the narrator did at the beginning, telling the ferrryman to 'go up on the wall . . . and walk around'. In taking the narrator's place, Gilgamesh demonstrates a changed perspective on his life, also shown in the address not to the poem's many readers, as at the outset, but to an ordinary man who helped in the last stage of the journey.[22] The wall between life and death makes the city wall less important. It is less a part of the wakeful hero's fame than of the world that perishes and yet continues: 'One league city, one league palm gardens, one league lowlands . . . three leagues and the open area(?) of Uruk it (the wall) encloses'.

The sense in *Gilgamesh* that sleeplessness and sleep play on the fault line between mortality and immortality is present in other ancient texts. Gilgamesh did not need to sleep when he did not know he was mortal, but this was in fact a temporary – that is, a mortal – situation. Latin gives a word for wakefulness that we have retained in form and meaning, possibly because it connotes light and activity: *vigil*. But in ancient societies vigil, too – staying awake purposefully to keep watch for spiritual or human enemies – often served a liminal function. It may have been part of an initiation ritual like the Native American vision quest, in which a wakeful night will make the postulant's position in society or world view change.[23]

Enlightenment wrought by vigil is a border function more than a one-way street. Its process resonates with insomnia's borderline activity, where sleep is desired, but something unreachable within has it elude us at the border. One darkness forestalls another. Insomnia often occurs when night harbours a surfeit of daytime matters. Night's restorative powers are depleted when night work in the form of unspecified anxiety is borrowed for the day. Such borrowing normally occurs unconsciously, which makes the inability to sleep, read as a response to this borrowing, also unclear to the vexed sleepless consciousness. Darknesses converse with each other, and we lack the means to comprehend them.

More mundanely, vigil is required in war, as is testified repeatedly in Homer's *Iliad*. The chief difference between the ancient and modern meanings of the term, however, centres on awareness of night's dark agency. Recall that for the ancients, physical and spiritual enemies may take the same form. A common device in Greek tragedy and present also in Homer, with resonance from *Gilgamesh*, is the marking of the end of a hero's madness by a sleep. So while vigilance as wakefulness can connote spiritual and physical readiness, it can equally connote vulnerability, invasion by threatening forms. Its doubled, heterogeneous nature is no doubt the reason why the Sumerian lament 'O Angry Sea' describes a protective god as active in both human and divine dimensions: 'A shepherd who would not lie down he installed over the sheep . . . /A shepherd who does not fall asleep he placed on guard.'[24]

In the ancient world, dark powers were frightening. They showed that the human was dealing with something that transcended and exceeded it, but not necessarily externally. To the ancient Greeks what was inside the body was as unknowable as weather.

> Innards, the equipment of consciousness, and the fluids they contain, the stuff of feeling, were dark. But *loss* of consciousness was also dark. Sleep and fainting were a pouring night, like death. The darkness of the living, passionate mind mirrored that of the underworld, world of the dead. Black was the colour of consciousness and passion, and of their opposite: non-consciousness, death.

For the Greeks, the seat of consciousness was the heart, not the brain.[25] Yet their more labile understanding of darknesses within and without is relevant to our sleeplessness. We seek oblivion, which, for rational subjects, is beyond us, outside. We cannot reach it because of something at the border. Something that resists the control of the conscious mind is working, but this something is not outside like a burglar, a visible enemy. It crosses back and forth, like Gilgamesh's sorrow or Achilles' rage. In the Greeks' world, however – and this is where the contrast between our world and theirs is marked – enlightenment depended on darkness not only because darkness is the human condition. It is also the source of enlightenment. The earliest Greek oracles were 'shrines to Night', and the darkened seer was everywhere, as heroes passed through underworlds, blindness and caves or spent nights in incubation, the special sleep undertaken in the temples of gods, in order to see clearly: 'What is dark and within can "indicate" what is wrong', medically and divinely, for '[i]n darkness we see what we cannot see in light'. Darkness is richly dynamic here, and there is a high degree of nocturnal literacy. Insomnia risks peril chiefly because it makes for a roiling confluence of inner and outer darkness: 'Daemonic madness-senders are "dark-faced children of Night".'[26]

Greek tragic madness can be 'the intensification of consciousness and its darkness',[27] like insomnia, an unnatural waking. At a further turn, and back in time, a Greek epic hero's failure can be represented by an insomnia-wrought sleep (as with Standard-Version Gilgamesh, from whom Homer is not far distant historically). This is the case in Book x of the *Odyssey*, where Odysseus and his crew have been sailing for 'nine whole days' and 'nine nights, nonstop'. On the tenth, sighting land, 'an enticing sleep' comes over him, 'bone-weary/from working the vessel's sheet myself, no letup'. The failure to remember sleep unsettles the order on board and off, as the crew mutiny and the heavens respond with a squall that takes the ship far from the sought-after homeland.

At such liminal moments, heroic sleeplessness may switch from command to peril. In both the *Iliad* and the *Odyssey*, Night is the marker to which men and gods must yield. Failing to do so risks a disturbance in cosmic and human order. In both epics, rosy-fingered Dawn is anthropomorphized, but Night is not. She does not participate in Olympian society, remaining 'mysterious, powerful and aloof'. 'Best . . . yield to night' is the only phrase both the *Iliad*'s sides recognize as marking a legitimate halt to fighting. Yet Night's power is far from abstract. Although she herself is distant, her relatives darkness and death are repeatedly figured as mist and vapour, substantial intermediaries the gods use to intervene in human doings. Dark vapour is like a veil, a garment. Richard Onians notes that 'the darkness which veils the eyes in swoon or death seems to be outside, to envelope [*sic*] the victim', and that '[d]arkness was ... not recognised as mere absence of light till a much later point.'[28] Failure to yield to such material forces in sleep carries more concrete risks than it does for us.

Zeus suffers from insomnia in Book II of the *Iliad*, but when, in Book X, Agamemnon cannot sleep and rises to find Menelaus also sleepless, it is clear that their being abroad at night is suspect. Nestor's cry, 'Who goes there? Stalking . . ./. . . through camp in . . . dead of night?' is answered by Agamemnon's 'war's my worry', and his fear that the watchmen may be sleeping and themselves attacked. The Achaeans fear spying by the Trojans, but they spy themselves and, worse, kill sleeping Thracians in a nearby camp. Sleepless projections cause a break with the code of honour. Later, however (XIX), Agamemnon will defend his feud with Achilles with the word *atê*, the 'madness of self-delusion' and its attendant ruin caused, as he claims, by larger nocturnal forces: 'I am not to blame!/Zeus and Fate and the Fury stalking through the night,/*they* are the ones who drove that savage madness in my heart . . .' (XIX, 100–02).[29]

The double absence – the absence of oblivion – of insomnia is figured in a number of ways in the *Odyssey*. Odysseus' identity is concealed in the opening lines, in which the hero is 'the man of twists and turns . . . / . . . heartsick on the open sea' (I, 1, 5), corresponding with his absence from his wife and family in Ithaca.[30] An opening with a missing hero is unprecedented in Greek epic and gives greater weight to other kinds of absence, but also to twisting thinking, connected with wakefulness, for Odysseus' motif in both epics is his cunning, the darkness of a man who is difficult to read. His wife, Penelope, shows this same cunning, as revealed in Book II by Antinous, a hopeful suitor. Many suitors have sought to take Odysseus' place, and Penelope, we learn in Book II, has been fending them off with secret nocturnal labour. By day she has been weaving a shroud for Odysseus' father, Laertes – 'for that day/ when the deadly fate that lays us out . . . will take him down' (II, 109–10) – claiming that she cannot marry until this is completed. But by torchlight at night she has been unravelling her work, spinning yarn and tale out in a statement of precocious mourning that is something else: the secret hope for the return of her husband.

Greek vase-painting showing Penelope with her loom.

Weaving thoughts are like insomnia, and the epic's texture is similar: moving forward and back in time like warp and woof on a loom. Penelope's night work aligns her with the assumed deceptiveness of women, where weaving tales and garments meet – a tissue of lies, a net of fictions – but is justified, in fact, because the suitors are themselves disturbing natural and cosmic order through their usurpation of the hero's home. Penelope uses sleepless lies for virtuous ends, like Sheherazade in *1001 Nights*, and reworks the alignment of femininity with wiles and waking. The wakeful night is a doubled exception – lack of oblivion – that makes others possible, the place where feminine virtue can abide with cunning.

It is in keeping with the *Odyssey*'s theme of absence and longing that this act lies outside the narrative. By the time we enter the story, Penelope's trick has been discovered, and she has little left with which to defend herself against the suitors. When Odysseus returns in Book XIII, ruses multiply, as he adopts a disguise to test the loyalty of his household. Penelope is said by Athena to have been 'wasting away the nights', and Odysseus asks her to 'weave . . . a scheme' to punish the suitors. But Penelope has her own test with which to ensure that the aged stranger is not a usurper in disguise and poses a contest among the men that Odysseus, if he is present, will surely win. And yet if her husband is not present, she will be bound to marry a usurper. This challenge is, in its way, heroic, for we are in no doubt that Penelope desires the return of her husband.

Insomnia and troubled sleep continue to figure the other absences that drive the narrative. Telemachus, off in search of his father, cannot sleep in Book xv for 'tossing with anxious thoughts' about him (7–9). Penelope, speaking unknowingly to Odysseus in Book xx, claims 'sleep would never drift across [her] eyes' if he would keep his comforting presence near her, but also that 'one can't go without one's sleep forever' (xx, 663–6). She knows that her last tactic has been reached. Unbeknown to each other, Odysseus and Penelope exchange insomnia that night, and this figures the future of their lost connection. Athena showers sleep on Odysseus ('What a misery/keeping watch through the night . . .'), but '[a]s soon as sleep c[omes] on him . . ./slipping the toils of anguish from his mind', Penelope 'aw[akes] and,/sitting up in . . . bed, return[s] to tears'.

In exchanging wakefulness for sleep at opposite moments, Penelope and Odysseus weave love back into the action. This can only be done unwittingly, for all love requires an instance of immeasurable trust in the beloved, like sleep, a fall into unknowing. Odysseus' absence has left a void at the heart of Ithaca, but the void will not disappear now he is back. Rather, it will again become the mutual exchange of lack of certainty that love is, sheltered by family and kingdom. Penelope and Odysseus have each posed for themselves a challenge of trust, a love risk, inseparable from the challenge to each other. The absence of sleep that runs from each to each in the time of trust and risk, the night-time, is the sign, invisible to them as yet, that this encounter with love's darkness will be rewarded.

In Greek epic, lovesick insomnia has political ramifications whether it is undergone by women or men. The sufferings of Queen Dido in Virgil's *Aeneid*, the Roman Empire's national text, were read in their own right throughout the Middle Ages in an ongoing engagement with history's fictions.[31] Dido is unlike Penelope in being a queen with her own standing, and her sleepless sorrow in Book iv is a foil for Aeneas' travels and the founding of Rome to which they lead. Insomnia brings Aeneas and Dido together without them knowing it, for the episodes occur on consecutive nights. The absence of oblivion in its proper place (sleep) figures a future empire missing a ruler and a hero whose goal is not yet reached, but not love's renewal as in the *Odyssey*, for love in the *Aeneid* is thwarted. The relay of insomnia between Aeneas and Dido, his circumstantial and hers deadly, spells the fate of their two cities: Carthage will fall after Dido, and Aeneas will go on to found Rome. In Book I, Aeneas, who with his Trojan countrymen has been wandering the seas since the defeat relayed in the *Iliad*, is buffeted by storms and loses many ships. It is this that keeps him awake all night with worry. Dawn finds him in Dido's city of Carthage. Both Dido and Aeneas are exiles, she from Tyre following betrayal by her brother, who killed her husband. She offers Aeneas and his men safe haven, but that night Venus has Cupid afflict Dido with love for Aeneas.

Dido's love now keeps her sleepless. She lies down on her bed, then leaves it again: 'he's not there, not there, but she hears him and sees him'. We move from the fateful late-night banquet to dawn where 'the queen, long stricken by grievous yearning, fosters the wound with her blood and is caught in the grasp of dark fire'.[32] That day finds Dido and Aeneas out hunting, sheltering in a cave while a storm rages. They apparently make love. Lightning flickers, a 'witness of wedding', and nymphs above 'cry out in pleasure' (168). But we do not see the lovers in the cave. Dido regards the event as a marriage, and it quickly becomes the subject of rumour, which leads to Aeneas being reminded of his duty: founding Rome. When Dido learns of his intention to leave, she wanders the night in a frenzy, but she cannot change his mind. That night also she does not sleep, 'love savag[ing] her' (532). Aeneas is woken by Mercury and spurred to leave immediately. Dido mounts the pyre she has built, falls on her sword and dies.

Borders are alive throughout the narrative: reason against passion, violence against restraint. Dido's insomnia-fuelled death awakens other borders: for Aeneas, 'between heart and head, affection and duty . . . fulfillment and . . . destiny', and for Dido, 'between loyalty to her late husband' and a ruthless love.[33] Aeneas loses sleep in a storm, then Dido loses it in ardour. The absence of sleep, the double negative that augurs the pair's distress, produces other absences that are also double negatives. We hear of but do not see the love act, mimed by nymphs; we do not see Dido's wound.

The pair have exile in common. As events unfold, the act in the cave is shown to be an exception. The negative of sleeplessness – the failure to reach oblivion – becomes for Dido another double absence: that of unrequited love and the death it leads to. She cherishes her unseen wound, but the only answer is to make it a real one. Thus her suicide and absence from the land of the living.

To an ancient audience, the illness that Dido suffered was real. Medea also suffers it in the *Argonautica*, an influence on Virgil's Dido. Eros shoots Medea full of a 'speechless stupor' and a 'wearying pain' that keeps her sleepless with love for Jason and leads to the murder of her children. Like Dido's, her sleepless love-madness shows her caught between worlds. To help Jason is to defy her family, figured dramatically in Book III as she wavers on the threshold of her chamber. Roman authors like Virgil inherited the tragic discourse of bacchic frenzy. Hippocrates, contemporaneous with the performance of Greek tragedy, described *phrenitis* (from which we get 'frenzy') this way: 'The blood heats the rest of the body. The patient loses his wits and is no longer himself . . . Patients with *phrenitis* are deranged, like melancholics, who also grow *paranooi* [delirious] – some rave (*mainontai*) – when their blood is corrupted by bile and phlegm.'[34]

To later medical thinkers, love was sometimes and sometimes not an illness, but lovesickness routinely involved insomnia. Galen (131–201 CE) treated a sleepless woman who turned out to be in love and concluded that this was a disorder of the soul, the nearest equivalent to our understanding of a psychological condition. Lovesickness crosses the borders of early medical explanations, sometimes seen as the result of illness, sometimes as the cause. Coming after Virgil, Galen's *Prognosis* depicts sufferers 'seeking to understand the inner body through description or dissection', but still draws on frenzy's porous darkness. 'As outer darkness fills everyone with fear,' he writes, 'so the dark color of black bile generates fear: it darkens the seat of reason.'[35]

Black bile and the humoural understanding of disorders such as insomnia attracted medieval people, who, looking to the ancients with their own concerns, replayed it. At this point we should remind ourselves that Dido's and Medea's lovesick insomnia was political as well as personal. While insomnia's political ramifications are discernible in the outcomes of the fall of a city and the destruction of a family, there is a closer, more heterogeneous connection. Insomnia, for these sufferers, came from outside with Eros' poisoned arrow. It was like one's enemies who could storm one's household or country. But that is also to fall into the modern tendency to remark clear distinctions. Lovesick sleeplessness invades like one's enemies because it shoots through the sufferer and condemns him or her to particular actions, as though an enemy had made one hostage from within. The pain is inside *and* outside, driving one to frenzy. For the ancients, 'there were good reasons to think of [non-human forces] as the main source of human feeling and experience . . . what we think of as our "own" emotions: these are the gods' best weapon against us'.[36] It is the gods who turn Dido's emotions against her so that they become her chief opponents. Feelings that keep one wakeful can be a coup, a betrayal whose first effect is to sunder imaginary borders. This makes for chaos in a kingdom.

Just before Dido dies, she lies on her bed and claims: '[A] great image of what I was will go to the earth below./I have founded a glorious city', but also, 'Happy I would have been . . ./If . . . the Trojan ships had never come to my shore!'. Her bed, her mind and her city are interconnected regions. *Atê* is relevant here as well as frenzy. What Dido suffers is not her fault, yet she suffers. By Virgil's time *atê* had come to mean 'madness', and tragedy had enacted it. But originally Night bore Conflict, who bore *Atê*, and *atê* crosses borders. It is 'ruinous recklessness', a 'disastrous state of mind'. It is both cause and consequence like love is.[37] Night's and Conflict's daughter was less visible by Virgil's time, but, like the sleeplessness she causes, a mad confluence of darknesses is her effect.

Speaking of insomnia today, we retain a vestige of this border-blurring function. We know medical problems occur within us, but often speak of sleeplessness as 'striking' unexpectedly. We say it visits us, even though we are heirs to a psychologizing understanding that tells us such sufferings are within. Perhaps this anachronistic image is a sign, like our word *insomnia*, of what we have lost, in this case a sense of the frightening dynamism of borders. Insomnia shows how unknown we can be to ourselves, and unknowable things often seem to come from outside. Caught in a resistance to dark striking that worsens the problem, we lack the nocturnal literacy the Greeks had, although it did not always help them manage it.

Nocturnal suffering as a peril of rulership also persists thematically elsewhere and down the ages. Ancient China offers two startlingly contrasting responses to this affliction. Chinese society has a long history of bureaucratic organization without the focus on public argument characteristic of ancient Greece. In China, 'one proved a point by history, not by logic'. A passage in the *Records of the Historian* (*c.* 100 BCE) shows the founder of the Zhou Dynasty, 'sleepless King Wu', who reigned from 1049/5 to 1043 BCE, being visited by his equally sleepless brother. They talk about 'how to secure heaven's support for the rising power of the Zhou' at a key moment in its history:

> When King Wu had arrived in Zhou he could not sleep (*bu mei*) at night. Dan, Duke of Zhou, went to the king's place and said: 'Why is it that you cannot sleep?' The king replied: 'I tell you . . . As until now I have not secured heaven's support how could I have time to sleep (*xia mei*)?'[38]

Remarkably, the benefits of sleep do not appear here. Sleep follows on success, not vice versa.

The chief quality of this type of insomnia is 'its effortlessness'. A good ruler easily stays awake, as 'the power of his virtue makes him "forget to sleep" (*ye ze wang mei*)', unlike ordinary people, although they, too, are enjoined to subdue their sleep needs. The Confucian *Book of Rites*, compiled in the first century BCE, states that 'if somebody stays outside at night (*ye ju yu wai*) it is legitimate to condole with him', so that 'merely by considering somebody's whereabouts at certain hours, it is possible to decide whether [he] is . . . in mourning'. While we cannot know whether such regulations indicate actual habits, what is striking is the way in which probable sleeplessness is streamlined in meaning. Early Confucian texts describe an extremely complex array of instructions for mourning, especially after the death of parents, which could last up to three years, in which 'the mourner should no longer sleep in his private chamber but spend the night outside, alone in a hut near the grave of the deceased, and should go without comfortable pillow or mattress'.[39]

But there is an equally streamlined tradition in China in which sleeplessness occurs in the opposite manner to that of the good king's or dutiful child's behaviour. This perhaps indicates the way in which both change and continuity in Chinese society require opposing polarities (yin and yang) to come into balance. The rivers-and-mountains (*shan-shui*) school of poetry began in the fifth century CE and was often taken up by rulers and statesmen. As David Hinton explains, this is true wilderness poetry, in which poetic language is a form of spiritual discipline shaped by the 'mysterious generative source' that is the wild natural world around one.[40] Poetic speakers are often to be found awake and abroad by moonlight. Tu Fu (712–70 CE) left the government in his 44th year after civil war broke out, but his lines mesh worlds. Remarkably again, insomnia seems to carry no furore or need for explanation as is common in Western texts:

> Faint, drifting from a city, a crow's cry
> fades. Full of wild grace, egrets sleep.
>
> Hair white, a guest of lakes and rivers,
> I tie blinds open and sit alone, sleepless.[41]

Meng Chiao (751–814 CE), a much blacker poet and a surrealist precursor, wrote:

> Lonely bones can't sleep nights . . .
> And the old have no tears. When they sob,
> autumn weeps dewdrops.[42]

This poem of Tu Fu's, however, brings remembered city and wilderness worlds into a larger confluence. Note how it turns the roiling darknesses of ancient Greece into something just as enigmatic, but without the striving across borders and exceptional states that modern-day Westerners have inherited. There are layers of kinds of living darkness, and they seem to open to each other:

Outside a lone city, our river village rests
among confusions of tumbling streams.

Deep mountains hurry brief winter light
here. Tall trees calming bottomless wind,

cranes glide in to mist-silvered shallows,
and hens nestle into thatch roofs. Tonight,

lamplight scattered across *ch'in* and books
all night long, I can see through my death.

But this is not poetry without peril. Tu Fu was repeatedly
driven from his mountain peace by renewals of fighting.[43] War was
within peace just as his city past was with him in the mountains, but
peace is bound to war because civil war knows no borders. One
exile resides inside another. For all that they were savvy political
agents, these poets appear close to an earlier understanding of
night, sleeplessness and (human) nature. Experts tell us that the
worst way to treat insomnia is with resistance, as Gilgamesh's
unexpected solution shows. And if insomnia still has echoes of the
ultimate sleep about it, improving nocturnal literacy can hardly be
wasted. The measure of that work is likely to remain unavailable,
whatever sleep scientists say. We could do worse than Fan Ch'eng-
ta (1126–93 CE), who entered government reluctantly at what in the
West was the point marking the shift from a darker age to a newly
imagined one of European dominance (which, as we know, brought
its own kind of darkness). Hearing rain, Fan's speaker gets up and
listens until dawn, 'hearing each sound appear and disappear./I've
listened to rain all my life. My hair's white now', he says, 'and I still
don't know night rain on a spring river'.[44]

Chapter Two

Love, Labour, Anxiety

It is appropriate to begin this chapter with reference to a trinity. The European Middle Ages, so named in the fifteenth and sixteenth centuries to figure the time between the fall of Rome and the rebirth of its ideals in what was later called the Renaissance, form a historical midpoint in the emergence of European modernity. The assumption of European centrality performed by the term is not incidental, for Europe's emergent market economy was to have decisive importance for the rest of the world. And intermediacy – an idea with clear relevance to insomnia's habitation of the border between waking and sleeping worlds – generated significant changes in the social and intellectual world view of Europe during this period.[1] Perhaps it should not surprise us to find the beginnings of the vexing of sleep's conditions here.

In medieval and early modern Europe, love, labour and anxiety performed an increasingly complex navigation between opposing, yet continually evolving, worlds. Merchants, who were still religious men, were also the people with the greatest burden of conscience regarding the contradiction between an increasingly important worldly, urban time and an eternal time that was the larger set: God's time, the time of Providence. The poet Geoffrey Chaucer went between worlds for a living as a diplomat – the work of words – while doing his poetic writing in his off-hours. The insomnia that opens his *Book of the Duchess* is an instance of the material ambiguity of his position in what was already a dynamically changeful culture. For medieval Christians, love had to be negotiated similarly as sinful due to fallen flesh but allowable by the Church for purposes of procreation, a distinction impossible to acknowledge fully in practice.[2] Medieval romances, in which lovesickness and insomnia are themes, dramatize this intermediate region where people attempt to resolve impossible contradictions in their lives.

While night was certainly the time in which evil forces were thought to flourish, other more concrete aspects of medieval life in Europe led, when not to outright disruptions, to an over-determination of the conditions for sleep. In households of the feudal era, the distinction between bedrooms and other rooms was not clearly marked, and beds were frequently shared. Until the late Middle Ages, peasant houses in France consisted of two main rooms, one with a hearth and a second functioning as a bedroom, to which were added buildings for livestock. Vermin and animal noises were customary irritants on the night's journey towards slumber.[3] Nor did high-ranking people sleep alone. Those who had them slept in close proximity to their valets or chamberlains, while aristocratic fathers insisted their daughters' virtue be closely guarded. In fifteenth-century Tuscany the bedrooms of wealthy people seem to have been 'in constant use for a variety of purposes' during the day, as Charles de la Roncière notes. By night, the closely guarded master bedroom was a place of both rest and vigilance, being also 'the strongroom where valuable treasures were kept'.[4]

Clearly, we are not yet in the realm of sleep as a private activity, or as a phenomenon clearly delineated from other social events. In medieval France, the king's bed became 'the symbol and setting of royalty', so that 'the sovereign ruled from a magnificent bed'. The beds of the seventeenth-century French aristocracy appear to have functioned primarily as theatres, with events such as 'lyings-in, births, christenings, marriages and deaths' serving as elaborate affairs for the receiving and entertaining of guests. It did not become 'bad form to sit on another's bed' until the mid-seventeenth century.[5] As to matters of comfort, even by the Tudor period, '[t]he bed was still far from being an efficient machine for sleeping in', despite the fact that

> [a]ll the necessary materials for making a comfortable spring mattress had been to hand for centuries, and there was no lack of craftsmanship: a swordsmith who could

make a fine flexible rapier might surely have been able to turn out coiled springs . . . But no thought seems to have been given to such possibilities.[6]

It seems that sleep, for medieval and early modern Europeans, was not particularly valued for its own sake, nor was it expected to occur in one uninterrupted stretch. Timekeeping had its roots in the twelve canonical hours into which the Church divided each day, but these did not extend into the night. The night 'was divided . . . into *vigilae* or watches'. Not only was there a close association between night-time and remaining watchful for medieval Europeans, but the metaphor of the watch, of which three became enshrined in the Christian liturgy, was extended to the three ages or stages of a person's life and, indeed, to its entirety, understood as a continual readiness for death and divine judgement.[7] Further-more, a commonplace interruption of sleeping time was experienced by Western Europeans until the close of the early modern period, one that has been surprisingly unaddressed by historians. This was the custom of sleeping in two main intervals of the night, of similar duration, 'bridged by up to an hour or more of quiet wakefulness' that bore the generic name 'watch' or 'watching'. According to E. Roger Ekirch, who finds reference to the two sleeps in several languages and a variety of sources, people often woke from their first sleep before midnight and spent the interval in a variety of ways: lying quietly, praying or performing tasks left over from the day.[8]

Ironically, the fact that medieval and early modern Europeans did not give sleep so much importance in its own right, or expect it to be as continuous as we do, may have helped protect them from insomnia as we understand it. Sleep researchers indicate that insomniacs characteristically under-recognize how much sleep they actually get, a state that of itself causes anxiety, often leading to further problems in sleeping.[9] In an individualistic culture such as ours, sleep is a key means of support for workaday selves. But in a communally oriented society with lower expectations regarding sleep quality and time, and with a long-held belief in the necessity of a watchful, prayerful attitude, interrupted or poor-quality sleep might not so readily produce the anxiety that leads to habitual sleeplessness.

Medieval Europeans did have other nocturnal foes to worry about, however. Arson, political conspiracy and robbery were feared, as were personal attacks. The cost of a world in which personal privacy is not highly valued is the constant threat of others laying claim to what is yours. Perhaps the most feared of all at night, though, were the Devil and his minions. Demonic appearances were associated with liminal regions and atmospheres: moonlight, twilight, fields and forests. Unexplained wakefulness, when not for the purposes of prayer or a by-product of other activities, was, like these environments, morally suspect. The hero of the twelfth-century French lay of Tydorel is 'a half-fairy whose eyes never close'; thus, he cannot sleep or dream. This lack of saving alternation makes him unfit for social life and positions of power, and he is eventually banished to a timeless realm.[10]

Demonic appearances occur in medieval French contexts at the point where the narrators of such events are either awakening or falling asleep. Making their entry at the threshold of sleep, demons are also able to go through closed doors, but as the centuries wear on they are increasingly seen to perform such acts by association with the porous bodies of women. Augustine's distinction between the flesh and the body led medieval Christianity to locate the source of human weakness and sin in the flesh, found to be 'restless, rebellious . . . intransigent' and feminine.[11] Augustine likened the flesh to a wife insufficiently under the control of her husband. Later, Bernard of Clairvaux depicted the will, corrupted by the flesh, as an infectious old woman whose threefold ulcer consisted of 'voluptuousness, curiosity, and ambition'. Thus the flesh, itself the site of the influx of sin, was marked by a continuous desire for physical fulfilment, knowledge and social advancement. Through the senses this feminine, flesh-corrupted will was seen to continually 'infect the soul'.[12] It was to this feminine restlessness that prayerful vigil was opposed.

As the doubled absence, the lack of unconsciousness, that produces an excess of anxiety and thought in the night-time, insomnia has connections with the assumed fleshly porosity of women. The medieval forest was feared as the haunt of demons because its opacity doubled the darkness of night, so that further darknesses might hide there.[13] As sources of border-crossing on which life depended, female bodies also signified the return to the earth in death, birth's fearsome double, both processes opaque to human understanding. Both the crossing into and out of existence that female bodies connoted were echoed by the everyday activities of waking and sleeping. Yet, unlike the dark forest in the unknowable night, women's bodies were themselves products of the mysterious crossing into life at the same time as they enabled that crossing for others. Their opacity, and its connection with waking and sleeping, and with birth and death, was rendered mobile. According to medieval theologians, female bodies combined opacity with a dynamic liminality and restless energy, and were increasingly seen as subject to demonic forces as a result.

St Bernard, along with St Francis and his followers, was influential in the later development of an enthusiastic form of popular piety that emphasized the humanity of Christ, and indeed his femininity, at such liminal moments as his birth and death, the Nativity and Passion. This is a peculiarly restless kind of devotion, in which Christ's mother, Mary, takes on the burden of her son's physical suffering at the moment of his death, enduring in addition the pains she did not endure at his birth. Christ is feminized through his portrayal as physically passive, boundary-less in his bleeding and nourishing in the form of the Eucharist.[14] The suffering Mary, herself imitating the suffering Christ, became the model for medieval laywomen who, by foregoing sleep and other physical comforts, hoped to redeem their previous fallen-ness as this active, flesh-focused piety got underway. Lay devotion transformed the more orthodox model of 'the dark night of the soul' – a communion with the divine about which the soul knows nothing, and in which both participants' realities remain mysterious – into a 'feverish intensity', a waking consciousness of fleshly suffering as redemption.[15]

The Prussian mystic Dorothea of Montau performed heroic nocturnal feats in the interests of sanctity, spending sleepless nights 'shuffling about on her knees, crawling, arching her body in the air with her forehead and feet on the floor . . . falling on her face with her hands behind her back as if they were bound, and so forth'. Pope Urban v habitually stayed awake to pray at night, while St Catherine of Siena 'eventually slept no more than half an hour every other day'. Fourteenth-century saints strove to make their beds as uncomfortable as possible when they did have to sleep. Lights were kept burning in the dormitories of monks, who were not allowed to sleep alone lest the Devil tempt them to sinful thoughts and actions.[16]

In India as in Europe, religious devotion in the language of the people also began to trouble the self-sufficiency of learned culture and to carve out an increasingly expressive middle ground between mythical divinity and courtly custom. The popular Hindu *bhakti* movements increasingly emphasized the mortal life of Krishna, an incarnation of the god Vishnu. The *Gitagovinda*, a twelfth-century work by Jayadeva, was the first Sanskrit poem to treat the love of Krishna and the cowherd Radha, who each, as we have seen, experience insomnia when apart. While it occupies an intermediate position between the reign of classical Sanskrit and the beginning of vernacular poetics, thus making for a historical parallel between Latin and the vernacular in Europe, the *Gitagovinda*'s treatment of Krishna's erotic disposition is not incompatible with its status as a poem of devotion, as would largely be the case in the West.

The poem was highly popular in its time, and its impact was governed by internal liminalities. Following a fifteenth-century commentator, Lee Siegel observes that the opening follows the classifications of Sanskrit poetics whereby the erotic mood of 'love-in-separation' is about to become 'love-in-enjoyment'. The framing parts of each of the poem's twelve cantos (*sargas*) typify Sanskrit court poetry, but the 24 songs of the cantos do not. These carry the impact of vernacular poetry, which, as in Europe at this time, demonstrates the general populace's growing desire to express spiritual love in human love's terms. The portrayal of the 'love-sports of the youthful Krishna' common to both courtly and vernacular forms is the means of this transition. Comparing the insomniac devotion of Krishna and Radha with that displayed by the twelfth-century southern French troubadour Bernart de Ventadorn, another critic notes that where 'the Bernardian *verso* is fuelled . . . by antithetical relationships' that never achieve fulfilment, the *Gitagovinda* follows the circular pattern of union, separation and reunion common to Indian erotic literature.[17]

As this tripartite schema suggests, while the love of Krishna and Radha is dynamized by several kinds of liminality, it is ultimately made meaningful by thirds. Krishna's adolescent love sports place him between child- and adulthood in an intermediate zone, while his love for the mortal Radha demonstrates the divine's human aspect, bringing a third dimension to their relationship. The poem's use of formal courtly codes to transmit the passionate vernacular is another pair enabling non-aristocratic people to recognize and express their devotion to Vishnu. Krishna's and Radha's insomnia opens a dimension of third-ness whereby insomnia – the absence of oblivion that sleep is – expresses their love and longing for each other. This dimension is materialized in the figure of the go-between who moves from Radha to Krishna and back again, conveying to each the extent of the other's nocturnal suffering.

The love relation, as we saw with Penelope and Odysseus, is a positive event born of a double negative: the exchange of lack of certainty that is the trust of coupled love. The *Gitagovinda*'s opening plays on another third intrinsic to Indian love relations and, like insomnia and trust, also an absent presence: the gathering monsoon weather:

> Clouds thicken the sky.
> Tamala trees darken the forest.
> The night frightens [Krishna].
> Radha, you take him home![18]

Monsoon clouds are traditionally the stimulus for the mood of love-in-separation in this period because the Indian spring rains make travel and war impossible and portend a time of festivals, domestic happiness and love-making. Thousands of verses play on the sadness of lovers who are away from home when the rain breaks, with no way to return. As we have seen, such lovers often suffer insomnia.[19] Until the rains fall, Krishna and Radha are also at this frontier between seasons.

According to Sanskrit rhetoricians, darkness typifies both fear and desire, and the symptoms – 'trembling, sweating, stammering, fainting' – of both are the same. The dark clouds, forests and night combine with dark-bodied Krishna – usually a dark blue – to create a scene of uncertainty and portent, of darknesses conversing with each other. Krishna may be feigning fear of the night to hide his desire for Radha, or Radha could be registering his adolescent sexual fear mixed with desire. But darkness is also doubled on behalf of the worshipper, since the poem's night scenes were doubled in performance. The *Gitagovinda* and its poet were claimed by the Sahajiya cult as its point of origin, and the text was performed nightly as part of a long tradition of such performances.[20] Listening to the *Gitagovinda* sung was the main way in which the story was transmitted in its time.

Krishna's and Radha's insomnia, then, where the border between night and day is troubled, also signals the inability of the poem to be contained and its status as a means of popular worship. In Part III, 'Bewildered Krishna', parted from Radha, bemoans his heart's 'sleepless state' at the same time as he 'wildly enjoy[s Radha] loving [him]' (6). In Books v to VIII he tosses and turns at night with Radha on his mind; her feelings are similar. In his devotion to Radha which causes suffering, Krishna becomes more human than in previous representations. But he is not only human. The term used for love's desolation in the poem (*viraha*) is also the term used in Bengali Vaishnava theology, the devotion to Vishnu of which the Krishna legends are part, to depict the soul's readiness for salvation.[21] Krishna is at once the human soul longing for Radha – and by extension for the divine – as well as being divine himself. His darkness within the forest in the dark, pre-monsoon season indicates the indistinguishable nature, but also the intercommunication, of other dark states: erotic and spiritual longing.

Paintings provided another means of transmission of the Krishna and Radha story, although representations of Krishna did not emerge until the fourteenth century and were initially rather basic. But in the time of the great Moghul emperor Akbar (1556–1605), many lavish illustrated manuscripts were being ordered, a practice continued by a local Indian ruler, Raja Sansar Chand. This resulted in the production of an illustrated *Gitagovinda* in the Kangra tradition of the eighteenth century.[22] One miniature shows Radha embracing the darkness of the night in Book VIII as painted by the master Manak, with Radha's go-between explaining to Krishna that this is because Radha is driven mad with longing.

Insomnia also features in the *Rasikapriya* of Keshavadasa, a sixteenth-century text about Krishna and Radha that goes further

Radha embraces the darkness of the night in the painter Manak's 18th-century watercolour illustration to Jayadeva's poem *Gitagovinda*.

than the *Gitagovinda* in juxtaposing worlds. Written in a Hindi dialect (Brajbhasa) at a time when the language was just beginning to achieve prominence in secular, courtly poetry, this text belongs to the *riti* tradition, which combines the higher register of Hindi diction with the classificatory methods of Sanskrit. As a new form of poetic expression adapting ancient forms, *riti* qualifies as one of Jacques Le Goff's intermediate operations, expressive of social and intellectual change. It is poetry in the vernacular for which Keshavadasa, acknowledged as the first poet of this kind, was seeking to attain classical status and permanence. Coming from a line of Sanskrit scholars, the poet was thus breaking with family tradition.[23]

Intriguingly, insomnia's first occurrence in the poem is in Book VIII, where it clearly departs from traditional Sanskrit method into vernacular invention, and thus where both Radha and the poet show anxiety. The anxiety concerns undue mixings and meetings, respectively of lovers and styles. At this point Radha, fearing that Krishna is making love with the other cowherd women, loses her appetite and her ability to sleep.[24] Burnt 'by moonlight', she, like Dido, moves 'from bed to ground, [and] from ground to bed' in torment. Sleep is depicted as a newly wed wife who can be brought

43

to bed only by arduous scheming. Her mistrustful demeanour suits both lovers' states.

Keshavadasa's intervention in Section V is to describe in concrete detail Krishna's and Radha's meeting places, which are not described in the ninth-century Sanskrit rendition of the story he has been following. The places themselves are also liminal, masked by other relationships or occasions: Radha's sickbed, a celebratory function, a servant's house. The act of writing in the vernacular within the framework of a courtly model constituted a 'linguistic and intellectual failing' in the poet's circle. His anxiety is shown in sections V and VI by the use of the qualifying phrase 'according to my own understanding' (or 'each knows as his wisdom shows') as a defence of innovation. Section VI concludes with an extra phrase: 'May master poets forgive [this poet's] audacity.' Keshavadasa's innovation is considerable. The places where Krishna and Radha meet are concrete, yet often involve deception. They are indexes of the larger function of the poem, which, while seeming to follow Sanskrit models, departs from them in the interests of common language, being steeped in a popular world view carefully protected and considered.[25]

A similar degree of carefulness is demonstrated in Persian courtly poetry of the twelfth century. Persian mystical poetry has been regarded as more authentic than its courtly contemporary by Western readers, while in European contexts the need for court patronage to sustain the work of writing is readily accepted. Yet, as rulers needed poets to ensure their lasting names, a complex relationship operated where poet and ruler each depended on the other for survival. The poet achieved influence, however, not only through verbal ingenuity, but through the art of hiding this ingenuity so that the ruler believed a change of heart had come from him rather than from his advisers. Where the role of the court poet met insomnia's doubled negation – an excess of thought resulting in the absence of oblivion – was in the subtlety and manipulation, the doubled-ness, through which the poet was advised to achieve influence over his ruler.[26]

One instance of sleepless activity expressing material dependence is found in a *qasidah* (panegyric) of Nizami Awhad al-Din Anvari (*d.* 1189–90?). Like the *Rasikapriya* of Keshavadasa, Anvari's *qasidahs* often include innovatively literal erotic episodes (*nasibs*) based on the stock trope of the distracted lover. In one such segment the poet is lying in bed when he is visited by his beloved, who chides him for idleness and sets him a task of nocturnal labour: to compose a *qasidah* to give to his patron the next day. In this and similar poems, the complaint of lovesickness serves a dual negative function, expressing the poet's suffering at his beloved's absence and providing the reason for his inability to write. Staying awake all night at his lady's command to write a poem for his patron, the poet emphasizes the trying physical conditions of his labour, where two negatives, lack of sleep and lack of love, nonetheless make a positive, the poem. While implicitly criticizing his own love obsession, the poet 'predispose[s] the patron to be sympathetic and generous' to his situation.[27] For just as the lover needs the beloved, so the poet needs an income, the provision of which comes from his patron. Here, lovesick insomnia carries the added meaning of the material costs of penning courtly praise.

Chaucer's early dream poem the *Book of the Duchess* also carries a message about the labour of love and writing. The poem is believed to have been written between 1368 and 1372 in memory of Blanche, the daughter of the first Duke of Lancaster and wife of the Earl of Richmond, John of Gaunt, to whom oblique reference is made.[28] It uses the framing device of a dream, common in the period, to express love for an unattainable lady, in this case because she is dead. However, the dream itself is preceded by other frames, the first of which is the narrator's complaint about his sleeplessness. In this, Chaucer was following the model of Jean Froissart's *Paradis amoureux* (1362),[29] but, like Keshavadasa, the English poet made a significant change. Chaucer's narrator is not, like Froissart's, shown to be unequivocally suffering from melancholia, which commonly causes sleeplessness. This role is given to the Black Knight he encounters later. Instead, the poem opens with an ambiguous statement of wonder regarding how, 'in the light of day', the speaker is still living, since he has suffered such trouble sleeping, he tells us, for the past eight years (1–15, 35–7).

This is one of Chaucer's typically uncertain narrators, whose 'distress and puzzlement' allow the reader – or, originally, the listener – to wonder in turn about the costs of love and writing depicted in the poem. These lines about insomnia, in their lack of clear cause, constitute an important key to the poem's meaning. In the period, dreaming was a figure for poetic inspiration – just as dream poems were a fit means of displaying literary skill – which means that the narrator, read as Chaucer, was experiencing a dearth of inspiration, a wakefulness that interfered with writing.[30] This is an ironic reversal of what fourteenth-century listeners would have recognized as the parallel of sleep with sloth, or *acedia*, much railed against in sermons and devotional writings, and against which prayerful vigil was recommended. 'Chaucer's point here', as one critic claims, is that 'good poets work hard at what they do' and that, contrary to non-writerly perceptions, '[f]alling asleep . . . is actually the first step towards fulfilling a poetic role', for lack of sleep means a reduction in material derived from dreaming.[31]

In courting sleep, the narrator reads Ovid's tale of Ceyx and Alcyone, which sets up his own tale of a grieving knight through its depiction of the loss of a beloved spouse. It also sends him to sleep and into his own dream vision, which forms the major part of the poem. In Ovid's tale, Morpheus, the god of dreams, sends the grieving Alcyone a vision of her dead beloved. The valley in which Morpheus dwells is the poem's true vision of idleness, where sleep and 'noon other werke' is done. This vision is unsuccessful, and Ceyx dies soon after, thus setting up a foil for Chaucer's own poetically more effective memorial offering. Faced, within his own dream, with the Black Knight's sorrowful story and likely insomnia – he is clearly suffering from love melancholy, as does the knight in the *Canterbury Tales*, whose sleep is typically disrupted[32] – the narrator offers the reader another angle on the cause of this suffering in addition to the one the Black Knight proposes.

On hearing the Black Knight invoke the metaphor of a chess game to depict the famously unpredictable nature of Fortune's dealings with him, as with all human beings, the narrator suggests that this view of things is unnecessarily negative (618–84, 740–41). In response, the Knight unfolds the tale of what he has lost in his queen, which forms the elegiac component of the poem. Guillemette Bolens and Paul Beckman Taylor indicate that this, however, is only one part of the Knight's and the narrator's interaction leading to healing. The second part 'is figured, not as an invention, but by the happenstance of the castle bell sounding that ends . . . [the] dream, and which wakes the poet' to the task of writing the poem.[33] It is only at this point that the Knight, going home to '[a] longe castel with wallys white' – the form 'Loncastre' commonly meaning 'Lancaster' – 'Be Seynt John, on a ryche hille' (1318–19), is identified as John of Gaunt. It is the sound of the castle bell that seals the effect of the dream's conversation as awakening to worldly responsibilities on both the Knight's and the narrator's part.

However, this castle bell was already secretly alluded to – albeit at one remove – at the outset of the poem, where it had a connection with the narrator's insomnia. While it is a bell that wakes the narrator at the poem's end, this bell would have undoubtedly been 'struck by a clock mechanism', as the verb *smite* shows, since church bells were made to sound quite differently, by being tilted to make contact with their clappers. Churches at this time did not have need of clocks, since the canonical hours were rung by their bells. As a new invention, a striking clock primarily demonstrated wealth and status in this period; churches could afford them only later. Bolens and Taylor locate the origin of the Chaucerian reference to a striking bell in Froissart's *L'Orloge amoureus* (1368), just prior to the likely composition of the *Book of the Duchess*.[34] Recall that Chaucer's poem begins by echoing, in standard medieval fashion, another Froissart poem, the *Paradis amoureux*, with the distinction of not giving a reason for the narrator's trouble sleeping.

Although Chaucer's poem does not begin with clock-watching per se – small personal clocks would become available only much later – it does begin with the heightened time-awareness of insomnia. The clock mechanism's striking a bell to wake the narrator indicates two kinds of time reference, one contained within the dream story, the other outside it. The first is suggested by the narrator's gentle rebuke of the Knight's view of capricious Fortune, in the course of which he refers to the Knight's losing 'twelve queens', a reference that has long puzzled scholars. Bolens and Taylor suggest that this reference may serve as a lexical bridge between two metaphors for Providence contained in the poem. The first is the Wheel of Fortune, to the capricious turnings of which the Knight refers his sufferings through the image of the game of chess whose outcome is unknown, thus making sense of the 'queens' reference. The second is the understanding of providential time as clock time, or the time God has measured and ordained according to the needs of each person, which unfolds according to the twelve segments into which a clock face divides each day.[35]

In his history of clocks and modern temporality, Gerhard Dohrn-Van Rossum cites an anonymous fourteenth-century author who depicts the heavens as a great flawless clock designed to serve the needs of human beings. With the clock's help, this writer suggests, people in cities and towns are not ruled by clocks as they were once ruled by the heavens, but rather use clocks to help rule themselves. This new measurable time, an indicator of early modern urban work-consciousness, provides the first glimmerings of the truism that time is money.[36] The time-marking clock bell that breaks through the poem's dream frame to awaken both Knight and narrator to their responsibilities belongs to the more ordered face of Fortune the narrator offers instead of the Knight's chess metaphor. Providence gives a degree of temporal control to humanity in God's service in this account, rather than reducing people to strategizing in a game of chance. But this bell, sounding from the Knight's castle, also returns the reader to the narrator's original condition, insomnia, through his waking in bed, emphasized by the doubled Froissart reference to love and clock bell that takes us back to the poem's beginning. The clock bell also takes us back to Chaucer's original departure from Froissart: his not providing an explanation for his narrator's insomnia. However, with the new understanding of Providence the narrator has offered the Knight now being supported by the clock bell's intervention, we are in a better position to give an account of this mystery, which will take us, rather as it took the narrator, beyond the framework of the *Book of the Duchess* to reflect on Chaucer's own time constraints and labours as an author.

The first point to note about Chaucer's work conditions is how varied and volatile they were. Born the son of a wine merchant who was also in service as deputy to the king's chief butler, the rapid rise of Chaucer's family exemplified the new mercantile possibilities of the European fourteenth century, with Chaucer himself entering the king's service as esquire in 1368. He retained this title after his move outside the household to hold a customs appointment and other jobs as clerk of works, justice of the peace and revenue manager while continuing to serve as a diplomat.[37] As we have seen, Chaucer's poetry writing was squeezed into the time left over from these financially necessary concerns.

Class-wise, too, Chaucer occupied a more than usually liminal place. The second half of the fourteenth century brought a significant destabilization of the received hierarchy of the 'three estates' that had typically dominated official discourse: those who ruled (kings and knights), those who prayed (priests) and those who laboured (peasants). In a sermon of 1375, Bishop Thomas Brinton figured four social estates: churchmen, kings, merchants and workers.[38] The new addition, merchants, demonstrates the growing importance of urban trade, but also the increase in importance of all kinds of middle groups in medieval European society. It was within this continually reconfigured middle group that Chaucer sat, but it is perhaps more accurate to say that he moved continuously across the borders between this group and others. His poetic work of importing French models and terms into English poetry – necessary to gain courtly legitimacy for English, the vernacular – was an after-hours version of his other job exchanging letters, the physical cross-Channel work of a courtly diplomat.[39]

While both diplomacy and writing vernacular poetry cross borders, it is part of their work to underplay these borders as well as the work that crossing them involves. Diplomatic errands smooth the way for higher powers who are then free to disregard the smoothing, and so, also, does courtly entertaining have its hidden cost. 'Summoning the illusion of a world without work', such as that depicted in the *Book of the Duchess*, 'was itself work', in short.[40] Insomnia, however, a resistance to the crossing into sleep resulting in the absence of unconsciousness, emphasizes both the sleep/waking border and the need to cross it. As such, it is the material flipside of the poet's twice-doubled work of underplaying the work of diplomacy and writing.

David R. Carlson notes that Chaucer himself, to use the terms he gives to the windy Eagle in *House of Fame*, 'could sit at his books only after his accounts were complete and all his other labors were done'. Reading and writing, bleary-eyed, at night, produced an insomniac narrator and an elegy without closure, just as 'in the Chaucer life-records the divorce between crown servant and court poet' appears falsely absolute, a distinction less clear in reality. 'Summoning . . . a world without work' is not only work, but over-work, it seems.[41] The site of the continuation between Chaucer's day- and night-time work is also the clock bell that replaces the dreamlike 'world without work' of the poem with the workaday pressures of Chaucer's present. The castle bell on its rich hill 'tolls for the *belle* White [Lady] the Black Knight has lost. And by the homophonous coincidence between Chaucer's English in *Duchess* and Froissart's French in *L'Orloge*' – that is, by the diplomatic crossing of upstart English verse with its courtly progenitor – 'the "belle" . . . who caused Froissart's sleeplessness . . . resurfaces . . . as the "bell" that wakens the dreamer' to another day's work and another night's trade-off between writing and sleeping.[42]

Broadly speaking, as the Middle Ages proceeded, Western Europeans found their lives increasingly governed by a variety of invisible intermediaries. The gradual emergence of a mercantile economy meant that it was future profits, themselves not visible, rather than approaching nightfall, that began to dictate the length of the working day.[43] Laypeople bought indulgences in the form of prayers from clerics, who performed this un-trackable task on behalf of departed souls. The Devil, who could take any shape or form and so become effectively invisible, became a much more constant presence than previously. Common to these examples is a symbolic function whereby one thing hides or stands for another, enabling the circulation of different elements within a system. Invisible intermediaries – good and bad – keep the system moving.

These changes caused considerable debate and uncertainty. Merchants were criticized because profits were seen to imply 'a mortgage on time, which was supposed to belong to God alone'. Time itself became over-determined, for 'natural [or meteorological] time, professional time, and supernatural time', while distinct from each other at certain points, had equal legitimacy. In addition, in the thirteenth century a decisive shift had occurred whereby penitence, previously subject to 'external sanction' from the clergy, had become a matter of internal contrition. The Fourth Lateran Council of 1215 made annual confession obligatory for all

'The Insomniac,'
illustration from a
14th-century
medical
manuscript.

Christians, while the mendicant orders – the Franciscans and
Dominicans – produced confessors' manuals oriented towards 'the
discovery of internal dispositions' rooted in the everyday conflicts
people faced.[44] The committing of unconsidered sins due to the
overlapping of different kinds of time and jurisdiction was one
such conflict, itself problematically open-ended.

The new confessors' manuals not only provided a forum for
the expression of anxiety regarding conflicts between different
kinds of time, but, since they were available to penitents, exacer-
bated it. Recall that insomnia is where two inscrutable agents, sleep
and night, find themselves in conflict at the border where the only
happy outcome is for each to yield some ground. Sleep occupies the
night even as night-time holds the sleeper. If we consider that the
material of anxious crisis in this period was the pressures wrought by
overdetermined time along with increased production of other kinds
of middle-ness – increasingly fine distinctions were introduced in

an attempt to 'clarify the relations of groups within the middle strata' of society, an activity itself required by crises of governance[45] – then we are close to finding ideal conditions for the production of insomnia.

While time-wrought anxieties about the end of time – questions of eternal doom and salvation – were pressing with new urgency upon late medieval Western people, the forces of darkness were being given increasingly mobile powers to corrupt and intervene in human actions. The Devil no longer tempted people by recourse to the seven deadly sins, which could be readily pictured and which functioned as external agents, but through offences that might result inadvertently and invisibly from a conflict over professional and supernatural allegiances. As with confessors' manuals, however, this new fear of the Devil was both remedy and poison. Accentuating the Devil's 'negative and baleful features' really began in the fourteenth century as part of the drive to get more laypeople to confession. Yet this worked best by creating a twofold, unresolvable anxiety: that the Devil was fundamentally inhuman, and that he 'could enter sinful bodies' readily to 'transform them in his image'.[46]

The Devil himself was seen as an insomniac, and required a corresponding vigilance on the part of Christians. In a Renaissance essay on demonology – the science of demons that began to emerge in the fifteenth century – Leon d'Alexis describes him as an 'angelic spirit' with 'a relentlessly active nature' who can neither turn to God nor 'find . . . rest and solace' in the contemplation of his own image. Thus, '[w]andering on earth in search of rest', he ceaselessly fastens on the affairs of human beings.[47] What is most unsettling about this new, labile Devil is that he was formed in the image of the early modern human being, itself increasingly subject to invisible manipulation by social forces. Whereas God, according to the Italian inquisitor Zacharia Visconti, speaks 'the "language of things" – that is, He expresses himself through the created world' – so that 'divine language at once makes and names reality, human language has no direct connection with the reality it describes'. This makes it liable to a third idiom, a 'language of the mind' spoken by demons or fallen angels, who, speaking through us, commit their evil deeds in the world.[48]

The Devil's manipulative lability, then, spoke to new anxieties about agency in the late medieval and early modern period in the West, where people were increasingly having to rely on networks they could not see.[49] But it was the change in the nature of the human being at this juncture from occupying a relatively static place in God's creation to a dynamic uncertainty of belonging that was the heart of the problem. Humankind had long been seen as an intermediate agent with a heterogeneous nature. 'Man's . . . particular distinction', as E. Ruth Harvey notes, 'is that he is the only one of God's rational creatures to obtain pardon for the sins he commits', since God 'takes into account the burden imposed on the rational soul by a body . . . possessed by the irrational desires of the beasts'. It was on 'the comprehension of man's middle state and hybrid nature' that 'moral doctrine and philosophy' depended,[50] yet it was this very middle-ness and hybridity that was now being mobilized in new and demanding ways.

There is a consensus among historians that the period was a time of new anxieties.[51] Anxiety is time-related, and is also central to the experience of insomnia. The *Oxford English Dictionary* defines anxiety as '"uneasiness or trouble of mind about some uncertain event"'. Man is anxious . . . because his existence extends into the *future*', itself 'inherently uncertain'. From the early fourteenth century, '[w]asting one's time became a serious sin, a spiritual scandal'. The Dominican Domenico Calva of Pisa developed an entire spirituality, using merchant vocabulary, 'of the calculated use of time'.[52] Yet despite the increasing presence of clocks and regulated work schedules, even Renaissance people 'continued to live with an uncertain time . . . a nonunified time, urban rather than national, and unsynchronized with the state structures then being established'. Where uncertainty about the future meets the need to fill up one's time with spiritually mandated effort, humanity's saving intermediacy breaks open. In Le Goff's words, 'the disturbance of mental structures opened fissures in . . . traditional forms of thought'.[53]

Ludovico Ariosto's epic romance *Orlando Furioso* (*The Frenzy of Orlando*), first produced in 1516 and revised continually until 1532, demonstrates this sense of cultural crisis through a near epidemic of sleeplessness on the part of its characters.[54] Relying on the dynamic polarity of Christian versus Muslim Moor provided by the Crusades of Charlemagne to frame its rendition of goings-on at the poet's base, the court of Este in Ferrara, the *Furioso* uses 'anachronistic fictions of chivalric heroism' – material from the past – to 'temporarily elud[e] . . . imminent [present and future] threats'. Like Chaucer, Ariosto's courtly position was 'never entirely secure', and he was forced to serve as a diplomat more often than as a poet, which he resented. The need to placate powerful figures makes his depiction of court life ambiguous and multilayered,[55] but the forces challenging this way of life from without are equally destabilizing.

The security of Estense Ferrara, on which the poet's livelihood depended, was not the only thing under threat. The Quattrocento's aristocratic humanism, hitherto supported by the Italian peninsula's political balance of autonomous states, was rapidly giving way to conflict and internecine strife. The 'Italian crisis', precipitated by the French invasion in 1494, consisted of a volatile mix of external threat and internal conflicts. The Estense court was precariously placed amid this challenge to geographical and social boundaries, 'near the point of encounter between the shifting macro-forces of France, Spain, the Emperor, Venice, Milan, and the papacy'.[56]

The insomnia of the poem's protagonist reproduces this sense of spatial insecurity, where the duty to defend Christendom – or Italy and the Estense region, in the case of the poet's times – conflicts with vexing private matters. Driven sleepless with unrequited love, Orlando leaves the Christian camp at midnight to search for his beloved in a forest. He eventually arrives at a meadow to find, in the form of inscriptions carved on trees, traces of her love for his rival. Fifteen cantos and various adventures later in Book XXIII, he is still pursuing sleep, when, giving full expression to his grief in the safety of a nearby shepherd's house where the same inscriptions are to be found, he is told the story of the lovers who previously slept there. Despite the torments of his prior sleeplessness, Orlando leaps from his bed on discovering that he is seeking peace in the very place where his beloved betrayed him. In Canto XVII, the poet asks why the Spanish and the French are subjugating Italy instead of the pagan enemy, and the message is similar: the worst evils are unsettlingly close at hand.[57]

To the confusion of spatial coordinates should be added temporal over-determination: the poem shows a strong consciousness of warring definitions of time. Its historical moment has been identified as one of prophetic tension, in which current events that appeared portentous – the wars, 'the discovery of America . . . the Lutheran Reformation, the expansion of the Turks', imperial rivalries, 'the great planetary conjunction of 1524, and the sack of Rome' – were filtered through a mix of contemporary political propaganda and medieval theories about the Last Judgement.[58] The nostalgic frame of medieval chivalric romance, itself looking back to the time of earlier Crusades, is continually riven by references to present threats that generate anxiety about the future. A case in point is when, in Canto XVII, Pope Leo X (during whose reign the first and second editions of the *Furioso* appeared) is challenged to refuse to 'allow Italy to be swallowed up in sleep', and instead to 'defend [his] flock from [enemy] wolves'. Elsewhere the poem is true to its title and to the 'ever busy and noisy movement' and 'frantic agitation' that form 'the rule of law in [its] world'. While several characters suffer sleeplessness as a result of fleshly desire and torment, there are also several for whom sleep (as for Italy) is ill advised in the face of present threats.[59] It should be recalled that essential to the Crusades was authorization by the pope that participants 'would be entitled to "indulgences" . . . remissions of the time to be spent after death in purgatory'.[60] Inherent in the frame of the *Furioso* is a legacy of aggressively won time (shot through with uncertainties about the Last Judgement) meeting profound instability in the contemporaneous time to which the narrative speaks.

Insomnia is also rendered structurally in the poem by means of *entrelacement*. Inherited from Italian and French chivalric sources, this method requires narrative sequence to be 'interrupted, separated, and recombined' with other sequences, creating a peculiar suspense for the reader, who must follow several plot lines before returning to the point of 'disjunction'. The proliferating plot lines mimic the proliferation of anxieties characteristic of insomnia and create a self-contained, contradictory world not unlike the insomniac's self-referential obsession, while the deferral of resolution mimes the sleepless state. Ariosto's innovative use of *entrelacement* has been seen as a structural means of responding to the poem's historical moment. In this reading, the continual disruptions of the method become charged with subversive intent, as the 'celebration of popes and potentates' yields to direct admonitions such as that we have seen directed to Leo x.[61] While Orlando's leaping from his bed to a further bout of intolerable sleeplessness dramatizes the disjunctive effect of *entrelacement* on the listener and reader born of the deferral of resolution, the method's impact goes further. It underlines a structural problem affecting the aristocracy and its superiors, where a backward-looking desire for slumber was riven by revelations of its place amid changing events.

Early modern England, too, showed increased doubts regarding 'the human capacity to perceive life truly', as well as a weakening of the belief that worldly matters are divinely governed. While disturbed sleep is not uncommon in Shakespeare,[62] the tragedies *Julius Caesar* (1599) and *Macbeth* (1605–6) showcase insomnia directly preceding or following murder, where the latter is both a political act and an intervention into divine order. Steven Mullaney's work on the marginal location of Renaissance public theatres suggests that they were sites where liminality itself was dramatized, where what took place was 'a performance *of* the threshold, by which the horizon of community was made visible, the limits of . . . containment . . . made manifest'.[63] Sleeplessness, then, was fit material for Renaissance playwrights. It dramatizes in the body of the sufferer a question at the threshold of communal recognition – like the incircumscribable, but real, conflicts of Ariosto's Ferrara – for in this period insomnia was yet neither a disorder of the individual distinct from his or her context nor yet entirely a pathology.[64]

Political interpretation is not only part of the performance context but also the central subject of *Julius Caesar*. The play's key dramatic act, Caesar's murder at the hands of Brutus, is the result of a fraught reading of the political temperature of Caesar's reign: the question Brutus answers with Caesar's death is whether such an intervention is justified for the good of the people. Historical views of Caesar suggest the impossibility of reaching a definitive judgement on the matter of whether he was 'a hero or a tyrant', and 'Brutus a patriot or an assassin'.[65] Given this uncertainty, it is fitting that Brutus should suffer insomnia on the night before the murder (II.I). His unsettled state of mind is mirrored in the stormy weather, and his musings indicate the anxious, paranoid thought patterns of the sleepless:

> Since Cassius first did whet me against Caesar
> I have not slept.
> Between the acting of a dreadful thing
> And the first motion, all the interim is
> Like a phantasma or a hideous dream:
> The genius and the mortal instruments
> Are then in council, and the state of man,
> Like to a little kingdom, suffers then
> The nature of an insurrection. (II.I)

Critics note that *Julius Caesar* marks a turning point in Shakespeare's work, whence he completes his English history plays, with their focus on development, and poses more existential problems for his characters.[66] And the later years of Queen Elizabeth's reign (she died in 1603) 'allow parallels between herself and a tyrannical Caesar'. Andreas Mahler is perhaps closest to the mark in describing the late 1590s, 'with the end of Elizabeth's reign inadmissibly drawing near', as disallowing dramatic closure in either the terms of the 'reintegration' plot of comedy or the 'elimination' plot of tragedy. A state of suspense is augured. This, he suggests, is the Shakespearean moment of 'experimentation'. Arguing that all 'Shakespeare's plots are plots of restitution' in which individuals who misjudge their place and threaten communal stability are made to know it, Mahler identifies *Julius Caesar* as the first experimental tragedy, in which restitution is problematized by the fact that the community surrounding the hero, whether Brutus or Caesar, is itself a group of conspirators.[67]

The conspirators meet at night, and so starts the seed of the thought pattern given full rein with Brutus' insomnia. While Cassius finds it problematic that Caesar lords it over the brotherhood, since this implies a reduction in all men's status but his (1.2), Brutus finds no cause to unseat him. 'Brutus's dilemma lies in the fact that the event to be feared' – Caesar's tyranny – 'seems imminent, yet has not come'.[68] Thus, Brutus must resort to anxious imaginings about the future, playing tricks with time, as he does on the sleepless night before the murder:

> . . . He would be crowned:
> How that might change his nature, there's the question . . .
> And since the quarrel
> Will bear no colour for the thing he is,
> Fashion it thus: that what he is, augmented,
> Would run to these and these extremities. (II.1)

Both Macbeth and Brutus can be said to murder time, because both intervene in the political present to halt, in Brutus' case, and to expedite, in Macbeth's, an imagined future course of events. In *Julius Caesar*, time is murdered not only in the sense that Caesar himself has ordered time – he had set the clocks of Rome and, immediately prior to the events of the play, had set the date with calendrical reforms – but because Brutus has to break with the providential time that mandates rulers and 'authorize himself' to murder Caesar. He instantiates an insomnia-fuelled hiatus, an experiment with time. And this step into subjective, insomnia-driven time, which turns on the impact of events imagined on a sleepless, stormy night, events that may yet not happen, then gives rise to Antony's revenge. For in committing the murder, Brutus in turn becomes the 'cause of disorder' he imagined Caesar was. In this play, every attempt at restoring communal, divinely ordered time 'turns out to have been a step into subjectivity', the subjectivity that turns around itself in the obsessive thought tracks of the sleepless. '[T]he world's time' and individual time, 'cyclicity and linearity[,] no longer tally, they have lost their divine synchronization'.[69]

In *Macbeth* this lack of synchronization is more profound, revealing a fundamental inefficacy in language, in the agency of the central characters and in the realm of politics itself. Immediately after the murder of King Duncan that will make Macbeth king, he claims: 'Methought I heard a voice cry "Sleep no more! / Macbeth does murder sleep"',[70] and this sleepless mandate spreads, crying:

> . . . 'Sleep no more!' to all the house;
> 'Glamis hath murdered sleep, and therefore Cawdor

Shall sleep no more; Macbeth shall sleep no more'. (II.3)

The lack of attribution for this terrible voice – Lady Macbeth's question 'who was it that thus cried?' remains unanswered – is matched by the strange unnameability of the murder.[71] Yet this unnameability gives to the act a fearsome agency, for to name an event is to place it in time, within the order of words to which those who speak are subject. Macbeth's act violates this sense of communally efficacious time and, with it, the providential time that underwrites it, so that Macduff's cry 'O, horror, horror, horror! / Tongue nor heart cannot conceive nor name thee!' on discovering Duncan's corpse immediately becomes 'Most sacreligious murder hath broke ope / The Lord's anointed temple'.

The image of the broken temple suggests the Last Judgement, the end of time, when all souls are awakened, also invoked by Macduff when he calls Malcolm, Donalbain and Banquo to awake and 'see / The great doom's image!' The cycle by which day follows night is halted in its progress; the murder of the sleeping king breaks both the natural order of time and the divinely mandated order of royal succession.[72] Both generational and natural time ordinarily open onto an unseen, but expected future: the future king, the future daybreak. These two forms of oblivion – where continuity depends upon an act of trust, of not seeing – also inhere in the relation of sleep to night, in so far as that relation is a double darkness, an embodiment of trust in Providence.

Because it is itself unknowable, sleep carries the meaning of other unknowable things, yet in a safe way, for even when sleep is bad, we will awake from it, and when it is good, we know little of its workings. It is the saving double darkness of sleep (the night in which we sleep is dark, and sleep is dark to us) where sleep's unknowable relation to the darkness of night enables it to symbolize more threatening kinds of darkness, sleep as 'the death of each day's life' (II.3), for instance, which Macbeth has murdered. Generational and natural time have been confounded by prophetic time through his precipitous response to the witches' prophecy, and now he learns that the darkness built into the former kinds of time protects human beings from the higher stakes – the uncontainability – of the latter. He enters the wastelands of insomnia's demonically coded double darkness, the inverse of trust in providence or sleep's safe dying: absence of sleep, absence of the ability to forget and recover.

Thus the play's pairings are continually opening onto thirds that become unmanageable.[73] Whereas prior to the murder, ordained forms of time protected the characters from the anxiety-causing third of the trilogy past/present/future, now the future's fearsome capacity, indeed its agency, leaches into the present. By the same logic according to which, before the murder, Lady Macbeth felt 'the future in the instant' (1.6), and commanded her husband to act accordingly, now the future is all, as both Macbeths use the passive voice to speak of the murder and the train of events it has unleashed, in which their agency is swallowed: 'What's done cannot be undone', 'the wine of life is drawn' (v.1, 11.3).[74]

Alexander Leggatt describes this spreading inefficacy of agency as forming 'an anti-drama without actors in which things are done, but no one does them, things are said, but no one says them'.[75] It is a process equal to insomnia, where an uncontrollable mode of activity that ignores conscious directives – for instance, anxiety – takes over, usurping the relation of intentions to ends. In insomnia, we are brought to the end of our intentions, to their futility. And like insomnia, which makes us feel at once obsessed with our onward-rushing thoughts and yet at the same time insignificant – alone with our wakefulness, cut off from community – Macbeth's self-authored ambition has cancelled him out (11.2). He becomes an empty space at the heart of his realm, the nothing life now signifies, doubled in the figure of the 'poor player' he is for his subjects as well as for the audience of Shakespeare's play (v.5). By contrast, the act that ends insomnia is both a large and yet an act-less act, one that paradoxically forgets the future by enacting faith in it, by trusting it to be benign. Underplaying itself, sleep doubles darkness. The unseen future is laid to rest.

This requirement to trust intermediacy as a function, since sleep's benefits are gained at the price of our not knowing them, becomes increasingly vexed in the early modern period and, indeed, in the following centuries. Repeatedly we see intermediacy as the domain of warring forces, the diminishment of which reveals a void.[76] Those forces, as is usually the case when an unmanageable reality is threatening to undermine social relations – here, the sheer pace of change, soon to become global – would become increasingly polarized. As Donald Howard remarks, 'the fifteenth, sixteenth, and seventeenth centuries' in Europe 'were obsessed with death, with the vanity of earthly pursuits, with the mutability of the world itself',[77] yet people were involved in such mutable, death-tinged pursuits increasingly, not least in search of their own salvation. Increasingly, too, however, the rest of the world would be drawn into a conversation that, while bearing the name 'Enlightenment' in Europe and producing a downplaying of sleep's contract with darkness, would not rest from its own history easily.

Chapter Three

The Sleep of Reason

Perhaps no image better depicts the contradictory relationship between early modern Europeans and their nightly rest than Hendrik Goltzius's *The Sleepless Night of the Litigant*, an engraving from the 'Abuses of the Law' series. Dated 1597 and sixth in a series of eight, the image shows two mythical figures interfering with the litigant's rest. 'Restlessness' confronts him directly, while 'Anxiety' chases 'Sweet Sleep' from the room.[1] Seven of the eight prints include quotations from biblical wisdom literature, as does *The Sleepless Night*: 'But to the sinner he gives trouble and worry'; 'For they cannot sleep unless they have done wrong'; 'A man who neither day or night grants sleep to his eyes'; and 'For all his days are sorrow and his travail grief; even in the night his heart does not rest' (Ecclesiastes 2:26; Proverbs 4:16; Ecclesiastes 8:16; Ecclesiastes 2:23). The theme of worldly vanity with which Ecclesiastes opens – 'Vanity of vanities . . . All is vanity' (1:2) – was common in Dutch culture of the period, as were the contradictory messages concerning worldliness that run through the series as a whole. In portraying the litigant in the charge of Restlessness while the positive influence, Sweet Sleep, flees, *The Sleepless Night* indicates the specific mix of prosperity and anxiety that characterized the sixteenth- and seventeenth-century Dutch burgher class and made its existence one of negotiating contradiction.

Anxiety, central in the image, certainly had real-life sources. In *The Comedy of the Rich Man*, written by Goltzius's humanist teacher Dirck Volkertszoon Coornhert, 'Conscience and Scriptural Wisdom' contend for a rich man's soul with the character

Hendrik Goltzius, *The Sleepless Night of the Litigant*, 1597, etching from the series 'The Abuses of the Law'.

Overvloed, who complains that although she eats and drinks of the best, she is 'heartsick and troubled'. As Simon Schama observes, the situation of the Dutch in Baroque Europe was unique by virtue of its precocity. Because of its fortunate position as the centre of naval trade in the late sixteenth and seventeenth centuries, the Netherlands had become 'a world empire in two generations'. Being ahead of the rest of the world in terms of prosperity, but founded on humanist principles of sensual restraint, the Dutch, in Schama's view, led 'a double-life . . . fraught with agonies of anxiety, guilt, and self-recrimination as they tried to reconcile the available with the acceptable'.[2]

The litigant's sleeping chamber indicates that he belongs to the burgher class, and the 'Abuses' are in the style of the emblem books then in circulation, which contained woodcuts or etchings combined with proverbs, maxims and instructions for social behaviour. These and related moralizing literature turn on the paradox that afflicted the burgher. A balanced life is recommended, and it is this prudent negotiation 'between privation and excess' that will lead to health and happiness. In his *Schat der Gezontheyt* (Treasure of Health) of 1656, the popular physician and author Jan van Beverwijck evoked ancient prescriptions of dietary moderation as the way to avoid physical incapacities, including insomnia.[3] Biblical wisdom literature, too, including Ecclesiastes, taught that sleeplessness arose from anxiety, and that anxiety came from putting faith in material things. But what was one to do when one's faith itself generated ever-increasing riches?

The self-image of the Dutch burgher class as 'plain-speaking, soberly dressed and God-fearing' was informed by the Calvinist ideal, strong in the sixteenth- and seventeenth-century Netherlands, of perpetual striving for sanctification. Calvin and his followers believed that only an elect few were predestined to escape, in the afterlife, the 'absolute depravity' of human beings, and that human activity could have no influence on divine decision. To compensate for anxiety over predestination, it became a 'duty . . . for believers to *consider* themselves among the elect few' and, through their works, to demonstrate their predestined status as an enaction of the faith that came from divinely granted grace. As Max Weber put it, '*Restless work in a vocational calling* was recommended as the best possible means to *acquire* the self-confidence that one belonged among the elect. Work, and work alone, banishes religious doubt and gives certainty of one's status among the saved.'[4]

Despite itself, however, a Calvinist world view generates prosperity, since diligence, which produces wealth, is the only reliable sign of predestination, and keeping money in circulation is preferable to retaining it.[5] But frugality of lifestyle combined with judicious spending is also the best way to generate wealth, which in turn leads to increased anxiety. In other images in the 'Abuses' series, the expense of litigation is shown such that, as in *The Sleepless Night*, wealth places the burgher at the heart of a vicious circle. The Netherlands' position as originator of the world's first international economy placed it at the heart not only of paradoxes such as that between conscience and complacency, but also of a form of exponential increase that can be mapped directly onto the structure and symptomatology of insomnia.

When sleep becomes particularly necessary, anxiety may find an inroad and, once felt, makes sleep harder to find, as anyone who has suffered insomnia can attest. Anxieties may then proliferate, taking on substance while forming a network of invisibly interlocking claims. The would-be sleeper tends to resist awareness of this anxious labour, well aware that it interferes with sleep. Yet worry's tendency to pick up both genuine and incidental causes and lines of argument means that the anxiety work that is resisted may grow more powerful to the extent that its networks are complex, invisible and seemingly arbitrarily connected. A split occurs such that the sleepless individual's unavoidable desire to reach sleep seems incompatible with recognizing the operation of the thought processes that forbid it.

This scenario is very close to the economic situation of the seventeenth-century Netherlands, where the invisibly dynamic networks of anxious thoughts equated with the increasingly complex trade networks that the nation pioneered and in which it participated. It was not only circularity and increase that the emergent international economy shared with insomnia, however. It shared a particular relation to historical cause as well, where the activity generated by the cause made it impossible to see how to resolve it. The source of the mind-split resulting in the cause of sleepless anxiety being hidden *by* the desire for sleep – just as the Calvinist drive to prosperity was hidden by the need to prove elected status – belongs further back, with the Protestant Reformation. Like the anxiety-causing times that produce both a greater than usual need for sleep along with the thought patterns that work against it, the Reformation made it impossible for Dutch burghers to see that the conundrum they faced was caused by it. It was impossible to recognize what had been gained from having human overseers – in the form of the one true Church and her priests – in place, that is, until this structure had been challenged and, as in the Netherlands, largely dismantled.

Where the pre-Reformation European Church saw signs of God's influence in human matters everywhere visible throughout creation,[6] the post-Reformation – and especially the Calvinist – world view posited a split between divine and human on the matter of signs of salvation, whereby nothing except the faith required for continued striving was to be trusted. Calvinism required the believer to take on two mutually exclusive roles at once: the striving sinner ignorant of God's plan regarding his or her eternal destiny, and the faithful believer whose trust in salvation provided rights to eternal bliss. But the split between these two roles required a mediator, lest unbearable anxiety fill the void left by the departure of priestly representatives of a more holistic view of the believer's future.

Ironically, in view of the fact that disgust with corruption and greed in the late medieval Church helped fuel the Reformation, the middlemen of the medieval Church were eventually replaced by the middlemen of post-Reformation commerce. And as European modernity proceeded, more and more daily operations came to depend upon invisible, but materially crucial, intermediaries: distant buyers of the objects of global trade, those to whom they sold the objects, and those who estimated the contributions of those buyers. Greater trust became necessary. Shared by sleep and trade is participation on an invisible level within a system or economy – for sleep, that of the body – where that system is itself part of other networks (chemical, seasonal, political) at work in the world. Both systems function only because participants demonstrate faith in the network or allow a darkness to fall on some part of reason. The wealth-generating split consciousness enacted by the Dutch burgher thus signals an important component of modernity, a precursor not only of the division of spheres that would characterize the Enlightenment but also of the reliance on invisible networks required in so many areas of contemporary life.

European split consciousness enabled by dark, increasingly distant mediation was given its most salient form in the Atlantic slave trade. Several aspects of Atlantic slavery are of relevance to insomnia. The devaluing of darkness involved where black bodies generated consumer products for far-off white markets was doubled when a number of those products – namely tea, coffee, sugar and tobacco – were stimulants, the accelerative or sleep-forestalling properties of which were recognized, but not, in the seventeenth and eighteenth centuries, well understood. Further, the measure of risk and anxiety intrinsic to modern systems of credit and speculation was first practised on a large scale in England and internationally through the trade. This means that the uncertainty created by debt – on a much larger scale, but not so different in kind from the uncertainty about the future that troubled our sleepless litigant – was generalized throughout the population.[7]

There had been many independent economies in the world before 1500, some linked by trade, but a worldwide exchange network did not appear until 1800. The Dutch played a significant role in establishing the early forms of this network through their two joint-stock companies, the United East India Company and the West India Company. In fact, the Dutch themselves became colonial mediators, assisting first Portugal and then England in settling slave-labour colonies. The English had become the leading European slave carriers by 1670 and held this position until 1807, when slave-carrying was outlawed by Parliament.[8] Because of the significance of slaving practices for the emergence and influence of European modernity, which itself created conditions amenable to sleeplessness, the rest of this chapter will focus on the situation in England in the seventeenth and eighteenth centuries. To this place and time we owe not only several causes of contemporary sleep deprivation, but, more importantly, the decline in nocturnal literacy that compromises our ability to recognize and ameliorate that state.

Like sleep in everyday life, enslaved African labour was vital to the success of the British economy in the seventeenth and eighteenth centuries, in such a way that its contribution was masked by forward speculation. The early industrialization of England, where specialization of manufacturing created a workforce 'capable of supporting increasing levels of trade with distant markets', and where paid wages enabled families low on the social scale to afford tropical groceries from the Americas and Asia – including, especially, sugar – helped support the trade.[9] The plantations were needed by Europeans for their economic well-being, but the plantations also needed European imports. Colonists exported tropical goods that helped transform the tastes of the European metropolis and imported staples they themselves, with land given over to export crops, could not produce. The crucial mediator of this mutual dependency was the enslaved black body. It was the base matter for financial speculation. Merchants who developed expertise in the management of credit underwrote the Atlantic trade. And the growth of a credit economy required, and produced, the imagination of a new social form: forward speculation in the face of risky sea voyages sustaining imports and exports that had become essential.[10]

Both coffee and sugar produce effects in the body that mirror their role in international trade as facilitated by the emergent British Empire. 'By the mid-seventeenth century' in England, thanks to its sugar plantations in Barbados, 'slave-grown sugar had entered the popular and mercantile imagination as the source of legendary wealth', and, along with tobacco, was 'quickly established' as a commodity purchasable by the poor on a daily basis. Refined sugar, we now know, enters the bloodstream of the consumer rapidly, producing swift energy release and a correspondingly quick demand for more of it. Coffee, for its part, speeds perceptions, and there is evidence that it may also lead people to believe their performance is more efficient than it is, because caffeine causes nerve cells to behave as if they are not fatigued when they are.[11] As a form of 'indirect stimula[tion]' with an accelerative effect that alters perceptions, coffee is a kind of credit-speculation agent in the body. And like sugar, coffee played an integral part in the growth of a credit society. Steven Topik notes that it was an unusual commodity in being produced for exchange rather than for use soon after gaining favour in the fifteenth century. That promissory perceptions on the level of biochemical process were matched by similar behaviours on the level of the national economy is clear from the way the stock exchange and the coffee house, as public institutions, arose together, not only in the same period, but often sharing the same physical space.[12]

Because they linked producers with consumers in Europe, Africa, Asia and the Americas into an early form of world economy, it has been claimed that seventeenth-century merchants who did business from the London Exchange and its nearby coffee house can be seen as 'precursors of modern multinational corporations'. In reality, of course, their work was much more haphazard than that parallel suggests. Merchants worked in partnerships and associations that

> formed and reformed for particular voyages and ventures.
> They collected, gathered, and processed information;

drew upon their talents, education, experience, and repu-
tations; connected their partners to relatives and their religious and business networks in distant ports; all in order to
operate together, and with greater chances of success, in
what was an extremely uncertain environment for international business.[13]

'Continuous chains of credit' were necessary for the many
tasks involved in global trading: the collection of cargo, the
maintaining of ships and hiring of crews, the delivery of slaves,
and buying and selling in distant markets. There are shades of
the exponential aspect of the litigant's nightly predicament here,
but also something new: a growing distance between the financial
results of speculation and the risky maritime ventures it underwrote. In 1694 the Bank of England, a private corporation, took
responsibility for the government's debt, and its notes soon became
currency as 'reserve assets' supplementing bullion. As the labour of
enslaved bodies increased in volume to satisfy consumer demand
for tropical products, the forms of wealth in circulation in Europe
became both more complex and more ephemeral. J.G.A. Pocock
points out that

[t]he National Debt was a device permitting English society to maintain and expand its government, army and trade
by mortgaging its revenues in the future. This was suffi-
cient to make it the paradigm of a society now living to an
increasing degree by speculation and credit . . . by men's
expectations of one another's capacity for future action
and performance.[14]

And although debt was to become a fact of life, by the close of the
seventeenth century there was disquiet at the fact that professional
armies increasingly protected ordinary citizens, a move that, since
self-defence was traditionally charged to each person, was seen as
potentially corrupting. Citizens effectively paid substitutes to
defend them while 'enjoy[ing] the benefits of an expanding culture and accumulat[ing] further riches as the means to further
enjoyment':

Not only must the speculative society maintain and govern itself by perpetually gambling on its own wish-fulfillments . . . but every man was judged and governed, at every moment, by other men's opinion of the probability that not he alone, but generations yet unborn, would be able and willing to repay their debts at some future date which might never arrive. Men, it seemed, were governed by opinion, and by opinion as to whether certain governing fantasies would ever become realized.[15]

It is worth noting the specific structural relations governing this process. These are of most relevance to insomnia, above all a structural event involving a stoppage at the border of two dynamic states, and a malady that became more widespread at exactly this juncture in European history. Money was increasingly borrowed to support the navy, which in turn supported British trade interests, and the emergent British Empire was an empire of the seas. The long and risky sea voyages required for trafficking in slaves were doubly disavowed: once by investment, but, prior to this, as the traumatic event the Middle Passage – the harshest and longest part of the Atlantic journey – was for slaves. Paul Gilroy claims the catastrophic Middle Passage as the black equivalent of Europe's dreams of 'revolutionary transformation'.[16] And just as revolution redefined the participatory parameters of the societies in which it occurred, so the Atlantic slave journey created new trading patterns – import and export, and forward investment – that fuelled the British, and eventually the American, economy. A process that, in the litigant's time, was enacted by the labour of each person – the cause of anxiety hidden by the continued need to prove predestination – was now split between peoples, and the cause, once again, was hidden by the process to which it had given rise.

We can now note further parallels between slave-trafficking and insomnia. There is border crossing that is, or is regarded as, essential, like the passage from waking to sleep, and, coupled with the desire for instant gratification, there is anxiety about outcomes, the pressing necessity of thinking ahead. Recall our chief observation about insomnia: that it is the embodiment of a double negative, the absence of unconsciousness. It is thus a doubled instance of something – lack of consciousness – that is naturally opaque to understanding, but on which we nonetheless depend. Profiting from slavery works similarly. Slavers and plantation owners effectively doubled or brought into concrete being the barbarity they saw in African people through the act of enslaving them, producing a doubled darkness or double negative in relation to the supposedly enlightening properties of civilization.[17] The doubling was entirely a production of Enlightenment process, which effectively recreated darkness in mythical forms. The growth of the new European metropolis, seen as a forward step, was fuelled by a backward one: enslavement. But once the barbarity of slave-owning and profiting from slavery disappeared within the civilizing mandate of the emergent British Empire, barbarity resided with the slave whose dark skin was the remainder of this process and the visible rationale for his or her enslavement. And because slavery, by definition, is labour without agency, or labour on behalf of the agency of others, the only kind attributable to the slave is the desire for revolt.

We begin to see that it is difficult to discover the exact contribution to European society of the regressive step of barbarity once it is attributed to black bodies, but also that the fact of this historical displacement twists dark contributions into something negative, and not only for white Europeans. Something measureless comes into play on the back of dark bodies as the result of enlightened calculation – or, better, as the result of serving as calculation's material cause – and this measureless something's darkness is, in turn, feared. Insomnia today cannot simply be disconnected from these historical conditions, where in the popular mind it is more difficult to credit dark activities, such as sleep, with positive contributions to well-being than to mystify and fear them. As William Dement's catch-phrase 'The brain never sleeps!' indicates, the fact that sleep's activity is dark to consciousness is routinely disavowed in Western culture.[18] Darkness is more active than white Westerners can either know or acknowledge, and darkest of all is the extent and nature of its contribution to our past.

Despite functional disavowal, there were numerous signs of the anxieties mobilized by slavery and its correlative, the empire, in the late seventeenth and eighteenth centuries. The fluctuations of public credit were famously feminized by the Augustan commentators

An anonymous painting of a London coffee-house, c. 1700.

Daniel Defoe and Joseph Addison as a reflection of the fact that society *was* increasingly governed by opinion rather than reason, or reason as 'the servant of the passions', including the fears that increased military spending. Coffee is an intriguing commodity in this respect, because as well as encouraging speedier thinking and mimicking the dark processes of the speculative empire, it was consciously associated with sobriety and thus with the figure of the merchant as a calculating man of business who was *not* swayed by the fickle tastes of the day. Wolfgang Schivelbusch goes so far as to claim that coffee 'achieved chemically and pharmacologically', in the body, 'what rationalism and the Protestant ethic sought to fulfill spiritually and ideologically' in the body politic. That is, it stimulated energy in ways both pleasurable and useful.[19]

At its point of English origin in the 1650s, the coffee house was amenable to London's Puritan authorities, who were set against the '"growing evil" of taverns and ale houses'. The first London coffee house inhabited a 'network of lanes and alleys' impassable to all but foot traffic, its spatial compression intensified by the 'fanatical environment of the Interregnum and Restoration'. Each disruption to civic order – and in 1659 the English republic entertained seven distinct governments – gave rise to a flood of publications that were read and debated in the coffee houses. Thus it was not only coffee that kept patrons awake at night; it was also the drama of political agitation and of news. By the late seventeenth century, England had thousands of coffee houses, and – because they fostered the circulation and discussion of printed material reaching a wide readership (pamphlets and books as well as news-sheets) – they became associated with the growing power of public opinion. Charles II's attempt to have them closed in 1675 having failed, the government sought to use them for 'contradictory purposes': sending spies into them, on the watch for seditious plots against the king.[20]

It was thought that, in earlier times, Muslim Sufi brotherhoods in the Near East had used coffee to keep them awake for their spiritual exercises, and, accordingly, various health benefits were claimed for it. But while the coffee houses were defended by their supporters as fostering a new political climate characterized by reason and public debate, coffee itself was also part of a pharmacological literature that both treated it as a powerful drug and mapped its functions onto political concerns about England's participation in world markets.[21] Significant here is William Harvey's discovery of the circulation of the blood in 1628, which made for a 'refurbishment of the ancient analogy between the body politic and the body natural'. Where previously it had been thought that 'a formed organ, usually the heart' was the most important component of the biological organism, Harvey performed a quantitative analysis of blood flow to prove that blood recirculated through the body rather than being continually manufactured. By analogy with trade – a key way in which the discovery was interpreted – this kept London, like the king and God himself, in place as central to the world economy – the heart of the realm and the country – but made the city newly dependent on the circulation of goods and money (or blood and nutrients). The fact that money was recirculated rather than being continually created meant that England would reap the perils, as well as the benefits, of the commercial activities it set in train.[22]

As a drug-food, coffee was seen as representing the unpredictability as well as the unavoidability of the market, and its potential for transforming tastes into dependencies. While Harveian circulation did not displace the older view of the body as a system balanced by the operations of the humours – a particular imbalance of which was seen to cause insomnia – Harvey himself argued that 'the entire body participated in this economy', rather than depending on a hierarchy of functions and parts. Similar mechanist or potentially mechanist discoveries such as the chemist Robert Boyle's conclusion that the universe consisted of matter in constant motion suggested that human physiology is 'never at rest', but continually subject to systemic fluctuations.[23] Volatility also belonged to the humoural understanding of the body, but as a principle of the erratic, non-duplicative nature of bodily reality. Now volatility began to be seen as a governing principle of human interactions, along with a speeding of perceptions and investment. Combined with mechanistic understandings of human process, the newly observed volatility in human beings and in the market was a deeply unsettling discovery, for it meant that unpredictability itself might be systemic. Such a contradiction in terms helps to explain why insomnia, too, as a response to latent conflicts, increased significantly in this period. The market, like coffee, stimulated spending – or thinking and talking in the coffee houses – in such a way that there was no way to temper resulting anxieties without the risk of producing more.

In Canto III of Alexander Pope's *The Rape of the Lock* (1712), it is coffee that inspires the Baron to steal a lock of Belinda's hair, while it clouds the judgement of the politician, possibly by inducing sleepiness the next day. Roger Schmidt points out that 'insomnia saturates [Pope's] work', and that he typically wrote in bed in the early hours, his wakefulness no doubt fuelled by the lively nocturnal action in the coffee houses he frequented, as was also the case with Samuel Johnson. Canto IV of the *Rape* takes the reader to the Cave of Spleen, an externalization of 'the English malady', a state of melancholy thought to have been produced by a surfeit of the humour of black bile. Spleen was also associated with general bad humour or irascibility, however, such as might inevitably result from lack of sleep. In fact, if one takes Schmidt's contention that a demise in positive attitudes to sleep began with the advent of the coffee house in English culture, then numerous other features of eighteenth-century life and thought become explicable.[24]

One such set of concerns appears at first to be paradoxical. Boredom, or dullness, in response to the excitement of the times became a fully recognized malady in the mid-eighteenth century. Once a general decline in the quality and quantity of sleep is factored in, the paradox makes more sense. Pope's *Dunciads* (1728–43) take aim at 'dulness', a distraction-induced state of mind that, he contends, leads men to become enthusiasts of many kinds of knowledge while being truly knowledgeable about none.[25] Such was the state of mind induced by popular-press-fuelled, gossip-laden conversations in the coffee houses late at night, or so it seemed to Pope and others; distraction, or poor concentration, is an inevitable result of compromised rest. Boredom also troubled Johnson and his biographer James Boswell, and the fact that it troubled them is significant, for it indicates the presence of submerged but pressing conflicts. Boredom is not the same as having a mind happily free of thoughts, but is, like insomnia, akin to having a mental itch one cannot reach, a state of unconscious enjoyment one can imagine, but cannot get to. And insomnia, while frequently companioned by anxiety and conflict, is reliably an experience of boredom.

Boredom is also like insomnia because it is a double negative, the absence not, as in insomnia, of actual unconsciousness, but of that which is wished for without being had: desire.[26] And a double negative, when it does not, as in the case of the love between Krishna and Radha considered earlier, produce a postitive, may instead signal something positively awry. The pathological double negative of sleeplessness indicates the pathology that may inhere in a more everyday version, where overstimulation of the mind and senses imperils the ability to discover what one wants, to recognize and direct desire. Insomnia's connection with boredom is thus a sign of the havoc that may be caused by the spectre of excessive satisfaction, a condition rampant in today's consumer culture, where the injunction to enjoy ourselves unstintingly is no longer primarily generated by individuals themselves, but is a cultural requirement difficult to ignore.[27] Insomnia's increase in the English eighteenth century in parallel with the emergence of boredom may also indicate the unconscious and unintended pressures of a nascent consumer society, the need people have for some things *not* to be available all of the time, or for occasions of release from the perception that they are.

Boredom, like insomnia, was also made worse by contemporaneous strictures against it, however. If space to imagine desire is what one needs, its refusal will weaken one's ties to a meaningful life yet further. James Harris, in 1744, published 'On Happiness' as one of his *Three Treatises*, and while he claimed that 'Satiety' caused 'Indifference' or boredom, he also argued that only a life of 'constant effort' could generate happiness.[28] Here we again meet the problem the Protestant work ethic set in train: most feared are goods and activities that are not brought about by one's own efforts. But increased leisure possibilities for all are exactly what a society of self-directed labour creates. Hence, the problem of what to do with the opportunities one has brought about when one's world view dictates that they are not to be entered into. Characterized by flatness, stupor and disengagement, boredom – the living product of this conflict – papers it over, just as coffee and sugar consumption did the traffic in slaves. Simultaneously, however, eighteenth-century boredom, a withdrawal of communicative energy, drew attention to itself by its oddness and apparent inexplicability within a citizenry increasingly publicly engaged. The frequent presence of the opposite frame of mind from what is promised by an emergent consumer society signals something problematic at its heart.

Like Harris, David Fordyce also claimed that 'the highest virtue' was brought about by the passions being kept awake. Boredom was regarded as a sign of 'moral failure' and, disastrously from the point of view of insomnia, was equated with what was seen as an excessive desire for sleep rather than a process of securing the rest the overstimulated mind and body might require. William Law's *A Serious Call to a Devout and Holy Life* (1728), which considerably influenced Johnson, makes sleep into the equivalent of a moral disorder:

> He . . . that chooses to enlarge the slothful indulgence of sleep, rather than be early at his devotions to God, chooses the dullest refreshment of the body, before the highest, noblest employment of the soul; he chooses that state which is a reproach to mere animals, rather than that exercise which is the glory of Angels . . . For sleep . . . gives a softness and idleness to all our tempers, and makes us unable to relish any thing but what suits with an idle state of mind.[29]

The American Evangelical movement known as the Great Awakening, a series of revivals that spread throughout the colonies, was the transatlantic cousin of this sort of personal morality. While the Awakening emphasized the perils of sleep both metaphorical and literal, it solved the problem of poor motivation by 'hammer[ing] religion into the imperial framework of commerce', as one historian puts it. Its leading proponent, the English preacher George Whitefield, claimed that 'devotion and business . . . go hand in hand', and initiated his first mission by 'hawking a shipload of manufactured goods' from England.[30] He marketed himself aggressively in the colonial press, which was on the point of significant expansion, so that he offered publishers 'rich returns' while he went about his own branch of business, saving souls and rendering them more profitable, in both spiritual and worldly senses. The Awakeners described salvation in market terms as a mutually beneficial transaction in a climate where the range of varieties of Christianity on offer was increasing. Precursor of the alliance between (corporate) wealth and (conservative) religion in today's United States, the Awakening offered a practical way to solve the historical contradiction of work-produced riches one was not supposed to love.

A notable aspect of this new climate, in England, too, was a 'shift from communal to personal interests'.[31] An unhappy side effect, however, was that cultural or structural conditions over which the individual may have had little influence were rendered the responsibilty of the individual. Difficulty getting up in the morning came in for repeated condemnation, although the causes were societal as much as individual, including, not least, the widespread Augustan tendency to rail against sleeping late itself. Putting pressure on oneself to sleep properly so as not to rise late almost guarantees insomnia. Johnson was his own worst enemy in this regard. As Boswell notes in his *Life*:

> He charges himself with not rising early enough; yet he mentions what was surely a sufficient excuse for this . . . 'One great hindrance is want of rest; my nocturnal complaints grow less troublesome towards morning; and I am tempted to repair the deficiencies of the night'. Alas! How

hard it would be if this indulgence were to be imputed to a sick man as a crime.[32]

The deep shame that attended the fact of sleeping late among metropolitans with some degree of wealth and leisure in the English eighteenth century shows them to have been caught in the cycle in which insomnia hides its cause. While late nights and stimulants were admitted to be double-edged swords, the value of unconscious labour itself – sleep – went unrecognized, and guilty concealment of the need for more sleep decreased that value's chances of recognition. Remarking that seventeenth-century poetry 'does not concern itself with the social surface in the way eighteenth-century verse does', Schmidt observes that one also does not find scenes of people actively 'struggling with sleepiness'. The 'lazy chair' and the 'easy chair', both of which were born in the eighteenth century, speak to both concerns. They are the first European chairs to have rounded rather than straight backs, which facilitate daytime napping and dozing. The Queen Anne wing chair, furthermore, evolved from a 'sleeping chair', but went a step further in the concern for appearances: its rounded shape facilitates napping while the wings hide the fact that one is doing so. Similarly, in a 1778 letter to Boswell, Johnson gives the following advice: 'When any fit of anxiety, or gloominess, or perversion of mind, lays hold upon you, make it a rule not to publish it by complaints, but exert your whole care to hide it; by endeavouring to hide it, you will drive it away. Be always busy.' Yet in the same letter he admits: '[M]y health is not restored, my nights are restless and tedious', without registering the correlation between a dissembling, conflicted busyness and an inability to sleep.[33]

Patricia Meyer Spacks notes that both boredom and depression, from which Johnson suffered, 'involve the horror of experienced helplessness'. Insomnia, too, is such an experience: one must perform helplessness as trust in order to fall asleep, and when one cannot, one is helpless in the face of the need to yield to helplessness. Johnson's writings show him to have been vexed by a desire for belief in divine purpose – for someone to be helpless before and to trust in – while at the same time fleeing perpetual doubt through busyness, a condition Boswell tellingly named 'perpetual vigilance'.

Another critic claims that Johnson 'is so much a sceptic that he will not repose even on the unrepose of scepticism', a state of mind that sounds like a recipe for insomnia. And while associated by others, and associating himself, with intellectual mastery, dialectical tension or inconclusiveness equally characterize Johnson's thinking. Indeed, the periodical essay itself, one of the English eighteenth century's – and Johnson's – favourite forms, is uniquely fitted to the practice of inconclusiveness, one-off attempts at a topic that need not be definitive, but that may produce further inconclusive attempts.[34] Given the contemporaneous concern with distraction, it may also have been the natural form for a metropolitan class of authors continually deprived of sleep.

But how were these swift and thoroughgoing social changes registered in the countryside? Were there equivalent or even more turbulent changes there? Rural Britain was far from sleepy in the eighteenth century, and the following chapter will take up the question of sleeplessness caused by new relations between human beings and nature – and not only in England – in greater depth. For now, though, let us consider the works of two women from opposite ends of the social spectrum to close our survey of England up until mid-century. Anne Finch, Countess of Winchilsea, published 'A Nocturnal Reverie' in 1713, while in exile in the countryside of Kent. As maid of honour to Mary of Modena, wife of the Duke of York, she had previously been one of a group of literary women in the court of Charles II, marrying Heneage Finch in 1684. After the Duke became James II and was deposed in 1689, the Finches refused to swear allegiance to the new sovereigns, eventually settling on Heneage's nephew's estate at Eastwell, where Anne maintained some literary and social connections.[35]

'A Nocturnal Reverie' is not the only poem in which Finch depicts insomnia, but it is the only one in which she renders it positively. One of the reference points for the 'Reverie' as an insomniac text is Milton's 1631 poem 'Il Penseroso', which uses a string of 'or' clauses to convey the effect of the sleepless mind swiftly turning. Both poems marked out new territory for poetic engagement. Where Virgilian pastoral takes evening as marking the limit of human activity, Milton, in 'Il Penseroso' and the later *Paradise Lost*, makes night into a place of activity. In *Paradise Lost* Eve's nocturnal curiosity is aligned with the tempting voice of Satan, but the speaker of 'Il Penseroso' chooses night as a time of study.[36]

Finch's poem, however, while responding to Milton, differs from both Milton poems. Where Milton's 'or's indicate the sped-up pace of the mind at night, Finch's poem inhabits one long, unbroken subordinate clause, beginning: 'In such a Night, when every louder Wind/Is to its distant Cavern safe confin'd', and sustaining its nocturnal premise through more resonances of natural and human activity than I have space to chart here. The experience of nature is rendered through a number of kinds of time that overlay rather than conflict with each other – present time, historical and mythic time, and 'the eternal time of religious meditation' – as well as awakening the reader's senses to the sights, sounds and smells that are available to the quiet inhabitant of the rural night world. Then, four lines from the close the speaker states: 'In such a Night let Me Abroad remain,/Till Morning breaks, and All's confus'd again.'[37] The effect is to re-route the natural environment of Eve's confusion from the night to the daytime, as well as to sustain as long as possible the mood of alertly quiescent observation – a mood perhaps only possible at night – carefully built up in the course of the poem.

Calling the poem a 'reverie' places a positive spin on insomnia by *not* emphasizing the struggle to sleep of the melancholy or spleen-affected speaker, or making the sleepless frame of mind as distant from the natural night-world as that of the thinker in Il Penseroso's tower. Christopher Miller points out that John Locke, in *An Essay Concerning Human Understanding* (1690), distinguished reverie from both recollection and contemplation as a peculiarly interim state for which the English language 'scarce has a name'. The speaker of 'A Nocturnal Reverie' is neither 'wide-awake' nor dozing, but Finch organizes what she observes 'with a lucid syntax of wakeful observation', and in this way 'makes the best of her own insomnia'.[38]

There is no chance of happily wakeful dreaming in Mary Collier's 'The Woman's Labour', however, and the poem itself gives the reason why. Published in 1739, Collier's poem responds to the work of another rural working-class poet, Stephen Duck, whose 'The Thresher's Labour' had appeared previously and which she had committed to memory. Duck was, like Collier, caught in contradictions. He educated himself late at night or between work breaks and eventually attracted aristocratic patronage, although this seems to have been a mixed blessing. 'The Thresher's Labour' begins in a countryside altered by capitalism, a world E. P. Thompson famously described as having shifted from an earlier 'task-oriented' – and worker-oriented – experience of time to that of time as measured by an employer. In the new temporality, '[t]ime is . . . currency: it is not passed but spent'.39 Finch's sense of several kinds of time cohabiting within and enriching the present moment is no longer possible, even to the extent it might once have been for rural labourers.

While Duck's poem details the disheartening experience of the thresher's time belonging to the employer, only daytime labour makes an appearance in his poem, and home is a place to return to, tired from work. Collier's poem, by contrast, consists of more than one homecoming from the same fields of labour, but each portends a new round of work, either lasting long into the night or beginning with a midnight early rising. The first heralds work on behalf of husbands, while the second – women workers having taken infants into the field either to assist or be attended to – is taken up with attendance on both children and husbands. Sleep is curtailed at both ends of the night, as the winter work of 'charring' (washing) involves getting up in the middle of it ('When bright *Orion* glitters in the skies') in order to complete the task before dawn. Collier uses what John Goodridge calls 'a piece of disharmony' not present in the male-authored rural labour poems he studies, by having the early women workers locked out of their workplace because the maid, 'quite tir'd with Work the day before,/O'ercome with sleep',40 fails to open it. The message: women of the same class suffer worse sleep deprivation than men.

The sleeplessness of Collier and the women who work with her is, unlike Finch's, not natural, but it is necessary. Indeed, the 'Mistress' who issues repeated commands in Collier's poem might have been Anne Finch if she had lived in Hampshire a few decades later. Night is continually 'com[ing] on' in Collier's poem ('Like you when threshing, we a Watch must keep;/Our Wort [ale being brewed] boils over if we dare to sleep' [234]), but there is hardly ever any *'Time to dream'* (134) – that is, to sleep. This means that work, or time as money, has so intruded into private life that such sleep as there is is likely to be of poor quality, semi-watchful. But not having time to dream also suggests that 'there is no utopian potential' for inhabiting the night as Finch does, for 'imagining that things might be otherwise'.[41] Where Finch is able to find in nature an imaginative extension of her own poetic reverie, a mode of quiet nocturnal conversation, the incessant rhythm with which day follows night offers no such respite to Collier's women, for whom unsought insomnia could not possibly be helpful.

Evening was associated with lyricism in the eighteenth century because, like the darkness, poetic labour is invisible work, often begun when others' tasks have ended, and so to write a hymn to evening was also to claim one's vocation as a poet. But this understanding of evening depends upon its status as a time of transition, as a nocturnal world fundamentally different from the day begins its reign. And the world Collier's women inhabited shares with our own the elision of this temporal point of changeover. 'When Night comes on . . ./that, alas! does but increase our Grief' (188–9) could serve as a mantra for those working double, and triple, shifts worldwide.[42]

In the following chapter we will consider others for whom sleep was a sometime luxury: soldiers, painters and hysterics among them. It is the dark night of empire to which Collier's endless round bears witness that we will find ourselves tracking, and this night, with its roots in the forgetting of laborious mediation, will face the consequences of that forgetting in increasingly violent, invigilating forms.

Chapter Four
The Night of Empire

From 1750 to 1900, world events began to speed up noticeably. The industrialization of Britain and its role as leader of a prosperous international empire, the invention of the railway, telegraph and telephone, of motion-picture film, and the growth in popularity of clocks and watches all seemed to bear out the view that human society was progressing on its enlightened course. Yet the period was also riven with conflicts, most of which centred on the question of the pace and nature of social change and drew attention to its unforeseen, darker aspects. It was in this period that darkness was associated with the forces of political revolution as ordinary people awoke to the realities of systemic exploitation. While the French were bringing down their monarchy, in Britain impoverished rural workers and craftspeople were engaging in rioting, machine-breaking and poaching game at night in attempts to ensure their livelihoods.[1] Britain lost its American colonies, and the Americans went on to deliver a society in which work and wakefulness would become central to an unprecedented degree. Japan adopted calendrical reforms that ushered in its westernization, a process that did not go unchallenged.

What those challenges revealed – and this claim will form the central argument of this chapter – is that the Western requirement that the present serve a bright, progressively oriented future involved not only the consigning of the past to darkness but also a disavowal of the dark processes of modernity. So it should come as no surprise that the period led to an increase in varieties of insomnia. In insomnia, we experience one kind of darkness, that of not knowing when sleep will arrive, as a barrier to our reaching sleep, the longed-for darkness that pre-dates modernity. But the processes and states valued in modernity – rational thinking, the present moment and planning for the future – are also, in their submerged relation to the past and their inevitable contingency, states of darkness. Modernity devalues dark knowledge and operations, naming them backward, primitive, irrational. And because this move creates a readily recognizable set of images – vampires, ghosts, the art and lives of so-called primitive races – the operation itself escapes notice.

The art, literature and imaginative thinking of the Romantic and industrial periods insist, however, on the dark materiality, the incalculability, of real historical relations. They refuse the fiction of abstract, empty time that enables the present to open seamlessly onto the future. Insomnia, the doubled darkness of not knowing how to fall asleep in the night-time, when, as Leon Zolbrod claims, 'the past is turning into the future', is a materialization of the darkness that sustains the work of reason. The sublime qualities of nature as described by Immanuel Kant, the thrilling horrors of the backward-looking Gothic as depicted by poets, novelists and painters, the new kinds of art produced in the attempt to come to terms with the chaos of international war, all testify to the material excess produced by modernity. It is an excess, as Adam Phillips notes, writing of the Burkean Sublime, that was regarded as 'the key to a new kind of subjectivity' in the period, albeit not always willingly.[2] For Burke in particular, the Sublime was the dark, disruptive moment that made order and continuity – the triumph of the daylight world – more necessary.

This was not yet the case, however, for Edward Young, whose long poem *Night Thoughts* was much admired on its publication in 1742. The night sky serves as a text in which the viewer – or the recalcitrant Lorenzo, who resists knowledge of the divine authorship of what he sees for 'eight long, tedious books' of the poem, finally to give way before the apocalyptic excesses of the ninth – can read God's intentions. Against its author's purpose, the poem became associated with the cult of melancholy such that Young himself was regarded as a figure obsessed with anguished feelings as he wandered nightly among tombs, and the poem inspired an emerging generation of Romantic thinkers and artists who were, willingly or otherwise, committed to night as the time of exploration. It was admired by Wordsworth, a notoriously unhappy sleeper. And within its own religious mandate, the poem is a breathless manifesto for the Sublime, the rush the natural world delivers as it manifestly surpasses our experience and understanding. Marjorie Nicolson claims that no one in the eighteenth century equalled Young in his 'obsession with the "psychology of infinity"', not exactly a soporific subject. The theme of the second book is Time, and the cure for its misuse is work, making Time a moving feast whose use

> . . . was doom'd a Pleasure; Waste, a Pain;
> That Man might *feel* his Error, if unseen;
> And, feeling, fly to Labour for his Cure . . .[3]

In Young, night happily serves as the backdrop for the laborious pursuit of salvation.

A factor complicating the poem's reception after 1795 was the illustrations that William Blake was commissioned to make for it, which frame the words both literally, in the sense that the space for written text is cut out of a larger, surrounding picture, and imaginatively, as a picture delivers a more immediate, and often simpler, message than several lines of poetry. Blake did not simply endorse the messages of the poem, but sometimes disagreed with them, requiring the reader of the Young/Blake text to make decisions of his or her own. The conflict thus created, which will be resolved in a different way by each reader, makes a dynamic three – Young, Blake and the reader – out of the more orthodox two of the narrator speaking to the passive Lorenzo as stand-in for the reader, and makes reading the poem a third-party struggle with two time zones. In this sense, reading *Night Thoughts* is akin to insomnia. Blake portrays Time, for instance, as a 'malevolent and relentless enemy of humankind',[4] such as might torment a would-be sleeper. This is the time of Romanticism, when Enlightenment conflicts begin to appear, while Young's Time is more ordered, his claims for it decisive. For Young in Book II, Time's lessons make it 'than Gold more sacred', and when 'Time turns torment . . . Man turns a fool', a lesson the coming decades would teach in a fashion more difficult to resolve.

Night is continually being proclaimed as the time of awakening in *Night Thoughts*, and in this sense, too, as in insomnia, it is impossible for its materiality to be ignored. Blake contributes to this effect. In Book VIII, just prior to the final vision, Lucifer is seen tearing a book with 'NIGHT' written on it. In this respect the poem – and the night it represents – becomes a disruptive third term unsettling another binary: that of God and Satan,[5] so that it is not light that conquers darkness, which would restate the binary, but a deeper darkness, akin to the original Chaos from which God, in the Hebrew creation myth, spoke. If Satan were to embrace the night, here depicted as a time of wisdom, he might cancel himself out, since he belongs to a more limited definition of darkness than that portrayed in Young's all-encompassing vision.

Young's serving as a mid-eighteenth-century precursor of Romanticism makes sense if we regard the Enlightenment as giving rise to an inevitable grappling with its darknesses, some of which – slavery, debt and anxiety – we considered in the previous chapter. Enlightenment rationalism was, after all, 'an anticipatory cast of mind'. Coming to terms with the 'concealment of darkness' that funded that forward movement, the utopian strand of Enlightenment had to awaken to this darkness. Marshall Brown calls this awakening Romanticism. However, the strain of Romanticism that sought union with the divine ran up against its unbearable nature: this is the lesson of the Sublime in works that follow Young's, that humankind can only bear so much reality. Of interest here are the German idealists Kant, Schelling and Hegel. What is fascinating about Romantic philosophers who privilege night and a kind of eternal awakeness, as does Schelling, for example, is that they ultimately become terrifying for human beings, even while artists and writers express a longing to become one with this kind of oceanic consciousness.[6] The coexistence of a longing to belong to something larger and the fear of truly doing so suggest that it is important that something in one's relation to the world perform an unseen and ungraspable limit function. This limit needs to be structural – that is, empty of content or otherwise opaque to understanding in order for it to save us from a greater opacity: our inability to imagine the consequences of our desires to become part of something larger. Such a function, it seems, is usually performed for us by sleep.

Caspar David Friedrich, *Two Men Looking at the Moon*, 1819, oil on canvas.

Schelling's 'World-Soul' is his attempt to replace the primacy of the moral will in Kant with the creative will, making Schelling the Romantic to Kant's quester after Enlightenment. Before reason enters by means of language – or the Word, as Schelling calls it – human beings exist in a 'night of the Self', an 'infinite lack of being', the kind of ever-wakeful night that preceded the Hebrew creation story. This is also the case for Hegel.[7] Samuel Taylor Coleridge's poem 'The Pains of Sleep' has been read as a typical Romantic engagement with this kind of thinking. The poem's first stanza indicates that while '[i]t hath not been my use to pray', the speaker nonetheless longs to be part of the 'Love' he feels within him and everywhere around him. Coleridge is famous, like Thomas De Quincey, for having tormented dreams accompanied, in Coleridge's case, by violent shrieking and partly brought on by his use of opium. Although his difficulty was not so much with falling asleep as with waking painfully from terrifying sleep, he dreaded sleep itself for this reason.[8]

The second and third stanzas of 'The Pains of Sleep' detail a horrifying experience of such pains. William C. Davis reads these as a 'perverted fulfillment' of the desire to be one with the World Soul or 'Love' mentioned earlier, to merge with an original awakeness. The speaker's own scream ('yesternight I prayed aloud / In anguish and in agony') wakens him and saves him from the unhinging sensation of oneness with others' deeds and sufferings: 'Longing for union with the Absolute results in the loss, not of a *limiting* materiality, but of a world of subjects and objects that can be divided into good and evil' – in other words, from the saving presence of the limit. 'Outside the body lies, not "absolute freedom", but absolute moral chaos.'[9]

'The Pains of Sleep' shows that there is a price to idealizing insomnia, that of undoing the saving limit to consciousness wrought by sleep and the unconscious. Ironically, although perhaps understandably, given the Romantic interest in the reversal of accepted categories, Coleridge's speaker goes to sleep and finds himself in the Schellingian state of – now perilous – awakeness. Compared to this, actual insomnia would be preferable. But insomnia itself creates, in the waking hours, exactly the same kind of sensation Coleridge's speaker undergoes in sleep. The day after a night of missed sleep, we also find ourselves losing our sense of boundaries, facing 'life-stifling fear', 'remorse' and 'woe'. Schelling himself admits that eternal awakeness is tantamount to death, that we can either be nothing – no self – and eternally awake or be more limited, but bearable, selves, by borrowing a shape that does not fit – language – to convey our being. For Schelling, it is as though we fall out of a state of perpetual insomnia to become human beings in the same way that, every night, we fall asleep. That is, the act that brings us out of the primal state of perpetual awakeness is, like the act of falling asleep, unpredictable, '*radically contingent*'.[10] The saving action of the limit must be, and remain, dark to us; it can never be in our power.

The radical contingency of insomnia is thus a paradox, but one with which the Romantics were familiar. This paradox of striving to yield, of actively preparing oneself for passivity, as the twenty-first-century branch of medicine known as sleep hygiene recommends, is also expressed in Wordsworth's sonnets 'To Sleep' (1807), which detail his experience of insomnia. The border between waking and sleep that troubles Wordsworth's speaker is figured by the contradictory status of nature. Post-Enlightenment, nature becomes over-determined because science begins to take over more thoroughly the limit function between human consciousness and what lies beyond it that was formerly in the charge of religion. This gives rise to a new kind of infinity, that of scientific progress.[11]

It is worth noting the parallel between scientific method and insomnia, for they are structurally close by virtue of the fact of deferral: a good scientist never comes to the end of experimentation, the sine qua non of his profession. Mary Shelley's *Frankenstein* (1818) is an obvious example of the perils that were seen to follow on science's usurping the role of religion, but Victor Frankenstein is initially inspired to further his electrical experiments by observing the thrilling sublimity of storms, and the story itself originates on a stormy summer night telling stories.[12] For Frankenstein, nature inspires science and in this sense awakens him to post-human possibilities, the chance of arriving at a liveable version of immortality or eternal awakening. But in the early nineteenth century, nature is also – as it is for us today in a yet more fraught fashion, after many more decades of the same contradiction – required to comfort, to make up for our response to its provocations. Given that human beings are also an evolving part of nature, it is not surprising that nature and sleep are often at cross purposes.

In the Wordsworth sonnet beginning 'O gentle Sleep!', sleep is first a meek dove that does not want to come to the speaker, then 'a Fly' bobbing above and beneath the surface of water.[13] Unlike Coleridge's speaker, Wordsworth's has 'no pain that calls for patience' and thus, having no reason not to fall asleep, is doubly frustrated. But at the same time, he is 'pleased by fits to have [sleep] for [his] foe', since nature's activity is an inspiration for the Romantic poet. The fact that the speaker cannot bend nature to his will – cannot set a dove free that does not want freedom (cannot make it fly), and cannot make the water swallow the fly that 'vexe[s]' it 'with mockery' – comforts him, for it means nature is a continuing resource for poetry. But this comfort comes at the price of awakeness. The first six lines of the second sleep sonnet enact the frustrating experience of being close to the edge of sleep, but missing it, that the first sonnet expresses in more restless fashion. The speaker lists nature's soporifics in a manner designed to calm, as soft sounds match states that seem to hold the would-be sleeper:

> A flock of sheep that leisurely pass by,
> One after one; the sound of rain, and bees
> Murmuring; the fall of rivers, winds and seas,
> Smooth fields, white sheets of water, and pure sky . . .

But consciousness intervenes:

> I have thought of all by turns, and yet do lie
> Sleepless! and soon the small birds' melodies
> Must hear . . .

This is the fourth night the speaker has spent in search of sleep without finding it, and he begs for the saving limit ('blessed barrier between day and day') that sleep provides.

Sleeplessness materializes time by catching us out with the unknown consequences of the way our thoughts, so often, ignore it, flying freely between memories of the past and hopes for the future. At times we try to comfort ourselves by thinking 'I *knew* this would happen' – a protest at the reality of the situation, because sleep is governed by a material contingency more complex than the mind can entertain. This is what makes insomnia so frustrating. We do not know the effects of borrowing unconscious recovery time to supplement a demanding day until we arrive at the withdrawal point of sleep's time. Sleep, like being one with nature, is impossible to have as experience. In fact, our need for sleep could be seen as the means by which we belong to nature, because it is the one time when we are not separated from what lies beyond consciousness *by* consciousness.

The insomnia that occurs in Book vi of Wordsworth's long poem *The Prelude* demonstrates the complexities of belonging to nature only through a missed encounter. Book vi contains an account of the crossing of the Swiss Alps that Wordsworth and his friend Robert Jones made in August 1790. While walking, the men cross the Alps, which they had long imagined and looked forward to doing, without noticing that they are doing so. The poem's lines, which have for some considerable time followed the pattern of the two men's walking, break off at the point when their 'hopes that pointed to the clouds' are dashed by the knowledge that they have already, unknowingly, '*crossed the Alps*'. They have missed out on the sublime encounter. Then, 'the verse seems to interrupt itself',[14] and there is a passage in praise of the imagination. At first this seems odd, given that it is imagination that has swept ahead of the men's experience and led to their disappointment. However, the passage figures the imagination's power arising not from overcoming a block to understanding, but from being paradoxically thwarted by the absence of such a block: 'I was lost;/Halted without an effort to break through'. The imagination is revealed in its full power at the site of its failure: the not noticing of an event – the actual climb past the highest point – because its effortful nature has been masked by an image suggesting greater efforts that has occupied the climbers' imaginations. The experience is close to the dynamic of sleeplessness, in so far as thinking ahead deprives the men of the experience they wished for and expected.

The passage in praise of the imagination includes the recognition that 'usurpation, when the light of sense/Goes out' can 'with a flash' reveal '[t]he invisible world' and the 'infinitude' that, the speaker declares, is the home of human being (VII). I find these lines evocative of the Kantian mathematical sublime, but also of insomnia, because, here, infinity or the sublime aspect of nature has passed the travellers by unnoticed – a fact that is retrospectively noted in this passage – just as the night that harbours us, another kind of invisible home, can be entered only by means of a fall from consciousness, a 'usurpation' of sense. In contrast to the Burkean Sublime, which, in both *A Philosophical Enquiry into the Origins of Our Ideas of the Sublime and Beautiful* (1757) and *Reflections on the Revolution in France* (1790), Burke depicts as tied to land and tradition, delivering a form of manageable terror grounded in the experience of the senses (and one suited to the landed structures of authority in England), the Kantian sublime delivers a shock of 'failed perception'.[15]

The paean to the imagination is followed by an account of the descent from the mountain, down 'a narrow chasm' through which the men 'journey several hours / At a slow pace'. The description of the downward journey corresponds to Kant's descriptions of the sublimity of nature;[16] here is the experience that had been hoped for, but that had been missed at the high point of the climb. But the account renders the terrifying tumult of nature from the viewpoint of eternity, so that the effect is one of paralysis overriding movement or, better, of nature in an infinite conversation with itself from which the human being is excluded while at the same time being physically present, a witness to his exclusion from the scene:

. . . The immeasurable height
Of woods decaying, never to be decayed,
The stationary blasts of waterfalls,
And in the narrow rent at every turn
Winds thwarting winds, bewildered and forlorn,
The torrents shooting from the clear blue sky,
The rocks that muttered close upon our ears.

The 'black drizzling crags that spake . . . / As if a voice were in them' and the reference to 'the great Apocalypse' give the descent a nocturnal character concomitant with the fall into dreams, or nightmare, once thought's interference has been taken care of. Yet one kind of exclusion – the Sublime – leads to another, since, spending the night at 'a dreary mansion . . . / deafened and stunned / By noise of waters', the men find it difficult to sleep. Although Dorothy Wordsworth's journal refers to the 'awful night' in question when she, William and Mary revisited the place in 1820, adding that the two men had earlier been 'unable to sleep from other causes', she does not say what those were.[17] On a deeper level, however, the absence of an explanation for the insomnia beyond the noisy tumult of nature pushes the cause back to the moment of the fall of imagination, since this is when the walkers learn, as the insomniac learns, that their expectations are at odds with a larger material reality of which their consciousness is merely a part.

The insomnia following the fall of imagination is akin to what the imagination supplies to enable us to respond to sublime incomprehensibility, which is in turn related to Kant's 'moral image of the world'.[18] The travellers being blocked from entering the state of unconsciousness repeats the way imagination previously blocked an encounter with sublime nature when it was expected, only to arrive when it was unexpected, on the walkers' descent. In this sense, insomnia is part of the education the Romantic poet receives from nature.[19] Kant's moral will gives us an image of the world in which acts with unimaginable consequences can be imagined, not by providing an image of all likely *outcomes*, which would be unimaginably infinite, but via the famous command to 'act only as though the maxim of your behaviour could be taken as the maxim for all'. In taking on Kant's maxim, we gain a picture of the world from which we are excluded, replaced by the fact of other people, a process that is also activated in democracy, where each individual's vote counts only by disappearing into the greater number.[20]

In his youth Wordsworth had been an enthusiastic supporter of democratic ideals as propounded by the leading thinkers of the events that became known as the French Revolution. But after the 'reign of terror' (September 1793 to July 1794), he became disillusioned. And yet, in this section of *The Prelude*, the Kantian sublime reveals its political aspect. The missed encounter with sublime nature on the mountain and its continuation in the ensuing insomnia are the activators of Wordsworth's later lines in praise of the imagination, and it is there that he realizes that what gives us our humanity is the particular way in which we respond to its limits, as he reflects back on the limit point of his own sublime experience. In the act of writing those retrospective lines, he also realizes, albeit on a different level of political participation, the democratic principle of the individual's – and of reason's – production by means of an event unavailable to consciousness. The disappearance of the individual voice into the greater number is the functional limit that produces democracy, and there can be no democracy without it. While this is an insight that post-dates Wordsworth's time, it has a correlative in sleep, without which there is no reason (or poetry, for that matter). 'Through sad incompetence of human speech, / That awful Power rose from the mind's abyss', but this same power teaches by natural example that not being able to grasp the consequences of our thoughts and deeds – as is really the case in a democracy, the youthful Wordsworth's waking dream – is the precondition of making the world the mark of the rightness of our actions.[21]

It is Romanticism's Gothic strain that provides the greatest number of causes and examples of sleepless nights, and these reflect fears and anxieties more than the workings of reason. The first wave of the European Gothic's popularity occurred in the 1790s (although the first recognized Gothic novel, Horace Walpole's *The Castle of Otranto*, had been published in 1765). There was a resurgence of interest in the 1890s, now known as the *fin de siècle*, and this is significant, because the Gothic is fascinated by the porousness of borders and the conflicts and contradictions that societies express, and attempt to suppress, by erecting them. Within European culture, centuries' ends are associated with millenarian prophecies of day and night being abolished by apocalyptic events. One of the meanings of the term *sublime* is 'rising from beneath a threshold',[22] and in the Gothic Sublime the heterogeneous ground beneath Enlightenment distinctions surges up to displace them.

Characters in Gothic fictions have their sleep disturbed by fearful tales, unexplained events and persistent anxieties, but Gothic novels were seen to have similar effects on their readers, particularly women. In this regard the association with ancient land signified in the term *Gothic*, used by rationalists to suggest the redundancy of rural world views and long-held superstitions, has both a feminine and a proletarian connotation. Women are susceptible to Gothic horrors because they are like the ancient land with its cycles of day and night, death and renewal. And while Gothic texts contain monsters, and readers of Gothic texts are monstrous – in the Gothic, monstrosity is catching – so are the peasant masses rioting in France to focus attention on their land-based way of living.[23]

The spirits in Gothic novels, like the Devil, never sleep, and have their human equivalent in the form of 'sleepless souls', as suicides were known from medieval times in Europe until as late as the nineteenth century (as Richard Davenport-Hines points out, suicide was classed as murder in England until 1879). In Metz and Strasbourg, the corpses of 'self-murderers were placed in tuns' and set afloat on a river, a physical 'recreation of the eternal wandering' to which their souls were condemned. Because they had not 'await[ed] death's summons', these souls, it was thought, could not enter the land of the dead and so would persistently return to plague the living.[24] Ironically, the suicide's wish to reach a state of sleep in death resulted in an eternal waking. According to English legislation of 1853, suicides were allowed to be buried only between nine in the evening and midnight, and in unconsecrated ground, so as to reduce the risk of spiritual contamination. They were buried at crossroads in the hope that the cross would ward off or confuse the Devil, or beneath cemetery walls so that the living could not accidentally walk over the earth that hid them.[25]

Although the Gothic satirizes the claim to be done with the past, Gothic tales and images also played a role in the institution of modern nation-states, by creating an archive of dark traditions the modern world could claim to have moved beyond. Japan adopted the Western equinoctial system of day and night – hours of equal length – at the end of 1872, before which time was understood according to a lunar system of variable times and seasons. In 1854 the Shogunate had been made to sign a treaty, under threat from American warships, inaugurating diplomatic relations between Japan and the rest of the world, following which the country underwent a civil crisis resulting in moves towards westernization under the young Emperor Meiji.[26] Although the Meiji era ran from 1868 to 1912, coinciding with industrializing processes taking place elsewhere, as the definitive time of westernization it was also Japan's first real engagement with the discourses of the European Enlightenment.

The works of Kawanabe Kyosai, a painter of satirical and comic demon pictures who used the names Seisei, meaning 'enlightenment', and Kyo, meaning 'wild' or 'crazy' (and one of whose 'art names' was Schuchu gaki, or 'Intoxicated Demon of Painting'), belong to this period. Kyosai allied himself with popular writers who 'lampooned the Westernizing pretensions of the Meiji era'. As well as churning out hundreds of pictures at a time for paying guests at *shogakai*, elaborate parties that sometimes lasted through the night,[27] Kyosai drew on centuries-old myths of the activities of nocturnal spirits as part of a widespread critical response to his country's sudden shift to Western values. He made several works

Kawanabe Kyosai, *Night Procession of the Hundred Demons*, 1879, ink and colour on paper.

relating to the 'Night Parade of One Hundred Demons', including *Night Procession of the Hundred Demons*, a tradition of nocturnal storytelling popular from the eighth century until the nineteenth. The *hyaku monogatari* (One Hundred Supernatural Tales) was a game that arose from evening gatherings to discuss current events and retell ancient stories. A hundred wicks or candles would be lit and people would take turns to tell of frightening encounters. After each tale a candle would be put out, making the room progressively gloomier, until all were in darkness, waiting for evil spirits to appear.[28]

Tsukioka Yoshitoshi's 'One Hundred Aspects of the Moon' (1865) represents the transition from the qualitative understanding of time's passing afforded by the lunar calendar to Western time by the way in which the moon centralizes the activities of particular individuals – a Western emphasis, reflected in realist style – in the series. Yet contradictions remain. *Rising Moon over Mount Nanping – Cao Cao (Nanpeizan shogetsu – Soso)*, from 'One Hundred Aspects', depicts Soso, or Cao Cao, the villain of the fourteenth-century 'Romance of the Three Kingdoms', on the night before a famous battle. According to ancient precedent, a full moon represented

Tsukioka Yoshitoshi, *Rising Moon over Mount Nanping*, 1885, woodblock print.

autumn, a time of 'contemplation and nostalgia' rather than action. In the story, Soso 'hears crows cawing and asks why they are making such an inauspicious noise in the middle of the night', to be told 'they cannot sleep because of the brightness of the full moon'.[29] This is a bad omen, but Soso ignores it and is defeated the next day.

The tendency of Japanese artists to portray people and situations as affected by the moon, rather than in sunlight, was matched in literature. Ueda Akinari's *Tales of Moonlight and Rain* (*Ugetsu monogatari*) (1776) pre-dates westernization, but the supernatural focus is continued in the work of Izumi Kyoka, a transitional figure who rejected the modern realist style. In Akinari's *Tales*, the climax of each story occurs at night, and protagonists are either 'up all night praying' or unable to sleep due to frightening events. In Kyoka's work, sleeplessness has much the same function as in the European Gothic, to indicate the dependence of the daylight world of rational values on the ambiguities of the night world of supernatural powers, which has a longer history. The narrator of Kyoka's most famous tale, 'The Holy Man of Mount Koya' (1900), has trouble sleeping, and so does the monk who tells him his story, both prior to telling it and within the narrative itself. On the journey he details, he meets a beautiful woman who has both maternal and deadly aspects. During a sleepless night in the mountains bright with moonlight, the monk faces a test of his vocation when he considers staying with this enchantress.[30]

The power of such tales to connect people with the ongoing histories of their communities, and to help them understand the arrival of foreigners, was contentious in the Meiji era. Unsurprisingly, perhaps, it was Westerners who were seen as demons. Riots that occurred during the time of Western reforms centred on stories such as that foreigners were drinking a dark red liquid that looked like blood and 'stealing fat', a rumour verified by the sight of hospital beds with their many tubes. Japanese ghost stories were collected and redeployed as part of the modernization process, indicating their importance as bearers of cultural meaning. Four years before the appearance of 'The Holy Man', Inoue Enryo, who became known as the professor of ghosts, published the first of eight volumes of *Studies in Wonderology* (*Yokaigaku kogi*), composed of stories collected on his travels through Japan. Inouye's *On Techniques of Memory (Kiokujutsu kogi)* (1894) and *On Techniques of Forgetting (Shitsunenjutsu kogi)* (1895) sought to reduce the 'multiple temporalities' in operation in rural regions by rendering ghost tales through the lens of ethnographic science. By contrast, the sleeplessness that characterizes Kyoka's Japanese Gothic is a sign of the interpenetration of the worlds of day and night, unified by traditions binding people to place, and serving as a resource for the dramatization and resolution of conflicts. In this context, insomnia attests not only to time's continuity but also to its material heterogeneity.[31]

Modernity, however, gives rise to insomnia on its own account, albeit for different reasons, and provides its own version of the continuity of past and future by flattening both out onto the same plane of production and consumption. As the present moment vanishes perpetually into the future of goals, outcomes and profits, its present materiality is rendered null or masked – darkened, in the restrictive sense – twice: once in its function as a product of the past, and a second time in its own production of the future, where it is replaced by 'progress' or forward movement. This doubled darkness of modernity gives it an affinity with insomnia. At its simplest, the present moment as outcome of the past can be seen as the day's work that physically depends upon a good night's sleep before it can have any meaning as regards future profits. As Marx observed, it is capitalism's Gothic genius to be, like Dracula, unsleeping. Not only does capitalism count on its workers having had a good night's sleep before they have had it, but it adds the future value of future sleep, required to keep the worker working reliably, into its forward accounting of time.[32] Capitalism is Gothic because it is only able to calculate profits by raiding future sleep time – like Dracula raiding the bodies of sleeping women – as a surplus it claims as owed, but without the benefit of which it could never have got started in the first place.

Nineteenth-century America bore the legacy of the Puritans, who had

methodized the English calendar, throwing out the irregular carnival of saints' days and replacing it with the clock-like rhythm of the weekly Sabbath, when men were to be as tireless and unbending in their rest as they had been during the week at their labours.[33]

We see here the paradox of striving at the task of restfulness that governs many attempts to simplify lives in the twenty-first century. In addition, however, 'Puritanism saturated its believers with an acute sense of the dangers of idleness', according to the Calvinist understanding that each moment must be 'accounted for in heaven'. Before long, fear of wasting time became more generalized in Europe and America. '[O]nly idleness dishonors', wrote Pierre Foissac in 1863, going on to claim that, despite sleep's 'value as a gift of nature', it was 'nevertheless an enormous waste of time, and the principal obstacle to the study of the sciences and to the achievement of works in a life . . . already too short'.[34]

Nineteenth-century physics realized 'energy as the universal force present in all matter, capable of converting itself into innumerable forms, yet inalterable and constant', and it was this enshrining of the principle of unlimited productivity that made fatigue both inevitable and inadmissible. Such widespread contradictory energies are prime conditions for insomnia. Marx's belief that capitalism would propel itself into the inevitable end of revolution is not immune from this tendency. He celebrated 'capitalism *as* modernity', its inauguration of the conditions for the state of all-around revolution he identified as freedom. Indeed, in Part 1 of *The German Ideology* (1845), he manifests something very close to an insomniac sensibility as he celebrates capitalism's imminent revolutionary dawn:

> We will sing of great crowds excited by work, by pleasure and by riot; we will sing of the multicoloured, polyphonic tides of revolution in the modern capitals; we will sing of the nightly fervor of arsenals and shipyards blazing with violent electric moons; greedy railway stations that devour smoke-plumed serpents . . .[35]

Medical practitioners routinely blamed the stimulations of the industrial age for increases in insomnia, but modern nervousness was understood to affect men and women differently. One nine-teenth-century doctor claimed that women required more sleep than men because of their greater 'nervous excitability', a not uncommon view at the time. Another connected insomnia to 'morbid states of the brain'; these, too, were considered to be more common in women.[36] As part of the nineteenth-century obsession with efficiency, women were also expected to save time in the home as part of the new educational curriculum of home economics. But at the same time, they were to create the sense of a domestic environment as a haven from the pressurized external world (a recipe for nervous anxiety coming straight from the home-advice manuals). S. Weir Mitchell apparently discovered his famous rest cure by accident in 1874 when he sent a woman with persistent insomnia and exhaustion, whose illness had proved resistant to tonics and exercise, to bed, and after ten days discovered an improvement. Given the conflicting pressures on middle-class women, however – a rest cure was not something the working classes could afford – the cure's effectiveness may have had as much to do with easing 'the demands of conscience' as with rest from physical activity.[37]

Charlotte Perkins Gilman presents a very different picture of the rest cure in her story 'The Yellow Wallpaper' (1892), where it exacerbates the protagonist's madness and insomnia. While the narrator has been instructed by her husband to lie down after meals and forgo taxing activities because she has been suffering nervous exhaustion, she claims she 'never sleep[s]'.[38] Eventually she begins to sleep in the daytime instead of at night, a sign of the reversal of her reason. Obsessed with the wallpaper in her room, she takes to watching it nightly and becomes convinced that it is moving. The bars of the paper's pattern suggest the confinement forced on her as on many such women, and her response is to 'get behind the pattern' at night, along with locking herself in the room in a dramatic overplaying of the terms of her cure.

In 1913 Gilman wrote in the *Forerunner* of the failure of her own rest cure 26 years earlier. She saw work as her salvation, claiming that going back to work meant 'recovering some measure of power'.[39] In rejecting the prescription for women's desire to contribute to society, however, which was to curtail it, Gilman took on the larger social symptom of glorifying work. Her situation was indicative of the paradoxes inherent in the condition of hysteria, often classified as nervous illness in the period, but better understood, as Freud learned, as a manifestation of society's conflicts regarding desire. Nineteenth-century middle-class women were required to work as hard on the home front as men did on the work front, but they were also required to mask this labour. Associated with the nervous energy and sense-rushing spectacle of the city as well as with the restorative qualities of home, dynamic and unresolved contradictions characterized women's lot. And while Gilman's solution was preferable to madness, it may also be described as a hysterical one, in so far as hysteria unconsciously takes social prescriptions for desire to extremes, and in this way unsettles the apparent naturalness of such constructions.[40]

Anton Chekhov, a writer and a doctor, expresses something of these contradictory energies in his story 'A Case History' (1898), where insomnia is the materialization of a surplus in industrial society, but a surplus of expectations rather than products. Dr Korolyov is called to attend a young woman, the heiress to an industrial estate on the outskirts of Moscow, who is suffering from a nameless illness, but he cannot find anything wrong with her. Staying overnight in the house, he cannot sleep and goes out walking. Passing the factory blocks, he thinks about the workers 'slaving away, without a break, in unhealthy conditions', likening their situation to an incurable illness.[41] While it is clear that their illness is caused by industrialization – 'As I see it,' he thinks, 'there's five factories turning out cheap cotton print for sale on the Eastern markets just to keep Miss Christina supplied with madeira and sturgeon' – there is something else he cannot pinpoint. What is it precisely that makes the workers' illness incurable? What is the force that drives the cycle?

The nocturnal life of the factory – metallic tappings and two lit, eye-like windows – appears demonic. Korolyov thinks 'about the devil, in whom he d[oes]n't believe', and decides he must be the 'mysterious force responsible for the way the strong treat the weak and the weak fall victim'. Back at the house, he finds the young girl, Liza, also not sleeping, and it emerges that she suffers from something similar. Terrified because she fears she is *not* ill (and therefore does not know why she is unhappy), she declares: 'I read during the day but at night-time my head is empty and instead of thoughts there are dark shadows.' Dr Korolyov realizes that Liza is ill at ease with her privileges, with the strain of doing nothing. 'You're unhappy being a factory owner and a rich heiress', he suggests;

you don't believe in your own rights, and now you can't sleep. Of course this is better than being contented, sleeping soundly and thinking all's well with the world. Your insomnia is something *honourable* . . . [our parents] never discussed things at night, but slept soundly. But our generation sleeps badly, we . . . feel we can find the answers to everything, whether we're right or wrong. The problem . . . will already have been solved for our children and grandchildren.

But Korolyov has explained the inexplicably unhappy state of the world to himself by thinking of a devil in which he does not believe, a connector between old and new worlds that is helpfully outside the doctor's experience. This is a luxury not available to Liza. Korolyov has work to do that gives him the impression – or illusion – that life's problems, like illnesses, are being solved, that people are becoming happier. Liza has no work, and finds in herself the embodiment of the industrial system's excess, not in the sense of her access to medical treatment and education, but in the form of the production of left-over desire.

Liza carries in her person an unmanageable excess of social and personal expectation. As a marriageable woman and therefore a commodity who lacks the power to act in the market, she accrues in her person the senseless build-up of others' hopes that Marx named surplus value and that Korolyov calls the Devil. The official reason for the workers' unhappiness is economic, but just as this does not explain why they should suffer to supply others, Liza cannot understand why she should not.

There is a senseless circularity to industrial production, and it derives from the same forward-counting of sleep time that Marx saw, calling the theft of this time surplus value to indicate its quantitative – that is, its content-less – character. Even so, when sleep time and dream time are counted ahead of time into the equivalences of economics, then a quantity of human desire – of which sleep and dreams are material residues – is being stolen. And just as the system borrows workers' sleep time in advance, so it delivers an unearned extra quotient of hope-and-dream-time to its wealthy heiresses. Liza cannot imagine a peaceful future because the futures of others are subsidizing hers in a way that no one sees, and that the system she and they are part of does not admit, because the repetitive cycles of production make their own sense, a senseless sense with material effects – and affects – to which Korolyov and Liza are alert.

Because the production and consumption cycles of the factory steal and deliver desire invisibly, however, masking it with the happy lure of their products, we can give Korolyov's devil its proper name: capitalism's unconscious. And it is because this aspect of the system's operation is a dark operation occurring in relation to the dark time of sleep time – the necessary time of the workers' restoration, the time when Liza's job is to be peacefully dreaming – that her response also belongs to the unconscious. As well as being terrified by not being ill, which causes the question of what she desires to rebound upon her, Liza is terrified 'because things can't possibly change', by the fact that the excess of desire she stands for is not one she can access or hope to alter. Her insomnia is a cultural symptom, then, the embodiment of an affective build-up at a visible point in desire's systemic workings.

If Liza were a British subject, we might call her unconscious conscience-strickenness a materialization of the night of empire. But if Liza's femininity disallows her Korolyov's means of keeping away the Devil – his medical profession, making the world better – less than a decade would have seen a reversal of their fortunes. World War One is the occasion of the empire's night, for it was there that men were workers in the industry machine at its darkest, noisiest and most demonic. Soldiers' testimonies and novelistic accounts portray lost sleep as a matter of course. Such is the way of wars.[42] But they also portray what Eric Leed calls the labyrinth of this war, the fact of one's location within a network, the strategic activities of which seemed dark to soldiers. The labyrinth was dark because its immediate purpose was invisible to the individual fighting man – indeed, often to entire regiments – as well as because it

French soldiers resting between sentry duties in a World War One trench.

was dark underground. But what happened in the trenches was largely opaque to the generals as well.[43]

World War One gave society a new kind of nervous illness, the appellation of which was never uncontentious. In Britain, when soldiers broke down for no immediately apparent physical reason, the diagnosis shifted from hysteria to shell shock to malingering and back again, depending upon the fate of particular battles in the army's larger plan and the army's response to the reports of its doctors. Sleep in the combat zone was obviously a rare commodity. But prolonged lack of sleep could be both symptom and cause of nervous breakdown. And while eyes can be closed to assist with sleep, 'the sound of the guns, composite and sourceless', forestalls it, as do smells, which lack a semantic field and so are apt to become overwhelming.[44]

War-wrought insomnia continued after the war as part of the symptomatology of what we now call post-traumatic stress disorder. But it was also a sign of war's strange historicity. For soldiers who participate in wars in defence of civilization are not on a long clear line, at one end of which is the war and at the other is civilization.

They are the frontline matter of the dream of a warless society. Even to call them the frontline matter is simplistic. They are the only matter; they are literally the bits of ground on which human beings erect their dreams of future happiness. Erich Maria Remarque made this clear by calling mud and dirt the soldier's 'only friend'. And for Ford Madox Ford flames performed the role of houses, becoming 'the settled condition of the night'.[45] It is the function of serving at one turn both the material and the symbolic defence of civilization that undoes the soldier and makes his return to civil life, with its clear day-and-night distinctions, difficult. But this is because those distinctions are a functional fantasy, like Japan's new time, making possible the apparent ease with which civil interactions are conducted. The traumatized returning soldier is, like Liza's unnamed illness, the sign that the world does not run, as we are encouraged to think it does, on energies produced by daylight.

Marco de Gastyne, 'THE ANGUISH OF THE POILU: "I can't sleep in this silence"', illustration for the magazine *La Baionnette*, December 1915.

Paul Nash, *The Menin Road*, 1919, oil on canvas.

The world runs by masking dark truths in hidden ways and then finds, as in the aftermath of war, that there is a limit to production by means of masking. As depicted in a French cartoon by Marco de Gastyne, nights become scenes of inexplicable disruption.

The paintings of Paul Nash form a bridge between the two eras briefly canvassed in this chapter. His pictures are reworkings of late eighteenth- and early nineteenth-century views about landscape, making him a respondent to Romanticism. While some of his images of World War One are almost peaceful, *The Menin Road*, which remembers the Passchendaele battlefield of 1917,[46] displays sky and land as machine-like mirror images. It is difficult to tell if the scene depicted is day or night. John Middleton Murry described it as 'phantasmagorical and mad', a nightmare vision, while Sue Malvern sees the drama of its sky as 'invok[ing] . . . the sublime or the awesome terrifying power of nature', a terror outside human control, but ultimately made bearable through the way the trees appear blue in the water's reflection of the sky, and the fact that plants are beginning to grow. The scene looks like dusk, a significant time on the Western Front because it was one of the markers of the twice-daily stand-to, a ritual performed in the morning and the evening.[47] But if it is dusk, the painting gives a probable picture of the kind of sleep that might be coming. It could almost be the

Will Longstaff, *Menin Gate at Midnight*, 1927, oil on canvas.

wasteland of Liza's father's factory with its nerve-shattering night sounds.

It is easy to see why a painting like *The Menin Road* could not have served the memorial function of Will Longstaff's enduringly popular *Menin Gate at Midnight*. Longstaff was smitten with insomnia the night after attending a ceremony dedicating the memorial, which is in the Belgian town of Ypres, to the soldiers who died there. He went back to the gate in the night and later claimed to have had a vision of the men, which he transferred to canvas in a single sitting back in London.[48] Dusk has now become night, and while only one side of the gate is visible, its slanted pit of shadow the sole sign of un-dug graves, we know it is a gate and that there is a way through it. We know this also because of the way the gate of death opens before a night-blue sky that soothes and promises in a way Nash's sky does not, its cloud movement pushing off past the right-hand side of the painting, dwarfing the number-less forms of ghostly soldiers that at first glance look like flowers in the ground below.

The gate, and the distant lights behind it, within the field of the sky's sweep and movement also echo with the disturbed nights of those who had not been to war, but who had lost sons, friends, lovers and fathers, and who, with the aid of spiritualists, sought traces of their loved ones at night in their own echoing houses. Particularly suited to the landscape of Australia where the painting is lodged, *Menin Gate at Midnight* is also a pastoral image, as far from the rush and clamour of the city as it is possible to get. As a landscape the picture remains double-coded, however, because the traumatic scenes its rural vista knew are historically linked to the industrial metropolis and the progressivist thinking that helped make the war inevitable, as well as to the tradition whereby the rural landscape, idealized, compensates for the city. In propaganda terms, soldiers died for their country in this war, in the elevated sense conveyed by this image. The irony is that they died while themselves being framed in scenes of chaos, of which their only civil intimation – albeit an intimation unavailable to most – would have been the night-lightening promise of the city.

Chapter Five
Cities That Never Sleep

Historically, cities have many connections with insomnia. With increased population come greater noise and entertainments, as well as crime and the fear of crime, leading to increased anxiety. And as anxiety about night-time public order becomes a matter for debate and conflict, as was the case in American and European cities in the industrial period, the night becomes an ideological battleground. Of course, in spiritual terms it always was, but industrialization increases the pressure of contradiction. While there is a long history of aristocratic people – who do not have to rise early for work the next morning – using the night for spectacular and sonorous entertainments, the nineteenth and early twentieth centuries brought unprecedented numbers of people from the countryside to work and play, by night and day, in the world's largest cities.[1]

Wolfgang Schivelbusch argues that it was the European Baroque culture of the night that 'spawned modern night life', beginning around 1700 in England with the creation of the pleasure gardens at Vauxhall and Ranelagh. The times at which the gardens came alive grew later and later, beginning at six or seven in the evening, but eventually extending until midnight, with the fashion for lateness indexed to social standing: the later one ended one day and began the next, 'the higher one's social rank'. Late-night culture was, of course, assisted by the coffee houses, and it was not only entertainment that pushed back the night. In 1755 Horace Walpole complained about having to sit, as a Member of Parliament, through debates in the house until midnight, before going home to change for dinner and a ball lasting until five in the morning. The gaming rooms of clubs in Pall Mall and St James's Street apparently accommodated parties of players 'through a night, the whole of the next day, the following night, and up to noon of the second day, tiring out three shifts of waiters'.[2] One wonders how much money was being made by then.

But it was industrialization and its companion democracy, this chapter will suggest, that gave us cities that may almost be described as laboratories of insomnia. This was not only due to developments like gas and electric lighting and the popularizing of nocturnal entertainment, but to the kinds of routine experience such cities require of their inhabitants. Even for Romantics like Blake and Wordsworth, cities could be touched by the Sublime, as sites of 'unlimited growth, endless activity, boundless variety, and infinite possibilities'. When a town or village grows too large, it becomes a city, but cities grow endlessly without change of definition; they are instances of 'circumscribed infinity'.[3] The paradox of this built-in illimitability is the cause of contests over the meanings of urban time and space, especially at night as we shall see, but it also makes a good working definition of insomnia. Sleeplessness causes thought to feel unstoppable – witness Charles Dickens in 'Lying Awake' (1852), increasingly frantic images transporting him around London – an effect that increases as the night wears on. Sleepless thoughts mimic the natural infinity of the dream world, which their pace and proliferation stop the insomniac from reaching. And yet the insomniac is equally pressured by circumscription, the agreed-upon time zone when most citizens sleep. Like the city that grows exponentially, creating material blockades – riots, crime and so on – to its idealized infinity, insomnia's mode of increase shortens the night.

If the irony of the city's planned excess maps neatly onto insomnia's foreshortened pace, just as important is another component shared by insomnia and the city, this one more spatial than temporal: the problematic of the individual in the mass. Charles Simic's 'The Congress of the Insomniacs', which opens:

Mother of God, everyone is invited:
Stargazing Peruvian shepherds,
Old men on the sidewalks of New York.

You, too, doll with eyes open
Listening to the rain next to a sleeping child . . .

likens a gathering of insomniacs to a miraculous birth, as perhaps it would be, insomnia's condition being that of profound solitude. Edward Hirsh, another insomniac poet, calls sufferers 'an unacknowledged community', but then glosses this community as a 'band of solitaries who never come together'.[4]

Hirsh is right to link insomnia to community, for while in insomnia we are focused on the lonely inscrutability of our suffering, and in the city on spectacle and the mass, urban life is akin to insomnia, because it is shared solitude writ large. Being alone in the midst of strangers is the source of the buzz and rush of any great world city, and danger, the threat of the unforeseeable, is key to it. Where there is constant negotiation over the right to belong and move freely within the urban environment – which is related to feeling safe enough to sleep in it – some way of balancing personal freedom with public safety must be reached. Jean Verdon writes of a 'legal night' belonging to medieval French cities that operated somewhat independently of the fact of darkness. Marked by the ringing of bells to signal the putting out of hearth fires – or curfews, from the French *couvre-feu* (cover fire) – the closing of city gates and, in some cases, the jurisdiction of laws against people meeting in groups, this night was designed not only to keep order but also to separate the city from the surrounding countryside as it entered the spiritually uncertain world of darkness. Peasants were seen by city-dwellers as natural insomniacs, like the Devil 'creature[s] of instinctual transgression'.[5]

This view of night-time as a space of rural transgression, however, derives wholly from the city. The construction and guarding of city walls creates the outside as a zone of menace even as it brings the outside in as part of the city's circumscribed infinity, its population growth and shifts in social classes. The besieging of the town of Châtellerault in 1370 led to noblemen guarding the walls by day while people of 'low degree' were physically locked into their guard posts at night, forced into sleeplessness. In 1438 in Bressuire, too, households had to supply members for the watch so that others could sleep soundly, but it was the poor who were 'established on the ramparts' while bourgeois others watched them. Contests over the meaning of night lighting became violent during the French Revolutionary conflicts, when lantern-smashing – presumably also a disturbance to sleep – created darkness in which to perform other anti-establishment acts, as well as serving as a protest against myths of Enlightenment equality that had not come to pass in practice. Sleep could also be disturbed by the very forces of law and righteousness, however. In 1623 Salzburg's bells tolled all night during the summer solstice due to fears of 'devilish activities'. London's watchmen, in place by 1640, would cry out the time hourly and periodically announce the weather. Although the irony of people's sleep being broken by loud 'paeans to slumber' was not lost on the authorities, it was felt that city sleepers ought to remain on guard for criminal attacks and fire.[6]

Within industrial cities, the lower orders became associated both with dark kinds of labour – work in sewers and sooty factories – and with untrackable activities carried on while others slept: not only prostitution, but sweated and subcontracted work beyond the relative safety and sanitation of the factory. Lighting increased rather than decreased fascination on the part of middle-class urbanites with the nocturnal underworlds of their cities. By 1867 the Parisian sewer administration was offering guided tours of 'the subterranean system' with sewer-men carrying guests in gondolas illuminated by large lamps. It was not the case that lighting abolished night, at least not at first, but rather that public lighting, first generated by gas, made night itself into a spectacle. Whereas electricity annihilates darkness, gas 'illuminates it', as Lynda Nead explains. Shopping until eight in the evening in West End London in the 1840s and '50s was not only about taking in dazzling window displays; against the gaslit darkness the finery of shoppers – privileged individuals – was also on display. Darkness does not give up its opacity to gaslight. Rather, its opacity is given a new social meaning through its interactions with light. As Schivelbusch puts it, 'the power of artificial light to create its own reality only reveals itself in darkness.'[7]

It is worth considering the politics of this illumination. The city's infinity is its population growth. In the nineteenth century, when technologies – the cinema, the railway, the telegraph – were produced by, and for, many users, this population began to take form as 'the masses'. And while in a city there are no individuals without the masses, it is individual desire that was increasingly given priority and associated with light. This material interaction between light and darkness in the newly spectacular city tended to hide itself, however. The working masses performed dark, invisible labour making glamorous things for wealthy individuals to shop for. This dark labour was complex, dynamic and layered, for while in itself – in factories and down mine-shafts – it was often lightless, dirty work, it did not only produce things but also the conditions of its own invisibility. Dark work makes it possible to disregard dark work because it makes the glimmer objects gain against the night.

It was not only lighting that fascinated city-dwellers. While by the late seventeenth century many European cities had some public lighting, many Americans and Europeans also had access to clocks on public buildings, and increasing numbers wore watches. Together, these inventions produced an interest in the varieties of street activity to be observed around the clock, so the 24-hour lifestyle of the twenty-first century is not entirely unprecedented. Indeed, it is likely that non-Western cities have behaved for longer than Western ones according to the 'polychronic time pattern' more of us now take for granted, partly due to less reliably centralized systems of public lighting. The six '"shifts" for street hawking and markets' noted by Josephine Smart in 1980s Hong Kong, for instance, ranging from six in the morning until two in the morning or later, might be the same in almost any era. Smart found people going to night markets in search of 'dentists, herbal medicine specialists, palmists, fortune-tellers, writers, singers and artists'.[8] An intriguing list, suggestive of the kinds of events – toothache, pain, anxiety about the future and entertainment to distract one from it – that have kept people awake for as long as cities have existed.

The artist William Hogarth, however, was well placed to observe the specific effects of the 'horological revolution' centred on London between 1660 and 1760, which resulted in the wide availability of accurate timekeepers. In contrast to the *points du jour*, the mythological tradition of painting the times of the day in a sublime or heroic setting, Hogarth's *Night* from the 'Times of the Day' series (1738) illustrates the particular qualities of the London

William Hogarth, *Night* from the 'Four Times of Day' series, 1738, etching and engraving.

night, alive with unpleasant activity. Time is now an 'artificial and tyrannical force dominating people's lives'. The figure leaning out of the chariot is a translation of Crispijn de Passe the Elder's Proserpina (the Roman name for Persephone, goddess of springtime) in his painting *Nox* (Night) of *c*. 1635. But where de Passe's image is captioned 'When Proserpina is covered with the black garment of Dis,/The friend of night, sleep, frees limbs from labor', the same is clearly not true of Hogarth's vision. Hogarth's Proserpina brings chaotic noise instead of sleep, and the broken chariot indicates the way that the natural night is broken by the unnatural turmoil of the city. The scene is Charing Cross, London's official centre at the time, and the *Night* scene is much more anarchic, even infernal, than the other three in the series.[9] What there is of the sky is hidden by man-made smoke, while except for one figure bravely sleeping beneath a makeshift shelter, the people pictured are all engaged in ignoble or painful – and certainly wakeful – activity: children wield dangerous weapons, a barber-surgeon gets to work, a chamber pot is being emptied and beer poured into a barrel.

The literary version of Hogarth's 'Times' was Thomas Legg's *Low-Life; or, One Half of the World, Knows Not How the Other Half Live* (1764), which presaged George Augustas Sala's *Twice Round the Clock; or, The Hours of the Day and Night in London* (1858). Sala was a protégé of Dickens, whose own 'Night Walks' (1860) indicates his habit of walking around London at night when he was unable to sleep, as was the case for a period following his father's death in 1851. There is a strange temporality and spatiality to 'Night Walks', which seems to be an amalgamation of several walks, with the walker being described as 'the houseless mind' or simply 'houselessness', driven outside by his inability to inhabit the night in sleeping. Things take on a hallucinatory quality, such as the ragged creature to whom Dickens reaches out to give a coin and who twists out of its garments and disappears, or the Courts of Law that whisper of 'the numbers of people they [are] keeping awake'. In 'Lying Awake' (1852), by contrast, the scenes the sleepless Dickens imagines are all too real, including the spectacular balloon ascents that took place at Cremorne Gardens, the successor to Vauxhall and Ranelagh, in 1852. In that year Mme Poitevin, an aeronaut, seated on a bull, was lifted into the air in what became a failed effort to outdo previous endeavours of the kind.[10]

Most of Dickens's writing is graphic, even cinematic, but that in 'Lying Awake' transmits the excitement one imagines feeling as part of Cremorne's crowds on a mid-century summer evening. It would not be at all surprising if people going to bed after watching the fall of Mme Poitevin and the bull had trouble sleeping. And the Gardens did promise 'exhaustless amusement'. Here, insomnia merely mimics the already frenzied pace of the city's entertainment. There is an echo of Hogarth also, for as Sean Shesgreen points out, in *Night* Hogarth was not imitating nature, but an imitation *of* nature performed by earlier artists, the sublime versions of the 'Times' (or *points*) in which night brought peace,[11] while Dickens was engaging in an authorial outdoing of the unnatural goings-on at the Gardens. Hogarth wished to show that the *points du jour* trend had become tired and to break the form open to the downward-hurtling course of the nocturnal city. And while one might imagine Dickens merely wished to get some rest, it is hard to shake the sense that insomnia's fevered increase was being helpfully spurred towards earnings. Insomnia is serial thinking, after all, and serial readership was the making of Dickens.

If Hogarth and Dickens rendered the increasingly hectic pace of modern urban nightlife, Edgar Allan Poe's story 'The Man of the Crowd' (1840) is tuned towards consumerism and thus to the question of the individual in the mass. Its narrator, watching from the windows of a London coffee shop one evening, is struck by one particular individual in the crowds flowing past. Observing him, the narrator finds 'confusedly and paradoxically within [his] mind, the ideas of vast mental power, of caution, of penuriousness, of avarice, of coolness, of malice, of blood-thirstiness, of triumph, of merriment, of excessive terror, of intense – of supreme despair', and finds himself 'singularly aroused, startled, fascinated' in turn.[12] Urban overstimulation or circumscribed infinity, indeed. As night falls, the narrator follows the man, who accompanies the crowd on a repetitive circuit, only moving elsewhere as the night deepens, the crowd thins and people begin to go home. The man does not notice his pursuer, and enters shop after shop, addressing all the objects 'with a wild and vacant stare'. His only relief seems to come from finding a new crowd – such as an audience exiting a theatre – to fall in with. The narrator follows the man past daybreak and all through the next day before finally, in the evening, confronting him, but gets no response, and concludes that he has encountered not a human being but a type: 'the type and . . . genius of deep crime'. The man not only refuses to sleep but 'refuses to be alone. *He is the man of the crowd*'.

Here is a version of the houselessness of Dickens taken further, where insomnia's singularity – an inability to inhabit the night unconsciously – drives the sufferer outside to be part of the unsleeping mass. Ernest Fontana sees the man of the crowd as a 'freakishly unique external man', his insomnia the sign of a lost subjectivity, a mass takeover and a text that thwarts reading.[13] This last claim refers to the striking image with which Poe opens and closes the tale. While the narrator first sees the man because he is distracted from his newspaper by the more engaging exercise of reading the crowd, our reading is prefaced by the statement 'It was well said of a certain German book that *"er lasst sich nicht lesen"* – it does not permit itself to be read' – and is ended by it too: 'The worst heart of the world is a grosser book than the "Hortulous Animae", and perhaps it is but one of the great mercies of God that *"er lasst sich nicht lesen"*.' That the unreadable book is a sign of the unreadable man is clear, and that this illegibility is criminal is also made clear at the outset. Yet, contrary to Fontana's reading of the sleepless man as the hollow shell of consumerist promises, a blank space at society's heart, the 'essence of all crime', Poe tells us, is not blankness, but opacity. How are we to interpret this?

The story certainly delivers a kind of phenomenology of insomnia. The narrator is driven by a set of conflicting impressions to follow a man who is himself feeding on the nocturnal energies of others. And just as the man thwarts the narrator by having neither a restful end nor a secret – so, no sleep, but *no reason for not sleeping either*, as in insomnia, this lack of reason being the most maddening thing about it – so Poe thwarts us by posing neither resolution nor revelation, but instead a doubled opacity, a statement in another language that translates as 'that which resists reading'. Or, as insomnia consists of three – the sufferer, the wakefulness and the night – and not only of two – the sufferer and the sleep he is not getting – we have a tripled opacity: a statement in another language that refers to something worse than a book that resists reading, the world's 'worst heart'.

Monika Elbert claims that the story details Poe's political ambivalence, and this provides a clue to the tale's opaque non-resolution, where Poe seems determined to pass on to us the un-plumbable relation of the man to his crowd and the narrator to his man, after having teased us into the expectation of a conclusion. Elbert notes that the presidential election of 1840 had caused debate about the nature of American democracy. The conservative Whigs sought to convince voters that they, and not the progressive

Democrats, were the true democrats. The Whig propagandist Calvin Colton maintained that democracy was the only viable kind of government and that Whigs and Democrats simply differed over how they defined the democratic individual. In a reversal of received ideas, the Whigs were artfully depicted as being 'of the crowd' while the Democrats were seen to be outside it.[14]

Poe's characters and narrators, Elbert maintains, 'are caught in the middle of this . . . phase' of political development. Furthermore, the American predicament is not to know the individual's role in history. Elbert suggests that 'the real demon' is 'declaring one's political affiliation and then finding behind the political system nothing which will sustain the individual'. However, we have seen how Kant's categorical imperative – '[A]ct only as though the maxim of your behaviour could be taken as the maxim for all' – actually performs the dark operation of democracy. To make any one of our actions into an advertisement for how everyone should go about things means we ourselves must momentarily disappear, replaced by the faceless crowd, but this is also what happens in every democratic process: the vote of each individual only has value as it disappears into the greater number.[15]

Democracy declares that we all have a say in the running of society. This seems enlightened: good daylight logic. But we also agree not to notice how this process works: by protecting the secret nature of everyone's desires. This crucial component of democratic workings seems less enlightened, however, and shares ground with more archaic models, for it logically means we could have a whole society of despots instead of, as in the old days, only one (and *that* conjures images of spying on one's neighbours, which could never be condoned by a democracy). The problem seems to be not so much that democracy is demonic because it is empty – freakishly external, to use Fontana's terms – but because it is secretly illegible, and that this secret illegibility is inseparable from the promise of transparency on which, to return to Poe's story and its disappointing opacities, democracy bases its sell. In closing the reader out of the ultimate meaning of the story, in asserting that there *is* no meaning while putting in its place an object – a book – that is made of the same material as the tale itself, Poe suggests that apparently neutral processes – democracy, writing – have a darkly illegible, material component. And if Elbert is right and the demon crowd-man partly represents democracy's hollow promises, then the tale also suggests that democracy is like insomnia, a materially inscrutable process in which the sleepless individual meets the night or the voting individual meets the mass, unable to tell when release will come, unable to ensure a non-despotic future.

The burden that belongs to the heart of the democratic social body is accrued individually, but cannot be given up individually, since to disclose one's vote does not affect its power, just as the wish to join the sleeping masses does not bring sleep before it is ready. Democracy needs not to care if all hearts are 'worst', or equally bad – the type of 'deep crime' – just as the insomniac must, in a sense, give up on the hope of sleeping. He or she needs to make a gesture that gets up and walks about, houseless like Dickens, or engage in some similar activity expressive of the limit point of ownership, of fevered counting. Paradoxically, but also logically perhaps, as the sleepless can attest, it is just this helpless democratic gesture, but only when it is truly democratic, that is founded in an acceptance of *not knowing* about sleep's processes and time scale that is most likely to result in the insomniac sleeping.

The need to accept the limit to reason of the body's secret knowledge about when it will sleep or, as with democracy, an opacity key to the system's functioning, can also be mapped onto social concerns about the future of urban labour in America in the 1880s. After the Civil War it became apparent that the American dream of the hard-working route to upward mobility could not be enacted by everyone: there was a limit to this infinity, for entrepreneurship, the pinnacle of the class climb, would always need labourers from whom to extract profit. Once the impasse making possible the dream of top rank for all began to be recognized, factory-owners and workers realized that payment by the day would not cause workers to work harder, since there was no higher place to which they could aspire. Many factory-owners turned to piece-work: 'The argument held that an industrial worker on piece wages was essentially in business for himself, an entrepreneur in overalls' and, thus paid, would be less inclined to shirk.[16]

Enter Frederick Taylor and his scientific methods of physical micro-management, designed to get maximum value from each worker. Piece-work meant 'carefully specifying hundreds of tasks', which meant employing more white-collar timekeepers. Yet in reality, when ambitious workers took their earnings above market rates, employers tended to respond by rate-cutting. This undid the rationale for piece-work, which led to new schemes designed to convince workers that they could improve their lot while not alarming the owners.[17] What was not admitted – and this truth is at the heart of insomnia – was that there was an unresolvable conflict driving the system. Like the dark point at which the individual joins the mass in the political transformations of democracy, what Taylor left out of his calculations in order to make those calculations – and thus stole from workers in a form of daylight robbery – was the workers' own relation to their work, the material component of all work that is not fully quantifiable, but which cannot be discounted. This unquantifiable, material relation between labourer and task, the discounting of which can certainly affect a worker's ability to sleep at night by making him or her *feel* discounted and thus frustrated, is of course what Marx called surplus value.

Taylor, then, was a kind of daylight insomniac, obsessed with eradicating every last heartbeat of a worker's unique relation to his body's labour. Anyone who has worked on an assembly line knows how time must be made to pitch and change with daydreaming or chatter if one is not to fall asleep or lose one's sanity completely. Small blackout moments drive production. Actual insomnia both mimics Taylorist paranoia about untrackable uniqueness with its clock-watching and twists it by playing back to worker measurement its greatest fear: time-wasting – and what else is insomnia? – the cause of which is not apparent. Worker time-study belongs, too, with other forms of standardization that govern the modern city. Railway Standard Time, adopted in 1883 in order to regulate the American railway network, was designed to systematize the national economy, so that those doing business by telegraph would not lose time and money.[18] Electric lighting is a corporate phenomenon because it is centrally governed and the same everywhere. It eradicates darkness in a uniform manner, unlike gas, which converses with the atmosphere in a differential dialect of haze and flicker.

'A levee at night – electric-light illumination', a wood engraving of New Orleans from *Harper's Weekly*, 1883.

Electric light and Railway Standard Time leach natural space and time of idiosyncrasy, and, like Taylorist method, both hide the fact that they are doing so. Electric light is as bright as, or brighter than, the day, and Standard Time is an encompassing civic fiction. In its unpredictability, insomnia brings that idiosyncrasy back to the insomniac's small world of one – no one knows when the sleep train will arrive, or the thought-light go out – yet, intriguingly, it also mimics industrial modernity, transposing into the night world operations that have become routine in the day. Like the factory-owner, insomnia thinks ahead and, once started on its labours, builds a senseless momentum. Like the bells and timers factory-owners installed to track worker productivity, insomnia refuses to allow us to be oblivious to our surroundings, to the fact of night. The clock's strike or digital display repeatedly jolts or frustrates us. The indifference of night – and sleeping others – to insomniac suffering provokes peculiar outrage in we moderns, accustomed as we are to micro-managing life's contingencies. But insomnia emphasizes night's opaque materiality by keeping us from becoming oblivious to it for reasons we cannot fathom and for a term whose length we cannot know. In this way, insomnia teaches about the limits, but also the conditions, of calculation.

In so far as Taylorist methods were effective, as Anson Rabin-bach maintains, it was because the ideological appeal of the system rested on its *'anticipated* economic and political advantages': sharper methods of measurement and their companion increased profits were always just around the corner. Thus the compulsive thinking ahead that characterizes both industrial capitalism and insomnia. Certainly, Taylorist methods – and indeed Railway Standard Time – were not accepted uncomplainingly by the public, but there was no getting away from them. The New York doctor George Miller Beard's *American Nervousness* (1881) partly blamed the tyranny of clocks and watches for the excessive stimulation that made modern urbanites unable to switch off, but he also claimed that '[m]en, like batteries' should be measured by their 'reserve force' and not by the energy they expend.[19] To understand the needs of the human being, one had to use the language of the machine. And yet to do so was to risk miscalculation by forgetting the limit point of mortality – figured in the nightly need for sleep, a constraint on productivity and measurement – that drives human endeavour.

The sociologist and philosopher Georg Simmel, resident in Berlin at a time when the city had sustained a 150 per cent population increase in half a century and had become a 'major economic and political force' in Europe, observed and lamented the effects of his city's success on its inhabitants. Over-stimulation, he claimed, 'agitates the nerves to their strongest reactivity for such a long time that they finally cease to react at all',[20] producing torpor instead of recovery. With hindsight, however, it is also possible to see the appeal of such a deadening of the senses to nineteenth-century Euro-American urbanites, as was shown by the popularity of Edward Bellamy's futuristic novel *Looking Backward, 2000–1887*, which features a hero afflicted with insomnia.

On its publication in 1888, Bellamy's novel became a runaway bestseller. Its writer was 'a little-known New England journalist and author of pale romances' when this utopian fiction 'propelled him . . . into the middle of the American stage'. It sold 60,000 copies in its first year, more than 100,000 the next, and was the second-best-selling work of fiction in the American nineteenth century. Subsequently, Bellamy clubs were formed, then a Nationalist organization consisting mainly of retired army officers.[21] The movement eventually produced a newspaper, and in 1890 Bellamy decided to enter politics by campaigning against the major parties for what was termed the Populist cause, but its future was undone by the Panic of 1893, the worst financial crisis America had known. *Looking Backward*'s hero, Julian West, is a chronic insomniac who routinely goes without sleep for two nights running. He has built a soundproof underground room in the basement of his house, and engaged the services of a mesmerist to help him lose consciousness. He wakes in 2000 to a world in which the problems of the 1880s have miraculously disappeared. The city is, to a contemporary reader wise to the history of Stalinism and other state-ist autocracies, terrifyingly organized. Administration has replaced politics. It is 'a consumptive, middle class utopia of youthful work followed by mature rest', yet the state is also run 'like a vast military complex'. There are no advertising, no legal system, no crime and no combat. There is no overt racism, but then, '[b]lacks are nowhere mentioned'.²² There is no insomnia either, but nor, since there is no conflict or contradiction, is there any evidence of desire. It is really as though the residents of the novel's not so very brave new world are sleeping.

Julian is wealthy and conservative. In 1887, when he falls asleep, he is engaged to be married to Edith Bartlett. He is also angry, because the building of a house the completion of which would enable him to marry Edith has been delayed by worker strikes. Thus Julian's insomnia is not only fuelled by the night noises of the city; it is also a sign of his own guilty conscience. He admits that he derives his living from the work of others, whose anarchic uprisings he fears. His conflicted feelings, resulting in insomnia, exemplify the widespread class antagonism and generalized anxiety of this period in American history. As Bryan Palmer demonstrates in his discussion of the Knights of Labor, a working-class organization formed in Philadelphia in 1869, night has long been the appropriate time for protests over increased capitalist inroads into workers' time, a contestation of the minimal value given rest.²³ But the key to the book's popularity is the ease with which it transmutes the unresolved nature of worker protest activity – exemplified in the Haymarket bombing of 1886, when Chicago anarchists detonated a bomb during a strike rally to which police responded with bullets – into a perfected human community delivered by a sleep. In this sense, Julian's insomnia signals the desire to fuse with the night and enter the benign torpidity of mindlessness.

Urban night life can be glamorous, but as insomniacs know, there is little glamour in sleeplessness. The poet James Thomson certainly knew this. Thomson suffered bouts of terrible insomnia, and his best-known literary legacy, the long poem 'The City of Dreadful Night' (1874), creates an urban vision of sleepless despair. The poem portrays an insomniac logic in the way its many voices emerge as though from darkness, while the narrator's voice all but annuls itself, as though he is trying to reach the state of nonchalance that, perversely, allows the sleepless to reach their goal. A striking feature of the poem is the way in which an air of rationality prevails despite the decadent subject matter.[24] While on the one hand this suggests insomniac exceptionalism – the poem's despairing voices exempt only themselves from inhabiting the world of sleep and happiness, and solipsistically fail to challenge that world's conditions – on the other it also suggests that the seeds of insomnia might lie in rationality, and in urban industrial rationality more specifically.

The poem's 'criticism of the anonymity of modern urban life', then, emerges in the form of that same anonymity writ darker, and indicates that the nocturnal urban spectacle itself may be the cause of lonely suffering:

> The City is of Night, but not of Sleep;
> There sweet sleep is not for the weary brain;
> The pitiless hours like years and ages creep.
> A night seems termless hell. This dreadful strain . . .[25]

For in the way the

> street-lamps burn amidst the baleful glooms,
> Amidst the soundless solitudes immense
> Of rangèd mansions dark and still as tombs . . .

so the city targets the individual consumer as its pace, set up to run for everyone, pressures him or her uniquely, '[e]ach wrapt in his own doom' (I). The singularity of insomnia is paradoxically expressed in the figure of a watch without a face or numbers, suggestive of a schedule running to no purpose, and a despair no spectacle could assuage (II). So we are back with Hirsch's community of solitaries, the paradox of shared solitude and shared insomnia, as

> Of fellowship in all-disastrous fight;
> 'I suffer mute and lonely, yet another
> Uplifts his voice to let me know a brother
> Travels the same wild paths though out of sight' (Proem)

Darkness makes insomnia possibly shareable, even while it obscures, as here, the causes of suffering. The complexities of the production of urban spectacle are dramatized more clearly, however, wherever disenfranchised groups achieve a space of visibility in the nightscape. This is the case with the femme fatale in the hyperactive night world of American 1940s and '50s film noir, who, post-World War Two, symbolizes not only the ambivalence that returning soldiers felt towards their wage-earning womenfolk but also the hero's war-born self-blindness and the urban nightscape to whose illusions he falls prey. In these films, as Nicholas Christopher observes,

> [o]rganized, crime, street violence, political corruption, poverty – the popularly lamented ills of urban life in the 1930s – are amplified, and augmented, by the far more corrosive acids of despair, dread, and paranoia, even while the national economy, fueled by breakneck military spending after the war is won, booms . . . Shellshocked, cynical, and worn-down, these returning veterans are either hypercharged and running on empty, or numb and cut off from themselves . . . Psychotic lapses, insomnia, and amnesia are widespread.[26]

Forward thinking and investment fail to mask or ameliorate the nightly suffering to which history has given rise.

If glamorous, deadly women are the mirror in which traumatized men see their own mortality in the post-World War Two American city, however, an image like Jeff Wall's *Insomnia* plays its

Jeff Wall, *Insomnia*, 1994, transparency mounted on lightbox.

ambivalence straight on to the viewer. Wall has indicated that the backlighting in his pictures has been intended less to emphasize their constructedness than as a 'preservation of some . . . literalism', resulting in the sense of mundane theatricality presented here. Everything in the picture is angled or awry, the partly opened cupboards and displaced chairs mapping the sleepless figure's trawlings through the scene. The table legs dividing the figure create a frame that opens off to the lower right-hand corner of the painting, as do the stove and the opened cupboards, but at an angle at odds with all the other angles, making for 'the estranging synthesis' Wall creates, as well as serving as an image of the insomniac's tortured thoughts.[27] The figure's head is cut off from his body by a leg of the table, emphasizing the terrible irony of insomnia where the body, exhausted, longs for sleep while the mind, frustrated, cannot yield. The most ordinary of human events, sleep, withholds itself, and the most ordinary domestic locale, the kitchen, becomes the stage set for an existentialist drama played by one.

While Wall's image might depict an inner-city or suburban scene, its starkness dissociates it from the rural. Yet, in its way, the picture is as crowded and unsettling as Hogarth's rendition of the denatured eighteenth-century London night. Wall's 'indecisiveness', his attraction to 'not choosing between fact and artifice', however, while suggestive of the reflection necessary for the practice of art, has been all but annihilated in the night worlds of many contemporary British cities. A relaxation of the liquor-licensing laws in Britain, which became fully operable only in November 2005, has already resulted in failure to connect this policy move with the government's stated enemy, 'anti-social behaviour' on the part of young urban drinkers in the nightscape, who keep many who would rather sleep awake.[28]

Some aspects of this development are by no means unprecedented, for the city night has long served as a field in which alternative lifestyles to the norm may come into their own, and, often, as an environment for the expression of progressive forces. And yet, in Britain,

Licensing de-regulation, combined with corporate technologies of profit maximization, has been accompanied by . . . harmful externalities, including the re-establishment of an almost medieval sense of exclusion and fear of the night that effectively place[s] much more of the central urban residential population under curfew.

Such overt contestations of the urban night do not provide an ideal environment for sleeping. And while control is being increasingly re-emphasized in almost every 'area of social life' today, in a world bound up in the uneven processes of globalization, there is one 'singular and startling exception': the economy.[29] Western policy-makers seldom blame economic deregulation for the real risks many contemporary commentators lay at its door, but an increasingly sleepless populace – which is, after all, an increasingly unwell and risk-prone populace – may yet force that connection on them.

Chapter Six
Wired

In lists of famous insomniacs, care-worn politicians loom large. Whether or not Margaret Thatcher did remark, as has been claimed, that 'sleeping is for wimps', it would seem that awakeness beyond the degree expected from the general populace is endemic to contemporary governance. The slogan of the American right-wing Freedom Alliance (founded in 1990 by Lieut. Col. Oliver North) – 'The Price of Liberty is Eternal Vigilance' – marries staying awake at night for religious reasons with the maintaining of American dominance-as-rightness on the world stage. The imagery of staying awake while others sleep as a praxis and sign of virtue is, as we have seen, of ancient origin, and if President Bush was quick to drop the language of the medieval Crusades in the post-11 September 2001 conversion of a situation of terror to a situation of war, similar terms, vigilance among them, have continued to do active duty.

In a column in the newspaper *African-American*, Roy Douglas Malonson describes the bombing of the Twin Towers as 'a wake-up call' for Americans who had been 'lulled to sleep by a misguided conviction that no dictator, terrorist cell, or suicide bomber was crazy enough to attack the most powerful nation in the history of the civilized world', and indicts 'those responsible for protecting our borders' for either sleeping on the job or being ineffective watchmen.[1] Malonson naturally prefers the language of wakefulness over that of light banishing darkness with its racist overtones, and warns of the upshot for African-Americans of America's continued retraction of civil liberties in the name of freedom. The warning enjoins African-Americans to practise their own kind of awakeness, where they might ordinarily sleep, in relation to the kind advocated by the post-11 September US government, lest they come under fire from that government's own newly mandated – in reality often racist – versions.

At the same time as greater vigilance is being required of the populations of many Western countries and their leaders, however, health professionals are campaigning for recognition of the dangers of insomnia and the role played in personal and communal safety by sleep. America's National Sleep Foundation runs a National Sleep Awareness Week coinciding with the return to Daylight Saving Time, when clocks 'spring forward' and North Americans lose an hour of sleep, with the overall aim of making 'sleep consciousness' a part of 'every American's health and safety plans'.[2] The irony, of course, is that sleep – unlike eating well, operating machinery or keeping to a budget – is the only needful human activity, life-saving surgery excepted, that relies on the complete extinguishing of consciousness. We might expect that making sleep consciousness a part of health-and-safety plans, therefore, is going to be ineffective if it does not take account of the definitional peculiarity of sleep, its work of restoring human consciousness and efficacy in direct relation to the extent to which its complete difference from these is allowed.

Many aspects of the 11 September strain of attention to vigilance overreach a concern with democratic alertness, such as that quite reasonably put forward by Malonson, to justify high levels of anxiety and paranoia and an increased intolerance of naturally occurring ambiguities in everyday action and speech.[3] It should perhaps be expected, then, that in November 2001 the Foundation's special 'Sleep in America' poll concerned with these events reported that the numbers of people who had difficulty falling asleep had almost doubled after the 11 September attacks from those reported previously. However, a report on the 2002 poll released in April of that year under the headline 'Epidemic of Daytime Sleepiness Linked to Increased Feelings of Anger, Stress, and Pessimism' contains the following by way of introduction:

> While many Americans enjoy the benefits of sufficient sleep, as many as 47 million adults *may be putting themselves*

at risk for injury, and health and behavior problems because *they aren't meeting their minimum sleep need* in order to be fully alert the next day. People in this army of the walking tired are more likely to sit and seethe in traffic jams, quarrel with other people, or overeat, according to the findings.[4]

The slippages within and between these discourses of health, governance and militarization are fascinating. At the same time as vigilance or unnatural awakeness is taken as a mandate for increasing measures of surveillance and aggression by the US government – as indicated by the Liberty-equals-Vigilance slogan – citizens are held responsible for their own ability or inability to sleep. In both Malonson's take on the latest American security measures and the 2002 National Sleep Foundation's findings, the responsibility for an unnatural degree of awakeness and an inability to sleep respectively shifts to the citizen, but in the latter case this citizenry is itself referred to as an 'army' who are failing to meet a need – 'their minimum sleep need' – as though it were a basic point of order. That the actions that follow on the failure to comply with minimum sleep need are themselves aggressive, whether in relation to others ('more likely to sit and seethe in traffic jams, quarrel with other people') or to the self ('overeat'), indicates the impasse reached, personally and politically, when the body's and the brain's last bastions of unconscious processing are ignored in favour of the logic of round-the-clock alertness. And to regard individuals' lack of sleep as separable from what Murray Melbin calls the West's centuries-old colonization of the night zone is problematic, to say the least.[5]

It is likely that insomnia will increase with the expansion of the 24-hour economy into more and more lives, and more of each life, because wakefulness and the wired world go together. The more interconnected we are, the more we communicate, and the more we communicate, the more we rely on our interconnected powers of thinking. In addition to work, many of our leisure pursuits, while seemingly soporific, actually undermine the likelihood of restful sleep, from drinking alcohol to surfing the net to watching thrillers on late-night television. At the same time, these are often required to enable the passage between our increased workday and our decreased sleeping night to occur at all. In some cases, our leisure and workday activities may be conflated by medium – many of us use computers or mobile phones at work, and go online or into txt-mode for personal, leisure-related reasons as well. Or our sleeping times may be disrupted by shift work necessarily done while others sleep or in cognisance of the fact – as in the financial sector – that at any moment somewhere in the world the populace is working and awake, and that there is no time to lose in speculating upon its – or its capital's – futures.[6]

Statistics taken from several sources do seem to indicate a gradual increase in the relatively well-off world's insomnia. It has been claimed that 'around one-third of adults in developed societies have some degree of insomnia each year and 10–15% of the population have insomnia at any one time', the standard figure in medical texts. However, the American National Sleep Foundation's 2005 poll found that over half of the Americans surveyed had experienced insomnia for a few nights a week or more in the preceding year, while another study reports that 75 per cent of Americans get less sleep than they did five years ago. A Japanese study found that between 1970 and 1990 'the average length of a night's sleep dropped by 30 minutes', and a 1999 New Zealand survey found that 37 per cent of adults felt they 'never or rarely' got enough sleep, while 46 per cent reported that they 'never or rarely' woke refreshed. Disturbingly, New Zealand's relatively small population may make this high figure the most reliable yet.[7]

Jim Horne of the Loughborough Sleep Research Centre in the UK raises important questions about these findings, however, indicating that 'claims that we sleep less nowadays' may result from 'misinterpretations of historic data', and that 'the public's understanding of the terms "tiredness" and "fatigue", which could indicate sleep debt, have much wider connotations'. Horne goes so far as to suggest that to advocate the need for more sleep wholesale may create 'more insomniacs, unfounded health worries and a greater demand for hypnotics', and that exercise could profitably be taken up during the time in which we are allegedly missing extra sleep. Horne's call for more detailed research into sleep that looks beyond its function to rectify sleepiness is a welcome alternative to the National Sleep Foundation's rather sensationalist claim that '[m]any problems and frustrations that have become part of the American way of life, from anger and stress to obesity, may have inadequate sleep and widespread sleep problems as contributing factors'.[8] The NSF's tagline, 'Waking America to the Importance of Sleep', indicates its preference for thinking about sleep in alarmist terms, which, given that public as well as personal causes of anxiety are on the increase, may not be a beneficial long-term strategy.

Horne's cautions are reasonable given another shared feature of insomnia and the 24-hour society seldom noticed by experts in the respective fields of sleep and culture: both insomnia and the 24/7-active world belong to a regime of desire whose key feature, over-production, hides their causes. As we have seen, a decline in what I have called nocturnal literacy – the ability to recognize the complex interaction of unconscious or invisible activities, from sleep and anxiety to offshore labour and foreign trade – has historically accompanied westernization. If we are '[c]olonizing the world after dark', as Melbin claims, our greatest problem may be that we are doing so invisibly. True excess is always made possible by forging a limit in dialogue with the field one is part of and then proceeding as though that limit did not exist. In the contemporary world there are few or no barriers to US trade, and in our own lives there are few or no barriers to ongoing activity. Insomnia produces a surplus of thought, and the wired world produces a surplus of information, images and interactive opportunities, and neither our world nor the insomnia it generates seems able to assist us with managing this ongoing surplus.

Medical texts are clear that insomnia, like the on-screen worlds we increasingly interact with, is a matter of perception as well as a physical process, in which it can be difficult to measure the influence of the former on the latter. Medically, insomnia is marked by 'subjective complaints about quantity and/or quality of sleep', leading to 'a feeling of being unrefreshed on waking'. While insomnia is certainly not an imagined disorder, the sleepless do tend to underestimate how much sleep they get. Poor sleep itself leads to faulty perceptions, to the inability to tell how far what we feel is responsible for what we think. Insomnia is also nosologically linked to anxiety and depression, states of too much identifiable feeling and too little, respectively, and there is a general lack of certainty about which gives rise to which.[9] Of course, once an individual has experienced a bout of insomnia, she or he is likely to become anxious about sleeping and depressed about missed sleep, which results in more insomnia and an increased perception of missing out that may not necessarily map directly onto the degree of sleep the sufferer is getting.

And yet, there is help available, because the historical cause of both kinds of excess – that of wakeful thoughts and twenty-first-century stimulations – is the original relation of co-dependence with the world that produced us. The limit to human wakefulness makes itself felt in the form of our biological clocks, which not only endorse the production cap integral to our nature, but reconnect us with our developmental past. In the globalizing economy, there is also a limit to taking for granted one nation's ability to control another on which it has become increasingly dependent. Thus commentators warn of American dependence on nations whose workings are opaque to the US – China, for instance – as were the African and Caribbean worlds that fed slavery for Western profit, albeit in such a way that Britain's and America's interests remained protected. Yet as Barry Lynn puts it, today's American 'corporations have built the most effective system of production the world has ever seen, perfectly calibrated to a world in which nothing bad ever happens. But that is not the world we live in.'[10] Forgetting the natural environment that formed us, like forgetting the traffic in human beings from which our credit systems came and the perils of the global system of wired-up interdependence, is to forget the restraints that have always shaped our seeming freedom.

The study of circadian biological clocks is relatively recent, emerging only around 1960. Our circadian clocks, which respond to light changes in the atmosphere, are effectively our bodies' living historical systems. They have evolved so as to prepare us for periodic events, such as sleeping and eating, that are necessary for our survival. There is evidence that we moderns may be wrong, too, to consider sleep as an exception to waking, because 'we are sustained during the day by brain mechanisms that *suppress* sleep and keep our bodies operating at full throttle. Then . . . as the next night approaches the systems are readjusted for slumber.' The fact that awakeness results from the suppression of the hormonal conditions for sleep leads some experts to suggest that instead of 'asking what the function of sleep is', we should ask why we spend so much time awake. Special cells in the retina detect brightness or darkness and transmit impulses to the SCN (suprachiasmatic nucleus) in the brain, which can be seen as the mainspring of the clock mechanism. When night falls, the sedative hormone melatonin, levels of which are low in the daytime and pass unnoticed, is secreted in greater quantities by the pineal gland in response to signals from the SCN. 'Melatonin synthesis switches on in the late evening (around 9–10 p.m.)' while 'synthesis stops around 7–8 a.m.', readying us for waking.[11]

While there are no scientific tests for measuring fatigue levels, there are tests that can be performed to assess levels of alertness, and it is predicted that companies will face increasing numbers of lawsuits in the future from workers whose well-being – and, in some cases, lives – are endangered by the sleep they miss due to the hours they are required to work. Shift workers are already recognized as a disadvantaged social group by doctors, because for biological as well as cultural reasons, it is easier to sleep continuously in the night than in the day. As body-clock specialists note, the largest nuclear accidents in recent history all occurred on the night shift, when our natural predisposition to alertness is compromised.[12]

Researchers at Loughborough have recently provided further depth to our understanding of compromised alertness, however: 'Our waking hours place particular strain on the frontal lobe of the cerebral cortex, the "thinking" part of the brain responsible for activities such as speech, temporal memory and innovative and flexible problem-solving thinking.' While many tests for sleep deprivation assess reaction time and proficiency, Jim Horne's and Yvonne Harrison's research shows that sleep loss negatively affects more complex, and arguably more important, tasks. '[I]nnovation, flexibility of thinking . . . risk assessment, appreciation of one's own strengths and weakness at th[e] current time (meta-memory), and ability to communicate effectively' are all compromised by insufficient sleep.[13]

The sleepless are also much more likely than the well-slept to persist with an ineffective strategy when another one is clearly called for. In temporal-memory tests where subjects' recognition of faces was tested by changing the context in which the faces appeared, Horne and Harrison found that when sleep-deprived subjects were asked how sure they were about their answers, they were much more likely than the non-sleep-deprived to give '100 per cent certain' ratings for incorrect responses. This 'unexpected exaggerated confidence' shown by the sleepless is now being explored further, as it may have implications for the veracity of test methods. 'If cognitive tests are rehearsed or repeated',[14] then the sleepless might appear more alert than they are, since sleeplessness increases the perception of certainty, but not, it would appear, its reasoned basis.

Increased attachment to a fundamentally mistaken frame of mind may well characterize the wider, wired society, however. To the extent that insomnia is a response to intrinsic limits resulting in altered perceptions, it has an unsettling daytime complement in the work environments of the 'new economy', in which greater freedom and flexibility, but also increased intensity and unpredictability, are key. A path-breaking research project carried out in Sweden, the findings of which were published last year, indicates that there is a new kind of tiredness abroad to match the changing work patterns of globalization. Ironically, it is a tiredness that makes it more, rather than less, difficult for its sufferers to fall asleep. The new tiredness is 'located in the head' and seems to be the result of a special kind of disavowal where structurally generated work habits are perceived to be under the control of the individual to an extent that may not be the case. In surveying engineers, teachers, waiters and domestic-nursing personnel, the project found a consistent ambivalence around the subject of increased workload, an unavoidable feature of the 'constant reorganization of workplaces' that is the contemporary norm.[15]

Despite these pressures, the average 'engineer, teacher, waiter, and domestic nurse assistant' surveyed all say that

> one of the things . . . they value most in their work is freedom . . . For all of them, the work amount has increased and they have to work faster and/or longer hours. The increase of tempo makes 'freedom and flexibility' even

more important, maybe even structurally necessary . . .
Under the headlines of freedom and flexibility it is expected
that one is (more) available and works more.

Sleeping problems are among a growing list of ailments that 'seem
to have become too common to be worth talking about'. The
authors of the study conclude that '[i]t seems as if today no major
group or class within our type of society is positioned to be ideologically in opposition towards the dominant economic ideology'.
As one interviewed boss expressed the problem, apparently without meaning to, 'People are not tired nowadays, are they? Why
should they be and how could they be . . . think of all the possibilities.'[16] Thinking of possibilities so as to forestall tiredness, however, is the opposite of what one has to do to fall asleep.

Having part of one's workload diverged to offshore outsourc-
ing, another current trend, can reduce job security and increase
anxiety, and when decisions about what we do are increasingly
made on the basis of desired profit rather than worker capability,
we are bound to be perpetually behind time. Yet while it has become
'normal to "have too much to do"' in almost all of today's work
environments,[17] the global reach of this intensification means that
the ambivalent nature of people's responses to the process may go
unnoticed. Because we are now so readily connected with each
other – so wired – there is no particular face we can put to these
changes. People's bosses are in service to the economy, which is
bigger than they are. In service to the faceless economy, we remake
our own just as quickly. Of necessity that face is brave and positive,
making it less likely that we will notice that how we are working
makes us sleepless, and that being sleep-deprived makes us prone
to depression, anxiety and, worst of all, an inability to take account
of or alter our way of thinking. So we remain attached, of necessity, to the belief that our workloads are under our control so long
as we perceive them to be offering us freedom.

The culture of intensifying work causes a conflict within ourselves, but the causal connector is not readily identified because it
is everywhere, where it appears as endless opportunity instead.
Opportunity, however, is not in itself a solution to conflicts, though
it may serve temporarily to displace them. It tends to be assumed

that our desire is of the same order as that of the global economy, which is voracious in nature and can turn itself to any object. Employees describe the 'hectic' nature of their work as 'positive', and call its 'feverish' pace 'exciting'.[18] It is exciting to be dealing with a continuing variety of different work challenges successfully, but in order to sleep, we need to know we are tired, and if neither we nor the system we inhabit can recognize tiredness, an increase in sleep problems, coupled with an inability to locate causes, will result.

Insomnia thus is a perfectly understandable response to a world in which life is 'all about getting a lot done', while at the same time we wish 'to be done with' each thing so as to 'move on to something else'.[19] By its nature sleep cannot always come in the time we allow it, because, to us, the exact nature of its contract with each day's energy expenditure is opaque. We cannot have sleep restore our energies if we are unwilling to embrace the original limit to capability to which its restorative power belongs. Sleep has its own phases and its own temporality. Its relation to our world is one we cannot fully master. And because our world has lost so much literacy in the workings of dark and unconscious agency as well as circadian mechanisms – the two are related to the extent that the latter belong to the long historical genesis we consider only when it suits us – a vexed wakefulness and a volatile ambivalence results. As the RETORT collective, responding to the events of 11 September in the US, put it, the 'consumer society manifestation' of modernity

is less and less able to offer its subjects ways to live in the present, and to have the flow of time be accepted and inhabited as it happens. And this is precisely because it stakes everything on celebrating – perpetuating – the here and now. Lately it has built an extraordinary apparatus to enable individuals to image, archive, digitalize, objectify, and take ownership of the passing moment. The here and now is not endurable, it seems (or at least, not fully real), unless it is told or shown, immediately and continuously, to others – or to oneself.[20]

In a penetrating analysis, Wayne Hope indicates that what is known in global networks as 'real time' manifests in a 'drive towards instantaneity' that 'never reaches full identity with itself'. And because the market takes form in the realm of images and screens – even numbers play on screens – in a similar way to which insomnia produces anxious thoughts, 'the defining characteristic of the market as an agent' is its desire, 'its lack of objectivity and incompleteness of being, its non-identity with itself'. In this continually uncompleted process, however, 'information and money are fused together' to generate ever more options for the wakeful who wish to avoid facing the matter of intrinsic limits. One outcome of this state of affairs is that '[p]eople who come closest to the momentariness of movement are now the people who rule . . . Domination consists in one's . . . capacity to escape and the right to decide one's speed.'[21] Privileged speeding may require speedy sleep, at which point we re-enter the system of money being made by escaping the present moment as the world's pharmaceutical giants thrive by helping those of us who can afford it to do precisely that. We can take a pill to sleep an hour from now, and another to shift the anxiety our chemically induced sleep may produce.

Unfortunately, one of the commonest medical responses to insomnia is still to prescribe sleeping pills. On the other hand, sleep-disorder clinics in the US more than tripled between 1989 and 1999, so it is to be hoped that people are seeking more than one kind of solution. Drugs to assist sleep, like drugs to treat other conditions that are inconvenient without being immediately life-threatening, are, however, part of a larger pharmaceutical picture. The drug industry has historically been reluctant to develop cures for conditions and countries where they are most needed, brand-name anti-retrovirals for the HIV virus and treatments for tropical diseases among them.[22] It is not too far fetched to link the West's declining nocturnal literacy skills with its drug industry's current neglect of sub-Sarahan Africa, given that imperial finance and Enlightenment beliefs – in many ways, global pharmaceutical companies are their latter-day representatives – were forged from the traffic in black bodies that gave us coffee, our first anti-soporific or night-banishing drug.

The other question that needs answering, of course, is to what extent sleeping pills assist those who take them to improve their sleep and overcome insomnia. But this is the kind of question it is hard to get clear answers to today. A number of recent studies have indicated the extent to which the global pharmaceutical giants insinuate themselves into the networks of medical practice, whether through subsidizing research, suppressing unhelpful results or providing incentives to doctors to use their products. Because insomnia is often either a by-product of or accompanies other medical conditions, including, especially, depression, the question of its treatment can be complex. For as long as we have industries whose profits depend on forging new disorders, however, it is in all of our interests to consider more holistic kinds of solutions.[23] The discourse of 'sleep hygiene', however unpromisingly named, is oriented towards the prevention of insomnia and focuses on steps the individual can take to avoid becoming dependent on sleeping pills. Many specialists recommend keeping a sleep diary along with following some simple rules. For example: use the bedroom only for sleep and sex; don't stay in bed when sleep eludes, but go into another room and do something relaxing until you feel sleepy; avoid caffeine for six hours prior to sleep time.

Another relevant context for improving sleep is the slow-living movement, a variant of the Slow Food movement, which, like attending to our circadian rhythms, 'connects a mindfulness in the present with a heightened awareness of historicity'. Slow Food and slow living, with their emphasis on pleasure and conviviality, also focus on the ethical implications of our shopping, consuming and time-spending choices, including matters such as supporting local food sources to reduce transport and greenhouse-gas emissions. When considered against the disastrous erosion of limits attending 'real time', in which fragmented and/or subcontracted workers monitored by global giants 'lose the capacity to shape rhythms of life for themselves', slow living may help us to sleep better not only because we have taken steps to change personal pace, but because we can rest more easily with the global implications of those choices. There is also a group – the International Dark Sky Association – which claims that 'light pollution', like other recent, rapid changes to our ecosystem, must be curtailed.[24]

Sleeping patterns do vary across cultures, of course, despite the levelling tendencies of globalization. The Mediterranean habit of taking a siesta after the midday meal answers an early-afternoon

A Tokyo 24-hour media café.

dip in energy levels that is the result of our circadian rhythms. Japan and China, too, have cultures of daytime napping. Chinese culture has become, according to one commentator, more, rather than less, tolerant of daytime napping as it has undergone modernization (or westernization), with its proponents defending napping as a 'continuation of daytime activities'. Whether or not this is a positive change remains to be seen. In Japan, daytime napping, or *inemuri* – literally, 'to be present and asleep' – is widely practised.[25] Japanese students are frequently encouraged to curtail night-time sleep in favour of sleeping during class time.

However, the slogan *yonto goraku*, or 'four [hours of sleep] pass, five fail', is context-specific. Japanese students are expected to take responsibility for their sleep time from an earlier age than are Euro-American students, based on how much study they need to do to get into a good high school and then into a good university. Because ambitious students attend extra classes (*juku*), their ordinary classes are often boring by comparison and provide good opportunities to catch up on lost sleep. 'The word *ganbaru* (fighting through, giving as much as one can)' refers to 'a subjective notion of time' that can be taken as lightly or seriously as a student wishes.[26] Quiet night-time conditions suit the need to memorize large quantities of material in order to proceed further with study, but *ganbaru* is also unsettlingly open-ended, since its principal requirement is overcoming one's limits.

There is evidence that short-term naps in the daytime do improve workplace performance, as long as they do not exceed 40 minutes, which compromises nocturnal sleep. However, defenders of the 'power nap' at work often fail to note that such endeavours form part of a continuing 'de-privatization' of sleep. Few of us would want our managers measuring our sleep time in the way they increasingly measure our work time, as could conceivably occur if more businesses were to provide sleep pods or sleep rooms for their workers to nap in, as some already do.[27] As work pressures become increasingly unpredictable in the climate of interdependency fostered by globalization, pressure to complete a nap quota form in the required manner is the last thing workers need!

Some professions, such as policing and detection, have affinities with insomnia that go beyond merely being called upon to work odd hours. As the popularity of film noir and hard-boiled crime fiction shows, we find compelling the idea that catching killers is best done by those who may themselves bypass the law and who can thus identify with others who do so. In Christopher Nolan's American remake of Erik Skjoldbjaerg's 1997 film *Insomnia* (2002), an ageing policeman, played by Al Pacino, investigates the murder of a teenage girl in the town of Nightmute, Alaska, under the unsettling glow of the midnight sun. During a chase scene early in the movie, the detective, Will Dormer, accidentally shoots and kills his partner, Hap, thus signalling the start of a long and downward spiral of sleeplessness, self-doubt and increasingly unorthodox engagements with the suspected killer, a crime novelist (Walter Finch) played by Robin Williams. Prior to the chase, Hap informs Will that a case involving a teenager's death – closed years ago, having resulted in a successful conviction – is to be reopened. It is a case in which Will, frustrated that a known multiple offender was going to escape justice yet again, planted false evidence against the accused that resulted in the conviction.

Finch immediately hones in on Will's double guilt, which feeds on and perpetuates his insomnia. In one scene Finch – who more or less admits his guilt in the matter of the teenager's death, although he does not regard his actions as criminal – likens himself to Will through the fact of the latter's not sleeping. Finch claims that he saw Will shoot his partner and, worse, attempt to cover it up, and declares that he and Will are 'partners on this' – presumably murder, but also, by inference, their guilt- and anxiety-ridden sleeplessness, not to mention the sense of artificial reality to which insomnia gives rise. The dramatic action of the film centres around Will's increasingly disturbed state of mind as, prompted by Finch's threats and his own insomnia-driven paranoia, he collaborates with the killer by misplacing evidence, writing himself into the scene of the crime.

The French literary critic and novelist Maurice Blanchot thinks along similar lines in *The Space of Literature* (1955) when he claims that insomniacs 'always appear more or less guilty' because 'they make night present', while other sleeping mortals innocently entrust themselves to the night in order that it may invisibly serve them in the ways daily life requires.[28] Two kinds of submissive activity – night's subservience to day, and the citizenry's subservience to sleep and night – are thus brought into the open by insomnia's own, less submissive activity. Those who cannot sleep in the time and space allocated to this necessary, 'natural' event effectively reopen the question of what nature, including human nature, is, embodying in their wakefulness both the rest of the culture's complete vulnerability – or its humanity – and its primitive, possibly ungovernable need.

Will's surname, Dormer, suggests the sleep that eludes him and that he relates specifically to his profession when he claims that '[a] good cop can't sleep because he's missing a piece of the puzzle and a bad cop can't sleep because his conscience won't let him'. The town of Nightmute suggests two further absences: that of darkness in summer in the far north of the globe, and that of speech, as neither the killer nor Will come clean to anyone else about their own or each other's probable guilt. Because it is always daylight, making even innocent sleep difficult, Will is suspended in indecision in the hope that each 'night' sleep may come and lead to a new perspective, but his growing terror and anxiety-driven actions chase it further and further away. The daylight also increases his paranoia because it is more likely, as he fears, that his actions are being watched and seen.

By contrast, Stephen King's novel *Insomnia* (1994) gives its hero, Ralph Roberts, and his companion Lois Chasse a chance to rise above their ordinary-citizen status and participate in an epic battle not only for the good of their town, but for the future of humanity. The novel draws on the association we have seen operating since at least medieval times between sleeplessness and melancholy or grief. It opens in flashback mode as Ralph, a 70-year-old retired citizen, is recalling the last four months of his wife's suffering from cancer before her death. During this time he had been shocked to observe a friend, Ed Deepneau, acting strongly and violently out of character, but had, in the press of events, forgotten the incident.

In the hot July of Carolyn's death, however, Ralph begins to notice a 'thing which had started ticking in the walls of their bedroom – and inside her – late at night'.[29] While he later identifies this ticking as the phantasmatic effect of his wife's cancer on him and their environment, its death-watch function doubles back once Ralph becomes afflicted with insomnia that causes him to awaken fifteen minutes earlier each night, so that, eventually, he ceases to sleep altogether. Like Will Dormer's insomnia, Ralph's makes him initially uncertain as to whether the strange events that have begun occurring in the town of Derry, echoing the incident of the previous summer, are real or products of his overextended imagination. It transpires that Ralph's similarly widowed neighbour, Lois, has been suffering from the same kind of insomnia, and that, like Ralph, she has kept quiet about her condition. The epic dimensions of the narrative begin with the discovery that Ed has begun to beat his wife and has joined with other townspeople to oppose the visit of a leading feminist spokesperson for a woman's right to abortion. Ralph and Lois begin to see 'auras' around people suggestive of their fates and frames of mind, and begin to interact with what turn out to be alien beings involved in the good-versus-evil dynamics of the battle the townspeople are playing out.

Like the film *Insomnia*, the novel exploits a number of borders essential to personal sanity and civic order, while pushing beyond them to ethical questions that render such borders both necessary and difficult to define. Both Ralph and Lois, being elderly and bereaved, have a proximity to death, while the focus of the anti-abortion and pro-women's-rights camps in the town is the question of when human life begins and what defines it. Bizarrely, both Ralph and Lois begin to look younger after a period of the usual insomniac daytime symptoms, as they are gradually educated regarding the interventionist role they are to perform. Initially thinking that his insomnia had made him vulnerable to the aliens' attentions, Ralph learns that even his sleeplessness was not under mortal sway. The insomnia is described by two of the creatures (named Clotho and Lachresis, two of the ancient Greek Fates responsible for spinning and measuring the thread of life) as the product of adjustment in earthly auras that 'alter the way [people] dream and . . . perceive the waking world', an activity in which 'madness is always a danger'.

One of the questions raised near the novel's end is whether the events that have been narrated really happened or whether they were a product of Ralph's grief-stricken, sleep-starved imagination. Sleep patterns in humans do change over the course of a life, with the amount of time spent in REM (rapid-eye-movement) sleep – the sleep in which our dreams' most memorable, uncanny events occur and we maintain heart rate and blood-pressure levels similar to those of waking – decreasing as we age.[30] The REM sleep phase is also believed to be the phase in which memories are consolidated. Losing REM sleep as Ralph does both naturally through old age and supernaturally by intervention, then, makes it more likely that he is losing his mind literally as well as figuratively, since he is forgoing the work of individual historical revision the unconscious brain and body perform while we sleep.

Gabriel García Márquez's novel *One Hundred Years of Solitude* (1967) tracks a specific thread of the colonial history that gave us ever-wakeful global real time, but also enacts in literary form the likely future of that system as a whole. Insomnia features significantly and repeatedly in the story, most notably in the form of the plague that afflicts the inhabitants of Macondo – the name of an old banana plantation with a slaving history – early on. '[T]he most fearsome part of this sickness', as is explained to José Arcadio Buendía, one of the protagonists,

> was not the impossibility of sleeping, for the body did not feel any fatigue at all, but its inexorable evolution toward a

more critical manifestation: a loss of memory . . . when the sick person became used to his state of vigil, the recollection of his childhood began to be erased from his memory, then the name and notion of things, and finally the identity of people and even the awareness of his own being, until he sank into a kind of idiocy that had no past.[31]

On one level, the insomnia plague figures the loss of memory that colonization visits upon indigenous cultures. Sleep, which passes quietly, is an instance of the taken-for-granted manner in which each culture inhabits and belongs to its world. South America's discovery by Europeans – whether as a result of Columbus's 1492 New World voyage or the American exploitation of Colombia through the banana industry – resulted in a terrible paradox not unlike insomnia's recognition of sleep's value.[32] The colonizing enterprise recreates the world it discovers as arcadia and marvel, bringing the relation of land and people to new awareness at the very moment it is being destroyed.

One Hundred Years of Solitude gives us the world as it would be if we never slept, which would be impossibly hallucinatory, but this impossible hallucination is precisely what the American United Fruit Company produced: '[F]oreign investment . . . creates boom conditions, leading to increases in local wages, and offers a seductive impression of progress and modernization', but it does not care about the future of the land or its people. Claiming to eradicate darkness and bring only opportunity, the progress narrative's descent into strike-breaking and murder in the 1928 Ciénaga massacre generated its own loss of memory as denials forced Colombians to contest the truth of the event. A world that never sleeps – that promises renewal without cost – does not have to be responsible for its actions, but García Márquez does not let his readers off so lightly. While industrial interests make Macondo, tragically, into a land of timeless magic in which portents of doom fail to register with the inhabitants, the reader observes the repetitions to which the characters are blind and carries this sense of doom throughout the narrative.[33]

Karl Polanyi described as 'disembedding' the process through which capitalism profoundly alters the 'basic elements of the species's life-world', leaving human beings without the 'protective covering' to survive the new, harsh conditions, the opportunities they are promised as a result.[34] The disembedded viewpoint may also be seen as the insomniac viewpoint, where the bed that once restored becomes a torment, and everything we know repeats itself intensified, powerless to return us to the unconsciousness we took for granted. Oblivion cannot exist in a lost paradise. The citizens of Macondo have never woken to their changed reality, but the reader as a knowing inhabitant of modernity must, and as we approach the story's close the double viewpoint of remaining wakeful while we simultaneously inhabit Macondo's dreams becomes one single viewpoint and one final act of readerly witness. The understanding of Aureliano Babilonia, who is finally deciphering his gypsy ancestor Melquíades's manuscripts, now approaches ours, as Aureliano learns that his life is not only his life but also that of the inhabitant of a fiction:

> Macondo was already a fearful whirlwind of dust and rubble being spun about by the wrath of the biblical hurricane when Aureliano skipped eleven pages . . . and he began to decipher the instant he was living, deciphering it as he lived it, prophesying himself in the act of deciphering the last page of the parchments, as if he were looking into a speaking mirror. Then he skipped again to anticipate the predictions and ascertain the date and circumstances of his death. Before reaching the final line, however, he had already understood that he would never leave that room, for it was foreseen that the city of mirrors (or mirages) would be wiped out by the wind and exiled from the memory of men at the precise moment when Aureliano Babilonia would finish deciphering the parchments, and that everything written on them was unrepeatable since time immemorial and forever more, because races condemned to one hundred years of solitude did not have a second opportunity on earth.

And what of twenty-first-century dwellers in the land of fictional freedoms? To us, Macondo's inhabitants seem wilfully blind to the price of forgetting history, but only because we are in a position to know better than they do, at least at the outset of the novel. And yet, global real time is a plague of its own, the very name of which falsely declares reality to belong to the fast-moving moment. It appears 'self-operating, self-defining, and ahistorical', though of course it is none of these things: 'Throughout the screened interiors of global financial activity, technological determinism and market determinism are mutually reinforcing.' To us, technologies are repeatedly described as neutral, equally open to various uses.[35] But the screened images and information that are the means of our interaction with them mask their conditions of production – and their outcomes – no less than the plague hides what is happening to the people of Macondo. The fact that we have created a present from which historical consciousness has largely disappeared is not accounted for. It is as though the world, as in Macondo, begins anew each day with infinite possibilities.

The wired world cannot help us manage contingency and dependence, the true price of interconnectedness, to the extent that these are what it imagines it excludes. In response to this world, insomnia is not only a nightmare mimicry of idealized instantaneity, however – too many thoughts occurring all at once, too quickly! – but also a form of historical consciousness, because in the absolute unknowing it calls us to – when will sleep arrive? We cannot know, or not to the minute – we are unable to continue worshipping 'the now'. Insomnia shows that although we can study the world repeatedly, we can never study it with our own being fully included, just as we cannot be awake and asleep in the same moment. The fall into sleep testifies to the limit in human imagination, materially, historically, representationally. We fall out of history as we know and study it into history as unconsciousness, into what remains of the long negotiation between adaptation and belonging to the world of which we are heirs.

And although the tedium of sleeplessness seems to call out for our usual distractions, the ungraspable reality of waking and sleeping can be a cure for contemporary banality. To the habitually sleepless, it is genuinely marvellous simply to awake refreshed. That the sleep scientist cannot always use the fruits of his or her knowledge to fall asleep shows that there is at least one thing we do each day that cannot be fully mastered, and in that resides its ability to renew us and remake us. While we can learn about the past, including our own past, we cannot, like Aureliano, map its connections with our present or grasp fully our own relation to the world without simultaneously disappearing. Fortunate for us, then, despite ourselves, that each night brings not only an end to the fiction of control of time, but a new chance to practise for oblivion.

References

INTRODUCTION

1   William C. Dement, 'What All Undergraduates Should Know about How Their Sleeping Lives Affect Their Waking Lives', Sleepless at Stanford, 1997: www.stanford.edu/%7Edement/sleepless.html

2   Roger Schmidt, 'Caffeine and the Coming of the Enlightenment', *Raritan*, XXIII/1 (2003), pp. 129–49.

3   Elizabeth Goodstein, *Experience Without Qualities: Boredom and Modernity* (Stanford, CA, 2005), p. 1.

4   Charles Simic, 'The Congress of the Insomniacs', in *Frightening Toys* (London, 1995), p. 71.

ONE: SLEEPLESSNESS IN THE ANCIENT WORLD

1   Stephanie Dalley, ed., *Myths from Mesopotamia: Creation, the Flood, Gilgamesh and Others* (Oxford, 2000), pp. 9–38; Scott B. Noegel, 'Mesopotamian Epic', in John Miles Foley, ed., *A Companion to Ancient Epic* (Malden, MA, 2005), p. 241; James B. Pritchard, ed., *Ancient Near Eastern Texts Relating to the Old Testament*, 3rd edn with supplement (Princeton, 1969), pp. 60–72, cited in Andrea Deagon, 'The Twelve Double-Hours of Night: Insomnia and Transformation in *Gilgamesh*', *Soundings*, LXXXI/3–4 (1998), pp. 469–70; Benjamin Foster, 'Gilgamesh: Sex, Love and the Ascent of Knowledge', in John H. Marks and Robert M. Good, eds, *Love and Death in the Ancient Near East* (Guilford, CT, 1987), p. 29.

2   Carl Kerenyi, *Zeus and Hera: Archetypal Image of Husband and Wife*, trans. Christopher Holme (Princeton, 1975), pp. 3–20, cited in Jules Cashford, *The Moon: Myth and Image* (London, 2003), p. 25; Joshua T. Katz, 'The Indo-European Context', in Foley, *A Companion to Ancient Epic*, pp. 22–3; Ruth Padel, *Whom Gods Destroy: Elements of Greek and Tragic Madness* (Princeton, 1995), p. 13.

3   Geoffrey Blainey, *A Short History of the World* (Ringwood, NJ, 2000), pp. 8, 67–9, 592; Anthony F. Aveni, *Empires of Time: Calendars, Clocks and Cultures* (New York, 1989), p. 33.

4   Martin P. Nilsson, *Primitive Time-Reckoning: A Study in the Origins and First Development of the Art of Counting Time among the Primitive and Early Culture Peoples* (Lund, 1920), pp. 13–16, cited in Cashford, *The Moon*, p. 41; Barbara C. Walker, *The Women's Encyclopedia of Myths and Secrets* (San Francisco, 1983), p. 83, cited in Cashford, *The Moon*, p. 42.

5   Blainey, *A Short History of Time*, pp. 7, 68; Aveni, *Empires of Time*, p. 108; Cashford, *The Moon*, p. 30.

6   Cashford, *The Moon*, p. 31.

7   Aveni, *Empires of Time*, pp. 107–8.

8   Aude Engel, 'Hesiod', in Patricia F. O'Grady, ed., *Meet the Philosophers of Ancient Greece* (Aldershot, 2005), p. 21; Hesiod, *Theogony*, trans. R. M. Frazer (Norman, OK, 1983),

pp. 116–17. See also Heinrich Zimmer, *Myths and Symbols in Indian Art and Civilization* [1953], ed. Joseph Campbell (Washington, DC, 1946), pp. 78–9, for the Indian tradition. The gods also name Night first in the Norse *Elder Edda*, trans. Patricia Terry (Philadelphia, 1990), p. 1.

9   *The Interpretation of Dreams: The* Oneirocritica *of Artemidorus*, trans. Robert J. White (Park Ridge, NJ, 1975), p. 4, cited in Vered Lev Kenaan, 'Delusion and Dream in Apuleius' *Metamorphoses*', *Classical Antiquity*, XXIII/2 (2004), p. 256. See also Alexandre Leupin, *Fiction and Incarnation: Rhetoric, Theology and Literature in the Middle Ages* [1993], trans. David Laatsch (Minneapolis, 2003), p. 70.

10 *The Interpretation of Dreams*, 4, quoted in Kenaan, 'Delusion', p. 256.

11 J. M. Roberts, *A Short History of the World*, 4th edn (Oxford, 1993), p. 42. Jack M. Sasson gives the most up-to-date list of versions, including novels, poetry, operas, a ballet, pantomime and a DVD, in 'Comparative Observations on the Near Eastern Epic Traditions', in Foley, *A Companion to Ancient Epic*, p. 231.

12 Maureen Gallery Kovacs, trans. and intro, *The Epic of Gilgamesh* [1985] (Stanford, CA, 1989), p. xxii; Noegel, 'Mesopotamian Epic', p. 239; Roberts, *A Short History*, p. 50; Robert Pogue Harrison, *Forests: The Shadow of Civilization* (Chicago, 1992), p. 14. Unless otherwise stated, quotations and citations from *Gilgamesh* are from Kovacs's translation.

13 The Standard Version of the epic consists of twelve tablets rather than eleven, which slightly alters the halfway point. Kovacs presents eleven tablets because of a widely shared view that Tablet XII does not belong in the epic. See Kovacs, *The Epic of Gilgamesh*, pp. 116–17.

14 John Gardner and John Maier, trans., *Gilgamesh* (New York, 1984), p. 84, quoted in Deagon, 'The Twelve', p. 467; Kovacs, *The Epic of Gilgamesh*, pp. xix, xxi; Foster, 'Gilgamesh', pp. 25, 30.

15 Kovacs, *The Epic of Gilgamesh*, p. 14.

16 Foster, 'Gilgamesh', pp. 25, 32.

17 Samuel Noel Kramer, trans., 'Gilgamesh and the Land of the Living', in Pritchard, *Ancient Near Eastern Texts*, pp. 47–50. This fragment is also known as 'Gilgamesh and Huwawa (Humbaba)' and 'Gilgamesh and the Cedar Forest'; see Kovacs, *The Epic of Gilgamesh*, p. xxiv; Harrison, *Forests*, p. 17.

18 Gardner and Maier, *Gilgamesh*, quoted in Deagon, 'The Twelve', pp. 466–7; see also p. 475.

19 Foster, 'Gilgamesh', p. 37, notes that Enkidu 'reverses the curse formula normally put on door stones to guarantee perpetuation of the builder's name', and that this 'may well have sounded humorous to an audience familiar with the genre'.

20 Sasson, 'Comparative Observations', p. 229.

21 Alexander Heidel, *The Gilgamesh Epic and Old Testament Parallels*, 2nd edn (Chicago, 1949), p. 144, cited in Deagon, 'The Twelve', p. 465; Jonathan Omer-Man, 'The Study of the Torah as Awakening', *Parabola*, VII/1 (1982), pp. 59–61; Mircea Eliade, *A History of Religious Ideas: From the Stone Age to the Eleusinian Mysteries* (Chicago, 1978), p. 79, cited in Thomas H. McAlpine, *Sleep, Divine and Human, in the Old Testament* (Sheffield, 1987), p. 139.

22 Foster, 'Gilgamesh', pp. 41–2.

23 Deagon, 'The Twelve', p. 466.

24 Unless otherwise stated, quotations and citations are from Robert Fagles, trans., *The Iliad* (New York, 1990). Thalia Papadopoulou, *Heracles and Euripidean Tragedy* (Cambridge, 2005), p. 68; see *Iliad*, XXIV, 747–94; R. Kutscher, trans., *Oh Angry Sea (a-ab-ba hu-luh-ha)* (New Haven, 1975), p. 144, quoted in McAlpine, *Sleep*, p. 198. See also Psalms 121:3–4: 'Behold, he who keeps Israel/will neither slumber nor sleep', quoted in ibid., p. 192.

25 Padel, *Whom Gods Destroy*, pp. 47, 65.

26 Ibid., p. 65; Ruth Padel, *In and Out of the Mind: Greek Images of the Tragic Self* (Princeton, 1992), pp. 47, 72. See also Augustine, *Confessions*, trans. R. S. Pine-Coffin (New York, 1961), quoted in Leupin, *Fiction and Incarnation*, p. 74.

27 Padel, *Whom Gods Destroy*, p. 66.

28 Lara Simone, '"It is a good thing to give way to the night-time": The Presence of Night in Homer's *Iliad*', www.columbia.edu/itc/ lithum/gallo/iliad.html; Richard Broxton Onians, *The Origins of European Thought about the Body, the Mind, the Soul, the World, Time, and Fate* (Cambridge, 1951), pp. 95, 422. Onians (p. 421) notes that 'the Latin word for "cloud", *nubes*, appears to mean "veil" (cf. *nubere*). Conversely for the Greeks a fine net was a "cloud"'.

29 Bernard Knox, Introduction to Fagles, *Iliad*, p. 54. As Padel points out (*Whom Gods Destroy*, pp. 175, 249), *até* is circular, like insomnia perhaps, where guilt and innocence combine. It is 'bewilderment caused by blindness or delusion sent by gods' and 'the punishment of guilty rashness', but also 'the consequences of such visitation'. Unlike its later use in tragedy to portend heroic doom, 'it is a way of *not saying* "guilty or not guilty?"' Like the insomnia with which Agamemnon indirectly compares it, *até* preserves the complexity of borders. It is a working, nocturnally coded stand-in, a mix-up, a punishment for exceeding borders in a way one could not have recognized and did not choose.

30 Laura M. Slatkin, 'Homer's *Odyssey*', in Foley, *A Companion to Ancient Epic*, p. 315. Unless otherwise stated, quotations and citations are from Robert Fagles, trans., *The Odyssey* (New York, 1996).

31 Marilynn Desmond, *Reading Dido: Gender, Textuality and the Medieval* Aeneid (Minneapolis, 1994).

32 Unless otherwise stated, quotations and citations are from C. Day Lewis, trans., *The Aeneid* (London, 1954). The second quotation is the translation by Michael C. Putnam, 'Virgil's *Aeneid*', in Foley, *A Companion to Ancient Epic*, p. 471.

33 Putnam, 'Virgil's *Aeneid*', p. 469.

34 Richard Hunter, Introduction to Rhodus Apollonius, *Jason and the Golden Fleece (The Argonautica)*, trans. Richard Hunter (Oxford, 1995), pp. xxx– xxxi; Apollonius of Rhodes, *Jason and the Golden Fleece*, Book III of *Jason*, p. 72; Vassiliki Panoussi, 'Polis and Empire: Greek Tragedy in Rome', in Gregory, *A Companion to Ancient Epic*, pp. 418–19; Hippocrates, *On Diseases*, 30 (*Affections. Diseases. Diseases*, trans. Paul Potter, vol. v, Loeb Classical Library [Cambridge, MA, 1988], p. 178), quoted in Padel, *Whom Gods Destroy*, p. 52.

35 Oribasius of Pergamon, *Oeuvres d'Oribase*, ed. U. C. Bussemaker and C. Daremberg, 6 vols (Paris, 1851–76), vol. V, pp. 413–14; Paul of Aegina, *The Seven Books of Paulus Aeginata*, trans. Francis Adams, 3 vols (London, 1844–7), vol. I, pp. 390–91; Caelius Aurelianus, *On Acute Diseases and On Chronic Diseases*, ed. and trans. I. E. Drabkin (Chicago, 1950), pp. 557–9, cited in Stanley W. Jackson, MD, *Melancholia and Depression: From Hippocratic Times to Modern Times* (New Haven, 1986), p. 354. See also Judith Perkins, *The Suffering Self: Pain and Narrative Representation in the Early Christian Era* (London, 1995), pp. 155, 157; Galen, *De locis affectis*, 3.10 (C. G. Kühn, ed., *Claudii Galeni Opera Omnia* [Hildesheim, 1965], vol. VIII, p. 91), quoted in Padel, *Whom Gods Destroy*, p. 52.

36 Padel, *In and Out of the Mind*, pp. 158, 157.

37 Translation in Panoussi, 'Polis and Empire', p. 417; Padel, *Whom Gods Destroy*, pp. 179, 205, *In and Out of the Mind*, pp. 101, 162–3.

38 Aveni, *Empires of Time*, p. 308; Sima Qian, ed., *Shiji* [1959], vol. IV (Beijing, 1989); *Yi Zhoushu*, in D. C. Lau and Chen Fong Ching, eds, *A Concordance to the* Yi Zhoushu (Hong Kong, 1992), 44: 20–21, quoted in Antje Richter, 'Sleeping Time in Early Chinese Literature', in Brigitte Steger and Lodewijk Brunt, eds, *Night-time and Sleep in Asia and the West* (London, 2003), p. 33.

39 *Liji*, in D. C. Lau and Chen Fong Ching, eds, *A Concordance to the* Liji (Hong Kong, 1992), 3: 7/14, quoted in Richter, 'Sleeping Time', p. 31. Also ibid., pp. 31–4, 40–41, note.

40 Aveni, *Empires of Time*, p. 310; David Hinton, ed. and trans., *Mountain Home: The Wilderness Poetry of Ancient China* (Washington, DC, 2002), p. xix.

41 'Opposite a Post-Station, the Boat Moonlit Beside a Monastery'; Hinton, *Mountain Home*, p. 115.

42 'Autumn Thoughts'; ibid., p. 147.

43 'Facing Night'; ibid., p. 112. Also p. 96.

References

44 'Night Rain at Luster Gap'; ibid., p. 263.

TWO: LOVE, LABOUR, ANXIETY

1 J. M. Roberts, *The New Penguin History of the World*, 4th edn (London, 2004), p. 489; Jacques Le Goff, *The Birth of Purgatory* [1981], trans. Arthur Goldhammer (Chicago, 1984), p. 7.

2 Jacques Le Goff, *Time, Work and Culture in the Middle Ages* [1977], trans. Arthur Goldhammer (Chicago and London, 1980), pp. 29–42; David R. Carlson, *Chaucer's Jobs* (New York and Basingstoke, 2004), p. 89; Tracy Adams, *Violent Passions: Managing Love in the Old French Verse Romance* (New York and Basingstoke, 2005), pp. 12, 31–2.

3 Raffaella Sarti, *Europe at Home: Family and Material Culture, 1500–1800* [1999], trans. Allan Cameron (New Haven, 2002), p. 121; Jean Verdon, *Night in the Middle Ages* [1994], trans. George Holoch (Notre Dame, IN, 2002), pp. 140–43, 160; Philippe Contamine, 'Peasant Hearth to Papal Palace: The Fourteenth and Fifteenth Centuries', in Philippe Ariès and Georges Duby, eds, *A History of Private Life, Vol. II: Revelations of the Medieval World* [1985], trans. Arthur Goldhammer (Cambridge, MA, and London, 1988), pp. 447–8.

4 Contamine, 'Peasant Hearth', p. 498; Georges Duby, Dominique Barthélmy and Charles de la Roncière, 'The Aristocratic Households of Feudal France', in Ariès and Duby, *A History of Private Life*, p. 62; Charles de la Roncière, 'Tuscan Notables on the Eve of the Renaissance', in Ariès and Duby, *A History of Private Life*, pp. 184–7. See also Lawrence Wright, *Warm and Snug: The History of the Bed* (London, 1962), p. 25.

5 Wright, *Warm and Snug*, pp. 57, 63; Luigi Grassi, Mario Pepe and Giancarlo Sestieri, *Dizionario di antiquariato: dizionario storico-critico di arte e antiquariato dall'antichità all' inizio del Novecento*, 2nd edn (Milan, 1992), under 'Bed', cited in Sarti, *Europe at Home*, p. 12.

6 Wright, *Warm and Snug*, pp. 71, 93, 96; Sarti, *Europe at Home*, p. 122.

7 J. A. Burrow, *The Ages of Man: A Study in Medieval Writing and Thought* (Oxford, 1986), pp. 66–8; David S. Landes, *Revolution in Time: Clocks and the Making of the Modern World* [1983] (London, 2000), pp. 55–6.

8 E. Roger Ekirch, *At Day's Close: A History of Nighttime* (London, 2005), pp. 300–01, 305–11.

9 A. Rechtschaffen and L. J. Monroe, 'Laboratory Studies of Insomnia', in Anthony Kales, ed., *Sleep Physiology and Pathology: A Symposium* (Philadelphia, 1969), pp. 158–9, cited in Francis Schiller, 'Semantics of Sleep', *Bulletin of the History of Medicine*, LVI/3 (1982), p. 394.

10 Verdon, *Night in the Middle Ages*, pp. 27, 35, 51, 64, 80; Ekirch, *At Day's Close*, pp. 172, 237; Danielle Régnier-Bohler, 'Imagining the Self: Exploring Literature', in Ariès and Duby, *A History of Private Life*, p. 330.

11 Verdon, *Night in the Middle Ages*, pp. 52, 56–7; Robert Muchembled, *A History of the Devil: From the Middle Ages to the Present* [2000], trans. Jean Burrell (Cambridge, 2003), p. 33; Peter Brown, *The Body and Society: Men, Women and Sexual Renunciation in Early Christianity* (New York, 1988), pp. 47–9, quoted in Karma Lochrie, *Margery Kempe and Translations of the Flesh* (Philadelphia, 1991), p. 19.

12 Augustine, *Enarrationes in psalmos*, ed. D. Eligius Dekkers and Iohannes Fraipont, CCSL, 40 (Turnhout, 1956), 16, p. 2037; Bernard of Clairvaux, *Sermo de conversione ad clericos*, 7, 12, in J. Leclercq and H. M. Rochais, eds, *S. Bernardi opera*, vol. IV (Rome, 1957), pp. 86–7; G. R. Evans, trans., *Bernard of Clairvaux: Selected Works* (New York, 1987), p. 83, both cited in Lochrie, *Margery Kempe*, pp. 20–21.

13 Verdon, *Night in the Middle Ages*, p. 64.

14 Richard Kieckhefer, *Unquiet Souls: Fourteenth-Century Saints in Their Religious Milieu* (Chicago and London, 1984), p. 90; Lochrie, *Margery Kempe*, p. 180; Caroline Walker Bynum, 'The Female Body and Religious Practice in the Later Middle Ages', in Michel Feher with Ramona Naddaff and Nadia Tazi, eds, *Fragments for a History of the Human Body*, vol. I (New York, 1989), p. 175; Hope Phyllis Weissman, 'Margery Kempe in Jerusalem: *Hysterica compassio* in the Late Middle Ages', in Mary J. Carruthers and

Elizabeth D. Kirk, eds, *Acts of Interpretation: The Text in Its Contexts, 700–1600* (Norman, OK, 1982), pp. 211–12; Jennifer Ash, 'The Discursive Construction of Christ's Bodiliness in the Later Middle Ages: Resistance and Autonomy', in Terry Threadgold and Anne Cranny-Francis, eds, *Feminine/Masculine and Representation* (Sydney, 1990), p. 86.

15 Susan Dickman, 'Margery Kempe and the Continental Tradition of the Pious Woman', in Marion Glasscoe, ed., *The Medieval Mystical Tradition in England* (Cambridge, 1984), p. 152; *The Dark Night of the Soul* (*c.* 1588) is a famous work by the sixteenth-century Spanish mystic St John of the Cross. It depicts the soul's journey as one of unknowing and emptiness on the path to spiritual bliss. See also Kieckhefer, *Unquiet Souls*, p. 3; Hans Penner, 'The Mystical Illusion', in Steven T. Katz, ed., *Mysticism and Religious Traditions* (New York, 1983), p. 90.

16 Kieckhefer, *Unquiet Souls*, pp. 26, 144; Duby, Barthélmy and de la Roncière, 'The Aristocratic Households', pp. 55-6; Verdon, *Night in the Middle Ages*, p. 149.

17 Lee Siegel, *Sacred and Profane Dimensions of Love in Indian Traditions as Exemplifed in the Gitagovinda of Jayadeva* (Delhi, 1978), pp. 21, 35; also p. 159, cited in Patrick Michael Thomas, 'The Mystic Erotic: Carnal Spirituality in Old Provence and Medieval India', *Neohelicon: Acta Comparationis Litterarum Universarum*, XXI/1 (1994), p. 218.

18 Barbara Stoler Miller, ed. and trans., *Gitagovinda of Jayadeva: Love Song of the Dark Lord* (Delhi, 1977). Unless otherwise stated, quotations and citations are from this edition.

19 Daniel Ingalls, ed. and trans., *An Anthology of Sanskrit Court Poetry: Vidyakara's 'Subhasitaratnaskora'* (Cambridge, MA, 1965), pp. 12, 130–33.

20 Siegel, *Sacred and Profane*, p. 35; Miller, Introduction to *Gitagovinda*, pp. 6–7, 16.

21 Siegel, *Sacred and Profane*, p. 39; Miller, *Gitagovinda*, p. 222, note.

22 Balraj Khanna, 'Krishna – The Divine Lover', in *Krishna: The Divine Lover* (London, 1997), p. 47; W. G. Archer, Introduction to M. S. Randhawa, *Kangra Paintings of the* Gita Govinda (New Delhi, 1963), p. 17.

23 Allison Busch, 'The Anxiety of Innovation: The Practice of Literary Science in the Hindi/Riti Tradition', *Comparative Studies of South Asia, Africa and the Middle East*, XXIV/2 (2004), pp. 45–6, 48. As Busch explains, 'Brajbhasa was the primary dialect of written Hindi prior to *c.*1900, at which point Modern Standard Hindi (Khari Boli) began to achieve cultural dominance' (p. 55, note).

24 K. P. Bahadur, trans., *The Rasikapriya of Keshavadasa* (Delhi, 1972), V, p. 73. Unless otherwise stated, quotations and citations are from this edition.

25 Busch, 'The Anxiety of Innovation', p. 46; Kesavdas, *Rasikpriya*, in Visvanath Prasad Misra, ed., *Kesavgranthavali* (Allahabad, 1954), vv. 7.1–3, quoted in Busch, 'The Anxiety of Innovation', p. 51.

26 Julie Scott Meisami, *Medieval Persian Court Poetry* (Princeton, 1987), pp. viii, 13–15.

27 Awhad al-Din Anvari, *Divan*, ed. Said Nafisi (Tehran, 1959), pp. 118–19, cited in Meisami, *Medieval Persian Court Poetry*, pp. 71–3.

28 Geoffrey Chaucer, *The Book of the Duchess*, in Helen Phillips and Nick Havely, eds, *Chaucer's Dream Poetry* (London, 1997), ll. 1318–19; Phillips and Havely, Introduction to *Chaucer's Dream Poetry*, p. 29. Unless otherwise stated, quotations and citations are from this edition.

29 Guillemette Bolens and Paul Beckman Taylor, 'Chess, Clocks and Counsellors in Chaucer's *Book of the Duchess*', *Chaucer Review*, XXXV/3 (2002), p. 283.

30 Phillips and Havely, *Chaucer's Dream Poetry*, p. 41; Lisa J. Kiser, 'Sleep, Dreams and Poetry in Chaucer's *Book of the Duchess*', *Papers on Language and Literature*, XIX/1 (1983), p. 4.

31 Thomas Brinton, *The Sermons of Thomas Brinton, Bishop of Rochester (1373–1389)*, ed. M. A. Devlin, vol. II (London, 1954), p. 462, quoted in Burrow, *The Ages of Man*, p. 67; Siegfried Wenzel, *The Sin of Sloth: Acedia in Medieval Thought and Literature* [1960] (Chapel Hill, 1967); Kiser, 'Sleep', p. 4.

32 *The Book of the Duchess*, in F. N. Robinson, ed., *The Works of Geoffrey Chaucer*, 2nd edn (Boston, 1957), l. 169, quoted in Kiser, 'Sleep', p. 5; *The Canterbury Tales*, in Robinson, *The Works*, I, lines 1361-4.

33 Bolens and Taylor, 'Chess, Clocks and Counsellors', p. 281.
34 Ibid., pp. 281–2; Landes, *Revolution in Time*, pp. 72–3; Gerhard Dohrn-Van Rossum, *History of the Hour: Clocks and Modern Temporal Orders* [1992], trans. Thomas Dunlap (Chicago, 1996), p. 62.
35 Phillips and Havely, *Chaucer's Dream Poetry*, pp. 83, note; 286, 281.
36 P. Heath Barnum, ed., *Dives et Pauper*, EETS, 275 (Oxford, 1976), 119, cited in Dohrn-Van Rossum, *History of the Hour*, p. 1; Le Goff, *Time, Work and Culture*, p. 50.
37 Paul Strohm notes that 'Chaucer's royal service may have commenced as early as 1366'. See Martin Crow and Clair C. Olson, eds, *Chaucer Life-Records*, from materials compiled by John M. Manly and Edith Rickert, with the assistance of Lilian J. Redstone and others (Oxford, 1966), p. 64, cited in Paul Strohm, *Social Chaucer* (Cambridge, MA, and London, 1988), p. 10; also Carlson, *Chaucer's Jobs*, p. 39.
38 Brinton, *Sermons*, p. 259, cited in Strohm, *Social Chaucer*, p. 3.
39 Carlson, *Chaucer's Jobs*, pp. 3, 41–2.
40 Ibid., p. 41.
41 Chaucer, *The House of Fame*, in Robinson, *The Works*, ll. 652–8, quoted in Carlson, *Chaucer's Jobs*, pp. 41, 89; Kiser, 'Sleep', p. 11.
42 Bolens and Taylor, 'Chess, Clocks and Counsellors', p. 284.
43 Le Goff, *Time, Work and Culture*, pp. 34–5, 48.
44 Ibid., pp. 29, 38–9, 117.
45 Ibid., pp. 111–12; Strohm, *Social Chaucer*, p. 7.
46 Le Goff, *Time, Work and Culture*, p. 39; Muchembled, *A History of the Devil*, pp. 23–4, 32.
47 Leon d'Alexis, *Traicté des energumènes*, fols 19r–v, in *Dämonie und Transzendenz* (Stuttgart, 1964), quoted in Armando Maggi, *Satan's Rhetoric: A Study of Renaissance Demonology* (Chicago and London, 2001), p. 1; Muchembled, *A History of the Devil*, pp. 35–6.
48 Maggi, *Satan's Rhetoric*, p. 2; see also Steven Connor, *Dumbstruck: A Cultural History of Ventriloquism* (Oxford, 2000), pp. 125–30.
49 Millicent Bell, *Shakespeare's Tragic Skepticism* (New Haven and London, 2002), pp. 6–7.
50 E. Ruth Harvey, *The Inward Wits: Psychological Theory in the Middle Ages and Renaissance* (London, 1975), pp. 2–3.
51 See the sources listed in William J. Bouwsma, 'Anxiety and the Formation of Early Modern Culture', in Barbara C. Malament, ed., *After the Reformation: Essays in Honor of J. H. Hexter* (Philadelphia, 1980), p. 216; also Donald R. Howard, 'Renaissance World-Alienation', in Robert S. Kinsman, ed., *The Darker Vision of the Renaissance: Beyond the Fields of Reason* (Berkeley, CA, 1974), pp. 47–76.
52 Bouwsma, 'Anxiety', p. 218; Le Goff, *Time, Work and Culture*, pp. 50–51.
53 R. Mandrou, *Introduction à la France moderne (1500–1640): Essai de psychologique historique* (Paris, 1961), pp. 95–8, cited in Le Goff, *Time, Work and Culture*, p. 49; also p. 32.
54 Ludovico Ariosto, *Orlando Furioso (The Frenzy of Orlando)* [1516], trans. Barbara Reynolds, 2 vols (Harmondsworth, 1975), VIII, 71; X, 18–19; XXIII, 122–3, 125, 132–3; XXV, 42, 65, 80; XXVII, 127; XXVIII, 17, 85; XXXII, 12–13; XXXIII, 59, 77; XLV, 102: XLVI, 80. Unless otherwise stated, quotations and citations are from this edition.
55 Albert Russell Ascoli, 'Ariosto and the "Fier Pastor": Form and History in *Orlando Furioso*', *Renaissance Quarterly*, LIV/2 (2001), pp. 487–8; Lisa K. Regan, 'Ariosto's Threshold Patron: Isabella d'Este in the *Orlando Furioso*', *Modern Language Notes*, CXX/1 (2005), pp. 51–2; Barbara Reynolds, Introduction to Ariosto, *Orlando Furioso*, trans. Reynolds, p. 18.
56 Ascoli, 'Ariosto', pp. 488, 498, 506.
57 Cited in ibid., p. 501.
58 Eric MacPhail, 'Ariosto and the Prophetic Moment', *Modern Language Notes*, CXVI/1 (2001), p. 30.
59 Eric Saccone, 'Wood, Garden, *locus amoenus* in Ariosto's *Orlando Furioso*', *Modern Language Notes*, CXII/1 (1997), p. 3; Ariosto, XXIII, 50; XLV, 5; XXXVIII, 30; XVIII, 180, cited in Daniel Rolfs, 'Sleep, Dreams and Insomnia in the *Orlando Furioso*', *Italica*, LIII/4 (1976),

pp. 461–2.

60 Roberts, *The New Penguin History of the World*, p. 525.

61 Elissa B. Weaver, 'A Reading of the Interlaced Plot of the *Orlando furioso*: The Three Cases of Love Madness', in Donald Beecher, Massimo Ciavoletta and Roberto Fedi, eds, *Ariosto Today: Contemporary Perspectives* (Toronto, 2003), p. 126; Ascoli, 'Ariosto', pp. 497, 507.

62 Bell, *Shakespeare's Tragic Scepticism*, p. 6. On disturbed sleep, see Simon B. Chandler, 'Shakespeare and Sleep', *Bulletin of the History of Medicine*, xxix (1955), p. 256.

63 Steven Mullaney, *The Place of the Stage: License, Play and Power in Renaissance England* (Chicago, 1988), quoted in Naomi Conn Liebler, 'Buying and Selling So(u)les: Marketing Strategies and the Politics of Performance in *Julius Caesar*', in Horst Zander, ed., *Julius Caesar: New Critical Essays* (New York, 2005), p. 173.

64 As Faye Getz indicates with reference to medieval medicine: '[T]he way in which the body worked . . . was ruled by several factors . . . conveniently distilled from the writings of Galen by Islamic commentators into the so-called nonnaturals: food, drink, and fasting; sleep and wakefulness; air; exercise and rest; excretion and retention, and the emotions' (*Medicine in the English Middle Ages* [Princeton, 1998], p. 87). Renaissance physicians taught medical humanism from within this long tradition. Too much or too little sleep was considered unhealthy, but not in itself a disorder. See Karl H. Dannenfeldt, 'Sleep: Theory and Practice in the Late Renaissance', *Journal of the History of Medicine and Allied Sciences*, xli/4 (1986), pp. 415–41.

65 Liebler, 'Buying and Selling So(u)les', p. 173; David Daniell, Introduction, in William Shakespeare, *Julius Caesar*, ed. David Daniell (Walton-on-Thames, 1998), pp. 22, 32.

66 Shakespeare, *Julius Caesar*, ed. Daniell. Unless otherwise stated, quotations and citations are from this edition. Horst Zander, '*Julius Caesar* and the Critical Legacy', in Zander, *Julius Caesar*, p. 3; Steve Sohmer, *Shakespeare's Mystery Play: The Opening of the Globe Theatre, 1599* (Manchester, 1999), pp. 17–18.

67 Shakespeare, *Julius Caesar*, ed. Daniell, p. 25; Andreas Mahler, '"There is Restitution, no End of Restitution, only not for us": Experimental Tragedy and the Early Modern Subject in *Julius Caesar*', in Zander, *Julius Caesar*, pp. 182–3.

68 Mahler, '"There is Restitution"', p. 187.

69 Shakespeare, *Julius Caesar*, ed. Daniell, p. 21; Mahler, '"There is Restitution"', pp. 190–91.

70 William Shakespeare, *Macbeth: Texts and Contexts*, ed. William C. Carroll (Boston, ma, and New York, 1999). Unless otherwise stated, quotations and citations are from this edition.

71 Alexander Leggatt, *Shakespeare's Tragedies: Violation and Identity* (Cambridge, 2005), p. 177.

72 As numerous commentators point out, the matter of royal succession was extremely topical in England in the 1590s, and *Macbeth* dramatizes the lack of certainty, combined with the pressing import, of the matter of who would succeed Elizabeth at her death. See Marie Axton, *The Queen's Two Bodies: Drama and the Elizabethan Succession* (London, 1977); Howard Nenner, *The Right To Be King: The Succession to the Crown of England* (Chapel Hill, 1995); William C. Carroll, 'Discourses of Sovereignty' and 'The Cultural Construction of Scotland', in Shakespeare, *Macbeth*. As Carroll notes, 'pro- and anti-Scottish discourses intensified' before 1603 as it became clear that James vi was 'the logical successor to Queen Elizabeth' ('Cultural Construction', p. 272). See also Lisa Hopkins, *Shakespeare on the Edge: Border-Crossing in the Tragedies and the 'Henriad'* (Aldershot, 2005), pp. 61–86, on the related matter of England's annulment of the border with Scotland.

73 Citing James Nosworthy, A. R. Braunmuller points out that 'triadic elements' in the play – 'the three sisters themselves . . . and their "Thrice to thine . . ." (1.3.33–4) or their three threes in "nine times nine"' (1.3.21) are associated with 'evil . . . usually satanic' contexts (J. S. Nosworthy, '*Macbeth, Doctor Faustus* and the Juggling Fiends', in *Mirror up to Shakespeare: Essays in Honour of G. R. Hubbard* [Toronto, 1984], p. 221, quoted in A. R. Braunmuller, Introduction to *Macbeth*, in *Macbeth*, ed. A. R. Braunmuller (Cambridge, 1997), p. 26. See also 1.2.37–8, 1.6.16, iv.1.2.

74 Also 1.5.65–6, 1.7.1–2, 2.1.62, 3.2.12; Leggatt, *Shakespeare's Tragedies*, pp. 185, 182.

75 Leggatt, *Shakespeare's Tragedies*, p. 185.

References

76   Bouwsma, 'Anxiety', p. 230.
77   Howard, 'Renaissance World-Alienation', p. 58.

THREE: THE SLEEP OF REASON

1   Hendrik Goltzius, *The Complete Engravings and Woodcuts*, ed. Walter L. Strauss (New York, 1977), p. 648.
2   Dirck Volkertszoon Coornhert, 'Comedie van de Rijcke-man', in P. Van der Meulen, ed., *Het Roerspel en de Comedies van Coornhert* (Leiden, 1955), pp. 23–4, cited in Simon Schama, *The Embarrassment of Riches: An Interpretation of Dutch Culture in the Golden Age* (New York, 1987), p. 8; Schama, 'The Unruly Realm: Appetite and Restraint in Seventeenth-Century Holland', *Daedalus*, CVIII/3 (1979), p. 121.
3   Schama, 'The Unruly Realm', p. 105; Wayne C. Martin, 'Bubbles and Skulls: The Phenomenology of Self-Consciousness in Dutch Still-Life Painting', in Hubert L. Dreyfus and Mark A. Wrathall, eds, *A Companion to Phenomenology and Existentialism* (Malden, MA, 2006), pp. 566–71; J. van Beverwijck, *Schat der Gesontheyt* (Dordrecht, 1656), cited in Schama, *Embarrassment of Riches*, pp. 158–9.
4   Schama, *Embarrassment of Riches*, p. 53; Stephen Kalberg, Introduction to Max Weber, *The Protestant Ethic and the Spirit of Capitalism* [1904–5], trans. Stephen Kalberg, 3rd edn (Los Angeles, 2002), p. xxxii. Although Goltzius is believed to have been a Catholic, allegorical imagery such as that in the 'Abuses' series served both Reformation and Counter-Reformation causes. In the 1580s Haarlem declared itself on the side of the Calvinists. E.K.J. Reznicek, 'Hendrik Goltzius', in *The Dictionary of Art* (Oxford, 1996); Grove Art Online: www.groveart.com.ezproxy.auckland.ac.nz/ shared/views/article; J. M. Roberts, *The New Penguin History of the World*, 4th edn (London, 2004), p. 578; Weber, *The Protestant Ethic*, pp. 65–6.
5   Hal Foster, 'The Art of Fetishism: Notes on Dutch Still Life', *Princeton Architectural Journal*, IV (1992), p. 15.
6   Lyckle de Vries, 'The Changing Face of Realism', in *Art in History, History in Art: Studies in Seventeenth-Century Dutch Culture* (Santa Monica, CA, 1991), p. 218.
7   J.G.A. Pocock, 'Modes of Political and Historical Time in Early Eighteenth-Century England', in Ronald C. Rosbottom, ed., *Studies in Eighteenth-Century Culture*, vol. V (Madison, WI, 1976), pp. 87–102.
8   Roberts, *The New Penguin History*, pp. 664–5; James Walvin, *Making the Black Atlantic: Britain and the African Diaspora* (London, 2000), pp. 15–17; also Johannes Menne Postma, *The Dutch in the Atlantic Slave Trade, 1600–1815* (Cambridge, 1990), p. 15; David Richardson, 'The British Empire and the Atlantic Slave Trade, 1660–1807', in P. J. Marshall, ed., *The Oxford History of the British Empire, Vol. II: The Eighteenth Century* (Oxford, 1998), p. 440.
9   Robin Blackburn, *The Making of New World Slavery: From the Baroque to the Modern, 1492–1800* (London, 1997), p. 16; Patrick K. O'Brien, 'Inseparable Connections: Trade, Economy, Fiscal State and the Expansion of Empire, 1688–1815', in Marshall, *Oxford History of the British Empire*, pp. 56–7; Sidney W. Mintz, *Sweetness and Power: The Place of Sugar in Modern History* (Harmondsworth, 1985), pp. 164–5.
10   Walvin, *Making the Black Atlantic*, p. 57.
11   Ibid., pp. 21, 91; Kenneth Pomeranz and Steven Topik, *The World That Trade Created: Society, Culture and the World Economy, 1400 to the Present*, 2nd edn (New York, 2006), p. 89; Jack E. James, *Understanding Caffeine: A Biobehavioral Analysis* (London, 1997), pp. 40–55, cited in Markman Ellis, *The Coffee-House: A Cultural History* (London, 2004), p. 148. While it is clear that coffee enhances the brain's 'overall arousal level' and 'delays the onset of sleep', the exact nature of its effect on the human brain is still being debated. Some studies suggest that while it 'improves mental ability on tasks requiring "speed"', it may degrade or have no effect on more complex reasoning tasks requiring 'power'. See Stephen Braun, *Buzz: The Science and Lore of Alcohol and Caffeine* (New York, 1996), pp. 133, 135.

12 Steven Topik, 'The Integration of the World Coffee Market', in W.G.C. Smith and Steven Topik, eds, *The Global Coffee Economy in Africa, Asia and Latin America* (Cambridge, 2003), p. 25; Blackburn, *The Making of New World Slavery*, p. 271; Ellis, *The Coffee-House*, pp. 166–81. From the late seventeenth century, the coffee houses of Exchange Alley, near the Royal Exchange in Cornhill, London, served traders from Europe and beyond who met to agree prices, 'settle bills and make deals'. The Alley itself had been opened in 1662 as a joint property speculation by a consortium of goldsmiths, bankers and merchants who sought to take advantage of its passage between busy streets, and the Exchange Alley Coffee House became an extension of the trading floor. See ibid., pp. 166–9.

13 David Hancock, *Citizens of the World: London Merchants and the Integration of the British Atlantic Community, 1735–85* (Cambridge, 1995), cited in O'Brien, 'Inseparable Connections', p. 60; Jacob M. Price, 'What Did Merchants Do? Reflections on British Overseas Trade, 1660–1760', *Journal of Economic History*, LIX (1989), cited in O'Brien, 'Inseparable Connections', p. 60.

14 O'Brien, 'Inseparable Connections', pp. 61–2; Roberts, *The New Penguin History*, p. 556; Pocock, 'Modes of Political and Historical Time', p. 96.

15 Pocock, 'Modes of Political and Historical Time', p. 95. See also *The Machiavellian Moment: Florentine Political Thought and the Atlantic Republican Tradition* (Princeton, 1975), chap. 13, cited in Pocock, 'Modes of Political and Historical Time', p. 97.

16 Roger Schmidt, 'Caffeine and the Coming of the Enlightenment', *Raritan*, XXIII/1, pp. 129–49; O'Brien, 'Inseparable Connections', p. 66; P. J. Marshall, Introduction to *The Oxford History of the British Empire, Vol. 11*, pp. 12–14; Stephen H. Gregg, Introduction to Gregg, ed., *Empire and Identity: An Eighteenth-Century Sourcebook* (Basingstoke, 2005), pp. 6–8; Paul Gilroy, *The Black Atlantic: Modernity and Double Consciousness* (London, 1993), p. 197.

17 Gregg, *Empire and Identity*, p. 9.

18 Juliet Flower MacCannell, *The Hysteric's Guide to the Future Female Subject* (Minneapolis, 2000), pp. 65–6, 72, 93–100, 106–9; William C. Dement, 'What All Undergraduates Should Know about How Their Sleeping Lives Affect Their Waking Lives', *Sleepless at Stanford*, 1997: www.stanford.edu/%7Edement/sleepless.html

19 Cynthia Wall, 'The Political World', in Alexander Pope, *The Rape of the Lock*, ed. Wall (Boston, MA, 1998), p. 388; Pocock, 'Modes of Political and Historical Time', pp. 98–9; Laura Brown, *Fables of Modernity: Literature and Culture in the English Eighteenth Century* (New York, 2001), pp. 95–131; Ross W. Jamieson, 'The Essence of Commodification: Caffeine Dependencies in the Early Modern World', *Journal of Social History*, XXXV/2 (2001), p. 281; Wolfgang Schivelbusch, *Tastes of Paradise: A Social History of Spices, Stimulants and Intoxicants*, trans. David Jacobson (New York, 1993), n. p., quoted in Braun, *Buzz*, p. 124.

20 Ellis, *The Coffee-House*, pp. 28, 42, 39, 68–9, 100, 103; Jamieson, 'The Essence of Commodification', p. 281.

21 Michel Tuchscherer, 'Coffee in the Red Sea Area from the Sixteenth to the Nineteenth Century', in Smith and Topik, *The Global Coffee Economy*, p. 51; Ralph S. Hattox, *Coffee and Coffeehouses: The Origins of a Social Beverage in the Medieval Near East* (Seattle, 1985), pp. 14, 26; Jamieson, 'The Essence of Commodification', p. 280; Ellis, *The Coffee-House*, pp. 131–5, 146; Richard Kroll, 'Pope and Drugs: The Pharmacology of *The Rape of the Lock*', *English Literary History*, LXVII/1 (2000), p. 103. Jürgen Habermas famously argued that the eighteenth-century coffee house provided the setting for the emergence of a rational, bourgeois public sphere. See *The Structural Transformation of the Public Sphere: An Inquiry into a Category of Bourgeois Society* [1962], trans. Thomas Burger and Frederick Lawrence (Cambridge, 1991); also Steve Pincus, '"Coffee Politicians Does Create": Coffeehouses and Restoration Political Culture', *Journal of Modern History*, LXVII/4 (1995), pp. 807–34. Habermas's findings have since been critiqued by Brian Cowan ('What Was Masculine About the Public Sphere? Gender and the Coffee-House Milieu in Post-Restoration England', *History Workshop Journal*, LI [2001], pp. 127–57), among others.

22 William Harvey, *The Circulation of the Blood and Other Writings*, trans. Kenneth J. Franklin

(London, 1990), cited in Kroll, 'Pope and Drugs', p. 99; Jerome J. Bylebyl, 'The Medical Side of Harvey's Discovery: The Normal and the Abnormal', in Bylebyl ed., *William Harvey and His Age: The Professional and Social Context of the Discovery of the Circulation* (Baltimore, 1979), p. 65; Andrea Finkelstein, *Harmony and the Balance: An Intellectual History of Seventeenth-Century English Economic Thought* (Ann Arbor, 2000), p. 102. This political analogy was also used by René Descartes, who first gave credit to Harvey. See *Discourse of the Method of rightly conducting one's reason and seeking the truth in the sciences, and in addition the Optics, the meteorology and the Geometry, which are essays in this Method* [1637], in John Cottingham et al., trans., *The Philosophical Writings of Descartes* (Cambridge, 1985), vol. I, p. 136, cited in Finkelstein, *Harmony and the Balance*, pp. 102–3.

23   Kroll, 'Pope and Drugs', pp. 100, 111; Robert Boyle, *The Origins of Forms and Qualities According to the Crepuscular Philosophy* [1666], in M. A. Stewart, ed., *Selected Papers of Robert Boyle* (Manchester, 1979), pp. 18–20, quoted in Finkelstein, *Harmony and the Balance*, p. 101.

24   '*Coffee* (which makes the Politician wise,/And see thro' all things with his half-shut Eyes)' (Pope, *The Rape*, 3:117—18). Elsewhere Pope wrote: 'I cannot sleep a wink./I nod in company, I wake at night/Fools rush into my Head, and so I write' ('Satire I: To Mr Fortescue', *The Poems, Epistles and Satires of Alexander Pope* [London, n.d.], quoted in Schmidt, 'Caffeine', p. 136; Lawrence Babb, 'The Cave of Spleen', *Review of English Studies*, XII/46 (1936), pp. 165–76; also Schmidt, 'Caffeine', p. 131.

25   Patricia Meyer Spacks, *Boredom: The Literary History of a State of Mind* (Chicago and London, 1995), p. 6; also Elizabeth S. Goodstein, *Experience Without Qualities: Boredom and Modernity* (Stanford, CA, 2005); Valerie Rumbold, Introduction to Alexander Pope, *The Dunciad in Four Books*, ed. Rumbold (Harlow, 1999), p. 3.

26   Adam Phillips, 'On Being Bored', in *On Kissing, Tickling and Being Bored: Psychoanalytic Essays on the Unexamined Life* (Boston, MA, 1993), p. 71.

27   See Todd McGowan, *The End of Dissatisfaction? Jacques Lacan and the Emerging Society of Enjoyment* (New York, 2004); Steven Connor, 'Defiling Celebrity': www.bbk.ac.uk/english/skc/defiling/DefilingCelebrity. pdf, pp. 14–15. The diminishing opportunity for privations that can help give shape to life is arguably one of the reasons so many people opt to suffer pain or go without things in the structured environment of reality television. Personal suffering – and, often, shame, which signals the conflict at work here – is mandated in a form for mass enjoyment.

28   James Harris, *Three Treatises* (London, 1744), pp. 130, 196–200, quoted in Spacks, *Boredom*, p. 35.

29   David Fordyce, *Dialogues Concerning Education*, vol. I (London, 1745), quoted in Spacks, *Boredom*, pp. 35–6; Schmidt, 'Caffeine', pp. 143–4; William Law, *A Serious Call to a Devout and Holy Life* [1728], ed. J. C. Reid (London, 1965), pp. 129–30; also p. 229. See also Richard Baxter, *The Poor Man's Family Book*, 6th edn (London, 1697), pp. 290–91, quoted in E. P. Thompson, 'Time, Work-Discipline and Industrial Capitalism', in *Customs in Common* (London, 1991), p. 392; Jack Lynch, 'Samuel Johnson, Unbeliever', *Eighteenth-Century Life*, XXIX/3 (2005), p. 13.

30   Boyd Stanley Schlenther, 'Religious Faith and Commercial Empire', in Marshall, *Oxford History of the British Empire*, pp. 141–2; George Whitefield, *Sermons on Important Subjects* (London, 1825), p. 654, quoted in Schlenther, 'Religious Faith', p. 141.

31   Schlenther, 'Religious Faith', p. 142.

32   James Boswell, *Life of Johnson* [1904], ed. R. W. Chapman (Oxford, 1980), p. 456.

33   Schmidt, 'Caffeine', pp. 145–7; Boswell, *Life of Johnson*, p. 1007; also pp. 787, 890, 1003, 1366, 1387; Samuel Johnson, *Selected Writings*, ed. Patrick Cruttwell (Harmondsworth, 1982), pp. 485–6, 491, 494–5.

34   Spacks, *Boredom*, p. 51; Boswell, *Life of Johnson*, pp. 329–30, quoted in Lynch, 'Samuel Johnson', pp. 2–3; Fred Parker, *Scepticism and Literature: An Essay on Pope, Hume, Sterne and Johnson* (Oxford, 2003), pp. 232–3, 238, 244. Parker also cites *Rasselas*, 'which famously ends in a "conclusion, in which nothing is concluded"'. John H. Middendorf et al., eds,

The Yale Edition of the Works of Samuel Johnson (New Haven, 1958–2005), vol. XVI, p. 175, quoted in Parker, *Scepticism and Literature*, p. 252; also Johnson's Sober, 'an acknowledged self-portrait', who fears going to sleep (G. B. Hill, ed., *Johnsonian Miscellanies*, vol. I [Oxford, 1897], p. 178); Middendorf et al., *The Yale Edition*, vol. II, p. 97, cited in Parker, *Scepticism and Literature*, p. 247.

35 Charles H. Hinnant, *The Poetry of Anne Finch: An Essay in Interpretation* (Newark, NJ, 1994), p. 32; Susan Stewart, *Poetry and the Fate of the Senses* (Chicago, 2002), pp. 260–61.

36 Christopher R. Miller, 'Staying Out Late: Anne Finch's Poetics of Evening', *Studies in English Literature*, XLV/3 (2005), p. 608. In other poems, for example, 'Ardelia to Melancholy' and 'An Invocation to Sleep', sleeplessness is a by-product of melancholy, and, as Susan Stewart notes (p. 264), these poems typically 'end in resignation or surrender'. See also Barbara McGovern, *Anne Finch and Her Poetry: A Critical Biography* (Athens, GA, 1992), p. 165; John Milton, 'Il Penseroso', in Douglas Bush, ed., *Poetical Works* (Oxford, 1977), p. 92; also Stewart, *Poetry*, p. 265; Milton, *Paradise Lost*, Book V, ll. 38–47; 'Il Penseroso', ll. 85–6, Bush, *Poetical Works*, pp. 94, 299.

37 Stewart, *Poetry*, p. 278; Anne Finch, 'A Nocturnal Reverie', in *Miscellany Poems, on Several Occasions* (London, 1713), l. 1, p. 291; l. 47, p. 293.

38 John Locke, *An Essay Concerning Human Understanding* (1690), ed. Peter H. Nidditch (Oxford, 1975), p. 227, quoted in Christopher R. Miller, *The Invention of Evening: Perception and Time in Romantic Poetry* (Cambridge, 2006), pp. 29–30.

39 E. P. Thompson, Introduction to Thompson and Marian Sugden, eds, *'The Thresher's Labour' by Stephen Duck and 'The Woman's Labour' by Mary Collier: Two Eighteenth-Century Poems* (London, 1989), pp. i–viii; also 'Time, Work-Discipline and Industrial Capitalism', in *Customs in Common* (London, 1991), pp. 358–9. Paul Glennie and Nigel Thrift have since qualified Thompson's claims ('Reworking E. P. Thompson's "Time, Work-Discipline and Industrial Capitalism"', *Time and Society*, V/3 [1996], pp. 275–99).

40 Mary Collier, 'The Woman's Labour: An Epistle to Mr Stephen Duck', in Thompson and Sugden, *'The Thresher's Labour'*, ll. 75–81, p. 17; ll. 105–14, p. 19; l. 143, p. 20; l. 152, p. 20. Unless otherwise stated, quotations and citations are from this edition. See also John Goodridge, *Rural Life in Eighteenth-Century English Poetry* (Cambridge, 1995), pp. 27, 53.

41 Carol Watts, 'Back to the Future: Revisiting Kristeva's "Women's Time"', in Roger Luckhurst and Peter Marks, *Literature and the Contemporary: Fictions and Theories of the Present* (Harlow, 1999), p. 173.

42 Miller, *The Invention of Evening*, p. 14; Watts, 'Back to the Future', p. 173.

FOUR: THE NIGHT OF EMPIRE

1 John Stevenson, *Popular Disturbances in England, 1700–1870* (London, 1979), pp. 155–9; John E. Archer, 'Poachers Abroad', in G. E. Mingay, ed., *The Unquiet Countryside* (London, 1989), pp. 52–79; Introduction and "Rural War": The Life and Times of Captain Swing', in Mingay, *The Unquiet Countryside*, pp. 1–8, 36–51; Trevor Wild, *Village England: A Social History of the Countryside* (London, 2004), p. 59.

2 Moishe Postone, *Time, Labor and Social Domination: A Reinterpretation of Marx's Critical Theory* (Cambridge, 1993), p. 5, quoted in Stefan Tanaka, *New Times in Modern Japan* (Princeton, 2004), p. 3; Leon M. Zolbrod, Introduction to Ueda Akinari, *Ugetsu Monogatari: Tales of Moonlight and Rain: A Complete English Version of the Eighteenth-Century Japanese Collection of Tales of the Supernatural* [1776], trans. and ed. Leon M. Zolbrod (Vancouver, 1974), p. 53; Adam Phillips, Introduction to Edmund Burke, *A Philosophical Enquiry into the Origin of Our Ideas of the Sublime and Beautiful* [1757], ed. Adam Phillips (Oxford, 1990), p. ix; Fred Botting, *Gothic* (London, 1996), pp. 1–11.

3 Stephen Cornford, Preface to Edward Young, *Night Thoughts*, ed. Stephen Cornford (Cambridge, 1989), p. ix; also Introduction, pp. 17–18; Marjorie Hope Nicolson, *Mountain Gloom and Mountain Glory: The Development of the Aesthetics of the Infinite* (New York,

References

1959), pp. 362–3; Young, *Night Thoughts* [1742], ed. Cornford (Cambridge, 1989), II, ll. 156–8. Unless otherwise stated, quotations are from this edition.

4 Edward Young, *The Complaint, and the Consolation; or, Night Thoughts* (London, 1796); Irene H. Chayes, 'Picture and Page, Reader and Viewer in Blake's *Night Thoughts* Illustrations', *Studies in Romanticism*, XXX/3 (1991), pp. 439–71.

5 Jeremy Tambling, *Blake's Night Thoughts* (Basingstoke, 2005), p. 63.

6 Marshall Brown, 'Romanticism and Enlightenment', in Stuart Curran, *The Cambridge Companion to British Romanticism* (Cambridge, 1993), pp. 31, 38, 45; Friedrich Schellling, *The Unconditional in Human Knowledge: Four Early Essays (1794–1796)*, trans. and ed. Fritz Martin (Lewisburg, 1980), pp. 184–5, quoted in William C. Davis, '"The Pains of Sleep": Philosophy, Poetry, Melancholy', *Prisms: Essays in Romanticism*, IX (2001), p. 54.

7 Peter Thorslev, 'German Romantic Idealism', in Curran, *The Cambridge Companion*, p. 79; Slavoj Žižek, 'Selfhood as Such in Spirit: F. W. J. Schelling on the Origins of Evil', in Joan Copjec, ed, *Radical Evil* (London, 1993), p. 8; Timothy Clark, *The Theory of Inspiration: Composition as a Crisis of Subjectivity in Romantic and Post-Romantic Writing* (Manchester, 1997), pp. 124–5; G.W.F. Hegel, *Differenz des Fichte' schen und Schelling' schen Systems der Philosophie* (Jena, 1801), reprinted in *Gesammelte Werke* (Hamburg, 1968), 4.16.1, cited in H. S. Harris, *Hegel's Development: Night Thoughts (Jena 1801–1806)* (Oxford, 1983), pp. 194–5.

8 Samuel Taylor Coleridge, 'The Pains of Sleep', in *Coleridge: Poems and Prose*, selected by Kathleen Raine (Harmondsworth, 1985), ll. 2, 5, 12, pp. 99–100. Unless otherwise stated, quotations and citations are from this edition. Neil Vickers, *Coleridge and the Doctors, 1795–1806* (Oxford, 2004), p. 154; Earl Leslie Griggs, ed., *The Collected Letters of Samuel Taylor Coleridge, Volume Two: 1801–1806* (Oxford, 2000), p. 982, cited in Vickers, *Coleridge*, p. 145.

9 Davis, '"The Pains of Sleep"', pp. 57, 59.

10 Žižek, 'Selfhood', p. 4.

11 Joan Copjec, 'Evil in the Time of the Finite World', in *Radical Evil*, p. xxv.

12 Introduction to Fred Botting, ed., *Frankenstein: Contemporary Critical Essays* (Basingstoke, 1995), p. 2.

13 'To Sleep' (three sonnets with the same title), in *The Poems, Vol.1*, ed. John O. Hayden (Harmondsworth, 1977), ll. 1, 3, 6–8, pp. 562–3. Unless otherwise stated, quotations and citations are from this edition.

14 J. C. Maxwell, ed., *The Prelude: A Parallel Text* (Harmondsworth, 1984), VII, 587, 591. This edition contains both the 1805 and 1850 versions of the poem. Unless otherwise stated, quotations and citations are from the 1850 version. Clark, *Theory of Inspiration*, p. 107.

15 Eve Walsh Stoddard, 'Flashes of the Invisible World: Reading *The Prelude* in the Context of the Kantian Sublime', *Wordsworth Circle*, XVI/1 (1985), p. 34.

16 Immanuel Kant, *Critique of the Power of Judgment* [1790], trans. Guyer and Eric Matthews, ed. Guyer (Cambridge, 2000), 28.5.261, p. 244.

17 Dorothy Wordsworth, *The Journals of Dorothy Wordsworth*, vol. II, ed. Ernest de Selincourt (New York, 1941), p. 258, quoted in Thomas Weiskel, *The Romantic Sublime: Studies in the Structure and Psychology of Transcendence* (Baltimore, 1976), p. 199.

18 The mathematical sublime arises when we try to comprehend something immeasurably vast as though it could be taken in as a single whole. We shelve an encounter that exceeds our understanding under the heading 'infinity' or 'too much', and thus make temporary sense of it. Kant, *Critique*, 26.5.251, p. 134; Paul Guyer, Editor's Introduction to Kant, *Critique*, p. xxxi. The dynamical sublime is the aspect of the sublime that relates to our moral development and translates the sublime encounter into the field, not of number or magnitude, which belongs to the mathematical sublime, but of relations, which connects the dynamical sublime to the moral will. In this aspect of a sublime encounter with nature, we discover our ability to discount some things – Kant names goods, health and life (*Critique*, 28.5.262, p. 145) – in the service of a greater purpose, even though it is not a purpose we can fully grasp or entertain. Our response to this law of relation is inspired by

the dwarfing of our own concerns by the surprising grandeur of nature.

19   As Clark notes (*Theory of Inspiration*, p. 94), Wordsworth was familiar with German
      Romantic-idealist thought as a result of his close friendship with Coleridge.

20   Immanuel Kant, *Foundations of the Metaphysics of Morals* [1785], trans. Mary Gregor (New
      York, 1996), p. 422; Dieter Henrich, *Aesthetic Judgment and the Moral Image of the World*
      (Stanford, CA, 1992), cited in Joan Copjec, *Imagine There's No Woman: Ethics and
      Sublimation* (Cambridge, MA, 2002), p. 172; Henrich, 'The Subject Defined by Suffrage',
      lacanian ink, VII (1993), pp. 56–7.

21   Weiskel offers support here: 'The fact is that the passage from imagination to symbol was
      occluded for Wordsworth, and yet the essential moment of his greatest poetry is right in
      the midst of this occlusion' (*The Romantic Sublime*, p. 172).

22   Jerrold E. Hogle, 'The Gothic in Western Culture', Introduction to Jerrold E. Hogle, ed.,
      The Cambridge Companion to Gothic Fiction (Cambridge, 2002), p. 14.

23   Observe the sheer number of times Emily St Aubert, the heroine of Ann Radcliffe's
      momentously popular Gothic novel *The Mysteries of Udolpho* (1794), loses sleep through
      fear, anxiety, new revelations or a nocturnal attempt to catch a villain at his evil labours
      (*The Mysteries of Udolpho: A Romance*, ed. Bonamy Dobrée [London, 1966], pp. 59, 160,
      169, 221, 325, 331, 341, 355, 360, 388, 412, 435, 466, 487, 518); Dale M. Bauer, Introduc-
      tion to Charlotte Perkins Gilman, *The Yellow Wallpaper* [1892], ed. Dale M. Bauer
      (Boston, MA, 1998), pp. 7–17; Fred Botting, 'In Gothic Darkly: Heterotopia, History,
      Culture', in David Punter, ed., *A Companion to the Gothic* (Oxford, 2000), pp. 3–14; John
      Paul Riquelme, 'Toward a History of Gothic and Modernism: Dark Modernity from Bram
      Stoker to Samuel Beckett', *Modern Fiction Studies*, XLVI/3 (2000), p. 586; Hogle, 'The
      Gothic', p. 4.

24   Richard Davenport-Hines, *Gothic: 400 Years of Excess, Horror, Evil and Ruin* (London,
      1998), p. 230; Michael MacDonald and Terence R. Murphy, *Sleepless Souls: Suicide in
      Early Modern England* (Oxford, 1990), p. 18; Arnold van Gennep, *The Rites of Passage*,
      trans. Monika B. Vizedon and Gabrielle L. Caffee (Chicago, 1960), p. 46.

25   Davenport-Hines, *Gothic*, pp. 229–30; MacDonald and Murphy, *Sleepless Souls*, p. 47.

26   Tanaka, *New Times in Modern Japan*, pp. 5, 65; Ikuko Nishimoto, 'The "Civilization" of
      Time: Japan and the Adoption of the Western Time System', *Time and Society*, VI/2–3
      (1997), p. 244, cited in Brigitte Steger, 'Negotiating Sleep Patterns in Japan', in Steger and
      Lodewijk Brunt, eds, *Night-Time and Sleep in Asia and the West: Exploring the Dark Side of
      Life* (London, 2003), p. 76; Timothy Clark, *Demon of Painting: The Art of Kawanabe
      Kyosai* (London, 1993), p. 13.

27   Clark, *Demon of Painting*, pp. 18, 20; Andrew Markus, '*Shogakai*: Celebrity Banquets
      of the Late Edo Period', *Harvard Journal of Asiatic Studies*, LIII/1 (1993), pp. 135–67;
      Clark, *Demon of Painting*, p. 17.

28   Midori Deguchi, 'One Hundred Demons and One Hundred Supernatural Tales', in
      Stephen Addiss, ed., *Japanese Ghosts and Demons* (New York, 1985), pp. 15, 18–19; Clark,
      Demon of Painting, p. 63.

29   John Stevenson, *Yoshitoshi's One Hundred Aspects of the Moon* (Leiden, 2001), pp. 53–4,
      59, 76.

30   Ueda Akinari, *Ugetsu Monogatari: Tales of Moonlight and Rain: A Complete English Version
      of the Eighteenth-Century Japanese Collection of Tales of the Supernatural* [1776], trans. and
      ed. Leon M. Zolbrod (Vancouver, 1974), pp. 99, 118, 163, 167, 188; Izumi Kyoka, 'The
      Holy Man of Mount Koya' [1900], in Charles S. Inouye, trans., *Japanese Gothic Tales*
      (Honolulu, 1996), pp. 63–4. Kyoka himself also had trouble sleeping. See Charles Shiro
      Inouye, 'Izumi Kyoka and Language', *Harvard Journal of Asiatic Studies*, LVI/1 (1996), p.
      13. Juliet Carpenter traces the figure of the enchantress to the folklore of the author's
      native region in 'Izumi Kyoka: Meiji-Era Gothic', *Japan Quarterly*, XXXI/2 (1984), p. 157.

31   Tanaka, *New Times in Modern Japan*, pp. 66–7; 70, note; 71; also Gerald Figal, *Civilization
      and Monsters: Spirits of Modernity in Meiji Japan* (Durham, NC, 1999).

32   'The prolongation of the working day beyond the limits of the natural day, into the night,

acts only as a palliative. It quenches only in a slight degree the vampire thirst for the living blood of labour. To appropriate labour during all the 24 hours of the day is, therefore, the inherent tendency of capitalist production' (Karl Marx, *Capital: A Critical Analysis of Capitalist Production* [1889], trans. Samuel Moore and Edward Aveling, ed. Frederick Engels, vol. I [London, 1943], p. 241); Peter Osborne, *How to Read Marx* (London, 2005), pp. 95–6; also Francis Hutchinson and Brian Burkitt, *The Political Economy of Social Credit and Guild Socialism* (London, 1997), p. 37; Philip Goodchild, 'Capital and Kingdom: An Eschatological Ontology', in Creston Davis, John Millbank and Slavoj Žižek, eds, *Theology and the Political: The New Debate* (Durham, NC, 2005), p. 133, both cited in my 'Watching and Learning', *Parallax (Pupils of the University Issue)*, XII/3 (2006), pp. 20–21; 25, note.

33 Daniel T. Rodgers, *The Work Ethic in Industrial America, 1850–1920* (Chicago, 1978), p. 9.

34 Ibid.; Pierre Foissac, *Hygiène philosophique de l'âme*, 2nd edn (Paris, 1863), pp. 194–200, quoted in Anson Rabinbach, *The Human Motor: Energy, Fatigue and the Origins of Modernity* (Berkeley, CA, 1990), p. 33.

35 Rabinbach, *The Human Motor*, p. 45; Osborne, *How to Read Marx*, p. 84; Karl Marx, 'The German Ideology: Part One' [1845], trans. Roy Pascal, in Robert C. Tucker, ed., *The Marx-Engels Reader*, 2nd edn (New York, 1978), pp. 191, 197, quoted in Marshall Berman, *All That Is Solid Melts into Air: The Experience of Modernity* (New York, 1982), p. 25.

36 Franklin H. Head, *Shakespeare's Insomnia, and the Causes Thereof* (Boston, MA, 1886), pp. 6–7; William A. Hammond, 'Insomnia and Recent Hypnotics', *North American Review*, CLVI (1893), pp. 18, 6–7, cited in Bonnie Ellen Blustein, 'The Brief Career of "Cerebral Hyperaemia": William A. Hammond and His Insomniac Patients, 1854–90', *Journal of the History of Medicine*, XLI/1, (1986), p. 36; A. W. Macfarlane, MD, *Insomnia and Its Therapeutics* (London, 1890), p. 50; Henry M. Lyman, AM, MD, *Insomnia and Other Disorders of Sleep* (Chicago, 1885), p. 39.

37 Maria Parloa, *Home Economics* (New York, 1906), p. 48, quoted in Michael O'Malley, *Keeping Watch: A History of American Time* (Washington, DC, 1990), pp. 188–90. See also Charlotte Perkins Gilman, *The Yellow Wallpaper* [1892], ed. Dale M. Bauer (Boston, MA, 1998) pp. 6–7; Rodgers, *The Work Ethic*, pp. 111–12.

38 Bauer, *The Yellow Wallpaper*, p. 52. Unless otherwise stated, citations are from this edition.

39 'Why I Wrote "The Yellow Wallpaper"', *Forerunner*, IV/10 (1913), p. 271, reprinted in Bauer, *The Yellow Wallpaper*, p. 349.

40 Mrs Henry Ward Beecher [Eunice White Bullard], *The Home: How To Make It and Keep It* (Minneapolis, 1883), cited in O'Malley, *Keeping Watch*, p. 190; Elisabeth Bronfen, *The Knotted Subject: Hysteria and Its Discontents* (Princeton, 1998), p. 39.

41 Anton Chekhov, 'A Case History', in Ronald Wilks, trans., *The Kiss and Other Stories* (Harmondsworth, 1982), p. 159. Unless otherwise stated, quotations and citations are from this edition.

42 A. P. Herbert, *The Secret Battle* [1919] (Oxford, 1982), pp. 32, 46–7, 64; Frederic Manning, *The Middle Parts of Fortune: Somme and Ancre, 1916* [1929] (London, 1977), p. 10; James Lansdale Hodson, *Grey Dawn–Red Night* (London, 1929), pp. 98, 156; R. H. Mottram, *A Personal Record*, in Mottram, John Easton and Eric Partridge, *Three Personal Records of the War* (London, 1929), pp. 59–60; also Eyal Ben-Ari, 'Sleep and Night-time Combat in Contemporary Armed Forces: Technology, Knowledge and the Enhancement of the Soldier's Body', in Steger and Brunt, *Night-time*, pp. 108–25.

43 Eric J. Leed, *No Man's Land: Combat and Identity in World War I* (Cambridge, 1979), p. 98; Edmund Blunden, *Undertones of War* (London, 1928), p. 90, quoted in Allyson Booth, *Postcards from the Trenches: Negotiating the Space Between Modernism and the Great War* (New York, 1996), p. 119; Peter Leese, *Shell Shock: Traumatic Neurosis and the British Soldiers of the First World War* (Basingstoke, 2002), pp. 22–3.

44 Ben Shephard, *A War of Nerves: Soldiers and Psychiatrists in the Twentieth Century* (Cambridge, MA, 2001), p. 44; David Trotter, 'The British Novel and the War', in Vincent Sherry, ed., *The Cambridge Companion to the Literature of the First World War* (Cambridge, 2005), pp. 38–9.

45 Cathy Caruth, Introduction to Caruth, ed., *Trauma: Explorations in Memory* (Baltimore, 1995), pp. 3–12; Erich Maria Remarque, *All Quiet on the Western Front* [1929], trans. B. Murdoch (London, 1996), p. 39, quoted in Vita Fortunati, 'The Impact of the First World War on Private Lives: A Comparison of European and American Writers (Ford, Hemingway, and Remarque)', in Joseph Wisenfarth, ed., *History and Representation in Ford Madox Ford's Writings* (Amsterdam, 2004), p. 61; Ford Madox Ford, *Parade's End* [1928] (Manchester, 1997), p. 291.

46 Sue Malvern, *Modern Art, Britain and the Great War: Witnessing, Testimony and Remembrance* (New Haven, 2004), pp. 63, 101.

47 Murry quoted without reference in ibid., pp. 96, 100–01.

48 Lee Kinsella, 'Will Longstaff', in Lola Wilkins, ed., *Artists in Action* (Canberra, 2003), cited in Betty Churcher, *The Art of War* (Melbourne, 2004), p. 16.

FIVE: CITIES THAT NEVER SLEEP

1 Joachim Schlör, *Nights in the Big City* [1991], trans. Pierre Gottfried Imhof and Dafydd Rees Roberts (London, 1998), p. 55; E. Roger Ekirch, *At Day's Close: A History of Nighttime* (London, 2005), pp. 210–18.

2 Wolfgang Schivelbusch, *Disenchanted Night: The Industrialisation of Light in the Nineteenth Century* [1983], trans. Angela Davies (Oxford, 1988), pp. 139–40; Thomas Burke, *English Night-Life from Norman Curfew to Present Blackout* (London, 1941), pp. 21, 38, 82.

3 Richard Shusterman, 'The Urban Aesthetics of Absence: Pragmatist Reflections in Berlin', *New Literary History*, XXVIII/4 (1997), p. 742.

4 Charles Simic, 'The Congress of the Insomniacs', in *Frightening Toys* (London, 1995), p. 71; Edward Hirsch, 'Sleeplessness', in Rod Townley, ed., *How Poets Use Dreams* (Pittsburgh, 1998), p. 62.

5 Jean Verdon, *Night in the Middle Ages* [1994], trans. George Holoch (Notre Dame, IN, 2002), pp. 2, 80; Ekirch, *At Day's Close*, p. 63; Schivelbusch, *Disenchanted Night*, p. 81; Piero Camporesi, *Bread of Dreams: Food and Fantasy in Early Modern Europe* (Chicago, 1989), p. 96; Natalie Zemon Davis, 'Proverbial Wisdom and Popular Errors', in *Society and Culture in Early Modern France* (Stanford, CA, 1975), pp. 255–7, 264, both cited in Bryan D. Palmer, *Cultures of Darkness: Night Travels in the History of Transgression* (New York, 2000), p. 33.

6 Verdon, *Night in the Middle Ages*, pp. 84–5; Schivelbusch, *Disenchanted Night*, pp. 100–06; Ekirch, *At Day's Close*, pp. 70, 79–80; Penelope J. Corfield, 'Walking the City Streets: The Urban Odyssey in Eighteenth-Century England', *Journal of Urban History*, XVI/2 (1990), p. 144.

7 Palmer, *Cultures of Darkness*, pp. 141, 147–8; Lynda Nead, *Victorian Babylon: People, Streets and Images in Nineteenth-Century London* (New Haven, 2000), p. 83; Schivelbusch, *Disenchanted Night*, p. 221.

8 Samuel L. Macey, 'Hogarth and the Iconography of Time', in Ronald C. Rosbottom, ed., *Studies in Eighteenth-Century Culture*, vol. V (Madison, 1976), pp. 42–4; Carlene E. Stephens, *On Time: How America Learned to Live by the Clock* (Boston, MA, 2002), p. 51; Lodewijk Brunt, 'Between Day and Night: Urban Time Schedules in Bombay and Other Cities', in Brigitte Steger and Lodewijk Brunt, eds, *Night-Time and Sleep in Asia and the West: Exploring the Dark Side of Life* (London, 2003), p. 172. When an American woman in Ruth Prawer Jhabvala's story 'An Experience of India' cannot sleep near midnight, she goes out walking to find shops open and plenty of social activity underway ('An Experience of India', in *Out of India* [Washington, DC, 2000], pp. 125–46, cited in Brunt, 'Between Day and Night', p. 176). Brunt notes that similar timekeeping is common in Bombay, with children playing cricket by lamplight when the air is cooler. Josephine Smart, *The Political Economy of Street Hawkers in Hong Kong* (Hong Kong, 1989), pp. 57–8, quoted in Brunt, 'Between Day and Night', p. 174.

9 Samuel L. Macey, *Clocks and the Cosmos: Time in Western Life and Thought* (Hamden, CT, 1980), p. 17; Sean Shesgreen, *Hogarth and the Times-of-the-Day Tradition* (New York, 1983), pp. 78, 107, 113, 146.

10 Michael Slater and John Drew, Introduction to 'Night Walks', in Slater and Drew, eds, *Dickens' Journalism, Vol. IV:* The Uncommercial Traveller *and Other Papers, 1859–70* (London, 2000), p. 148; Timothy Clark, 'Dickens Through Blanchot: The Nightmare Fascination of a World Without Interiority', in John Schad, ed., *Dickens Refigured: Bodies, Desires and Other Histories* (Manchester, 1996), pp. 34–6; Charles Dickens, 'Night Walks' [1860], in Slater and Drew, *Dickens' Journalism*, pp. 150–51; Dickens, 'Night Walks', pp. 154–5; Nead, *Victorian Babylon*, p. 115.

11 Nead, *Victorian Babylon*, p. 116; Shesgreen, *Hogarth*, p. 22.

12 Edgar Allan Poe, 'The Man of the Crowd' [1840], in G. R. Thompson, ed., *The Selected Writings of Edgar Allan Poe* (New York, 2004), p. 236. Unless otherwise stated, quotations and citations are from this edition.

13 Ernest L. Fontana, 'Literary Insomnia', *New Orleans Review*, XVII/2 (1990), p. 39.

14 Monika M. Elbert, '"The Man of the Crowd" and the Man Outside the Crowd: Poe's Narrator and the Democratic Reader', *Modern Language Studies*, XXI/4 (1991), pp. 16–18.

15 Ibid., pp. 18–20, 26; Joan Copjec, 'The Subject Defined by Suffrage', *lacanian ink*, VII (1993), pp. 56–7.

16 Daniel T. Rodgers, *The Work Ethic in Industrial America, 1850–1920* (Chicago, 1974), pp. 33, 36, 51; John A. Ryan, *Social Doctrine in Action: A Personal History* (New York, 1941), p. 199, cited in Rodgers, *The Work Ethic*, p. 52.

17 Rodgers, *The Work Ethic*, pp. 52–3.

18 Michael O'Malley, *Keeping Watch: A History of American Time* (Washington, DC, 1990), p. 99.

19 Anson Rabinbach, *The Human Motor: Energy, Fatigue and the Origins of Modernity* (Berkeley, CA, 1992), p. 242, emphasis added; O'Malley, *Keeping Watch*, p. 150; George Miller Beard, *American Nervousness: Its Causes and Consequences* (New York, 1881), p. 12, quoted in Rabinbach, 'Neurasthenia and Modernity', in Jonathan Crary and Sanford Kwinter, eds, *Incorporations* (New York, 1992), p. 178.

20 Elizabeth S. Goodstein, *Experience Without Qualities: Boredom and Modernity* (Stanford, CA, 2005), p. 267; Georg Simmel, 'The Metropolis and Mental Life' [1902–3], in Richard Sennett, ed., *Classic Essays on the Culture of Cities* (New York, 1969), p. 51.

21 John L. Thomas, Introduction to Edward Bellamy, *Looking Backward, 2000–1887* [1888], ed. John L. Thomas (Cambridge, MA, 1967), pp. 1, 70; Peter Beilharz, 'Looking Back: Marx and Bellamy', *European Legacy*, IX/5 (2004), p. 597.

22 Beilharz, 'Looking Back', p. 601; Martin Gardner, 'Looking Backward at Edward Bellamy's Utopia', *New Criterion*, XIX/1 (2000), pp. 22–3.

23 Bellamy, *Looking Backward*, pp. 105, 110. Unless otherwise stated, all quotations and citations are from this edition. Palmer, *Cultures of Darkness*, pp. 238–40.

24 Dafydd Moore, '"The Truth of Midnight" and "The Truth of Noonday": Sensation and Madness in James Thomson's *The City of Dreadful Night*', in Andrew Maunder and Grace Moore, eds, *Victorian Crime, Madness and Sensation* (Aldershot, 2004), pp. 119, 122, 125.

25 N. P. Messenger and J. R. Watson, 'James Thomson', in Messenger and Watson, eds, *Victorian Poetry: 'The City of Dreadful Night' and Other Poems* (London, 1974), p. 136; James Thomson, 'The City of Dreadful Night' (1874), in Messenger and Watson, *Victorian Poetry*, I, ll. 71–4. Unless otherwise stated, all quotations and citations are from this edition.

26 Nicholas Christopher, *Somewhere in the Night: Film Noir and the American City* (New York, 1997), pp. 38–9.

27 Jeff Wall, 'Frames of Reference', *Artforum International*, XLII/1 (2003), p. 191; Jack Bankowsky, 'Jeff Wall', *Artforum International*, XLII/1 (2003), p. 193.

28 Wall, 'Frames of Reference', p. 192; Phil Hadfield, *Bar Wars: Contesting the Night in Contemporary British Cities* (Oxford, 2006), pp. 3–6; Dick Hobbs et al., *Bouncers: Violence*

and *Governance in the Night-Time Economy* (Oxford, 2003), p. 277.

29 Hadfield, *Bar Wars*, pp. 259, 261; David Garland, *The Culture of Control: Crime and Social Order in Contemporary Society* (Oxford, 2001), p. 195, quoted in Hadfield, *Bar Wars*, p. 259.

SIX: WIRED

1 Roy Douglas Malonson, 'Terror Alerts Should Terrify "US"', *African-American*, 10 June 2004: www.aframnews.com/html/2004-06-10/wemust.htm

2 'National Sleep Foundation: Tackling American's Sleep Debt': www.sleepfoundation.org/site/c.huIXKjMOIXF/b.2428019/k.F850/National_Sleep_Foundation_Tackling_Americas_Sleep_Debt.htm

3 Sandra Silberstein, *War of Words: Language, Politics and 9/11* (New York, 2002), pp. 127–47; Amy Kaplan, 'Homeland Insecurities: Transformations of Language and Space', in Mary L. Dudziak, ed., *September 11 in History: A Watershed Moment?* (Durham, NC, 2003), pp. 55–69.

4 'National Sleep Foundation 2002 *Sleep in America* Poll Results Relating to September 11': www.sleepfoundation.org/site/apps/nl/content2.asp?c=huIXKjMOIXF&b=2428021&ct=3454757; 'Epidemic of Daytime Sleepiness Linked to Increased Feelings of Anger, Stress and Pessimism', http://www.sleepfoundation.org/site/c.huIXKjMOIXF/b.2417359/k.3028/Epidemic_of_Daytime_Sleepiness_Linked_to_Increased_Feelings_of_Anger_Stress_and_Pessimism.htm (emphasis added).

5 Murray Melbin, *Night as Frontier: Colonizing the World After Dark* (New York, 1987).

6 Carol Kaufman-Scarborough, 'Time Use and the Impact of Technology: Examining Workspaces in the Home', *Time and Society*, XV/1 (2006), p. 66; Penny Gurstein, *Wired to the World, Chained to the Home: Telework in Daily Life* (Vancouver, 2001), pp. 121–30; Melbin, *Night as Frontier*; Kevin Coyne, *A Day in the Night of America* (New York, 1992).

7 John Shneerson, *Sleep Medicine: A Guide to Sleep and its Disorders* (Malden, MA, 2005), p. 161; also Ruth M. Benca, 'Insomnia', in Alon Y. Avidan and Phyllis C. Zee, eds, *Handbook of Sleep Medicine* (Philadelphia, 2006), p. 38; William H. Moorcroft, *Understanding Sleep and Dreaming* (New York, 2003), p. 245; National Sleep Foundation, Press Releases 2005: www.sleepfoundation.org/site/apps/nl/content2.asp?c=huIXKjMOIXF&b=2428003&ct=3454153; Alistair Bone, 'Too Wired, Too Tired', *New Zealand Listener* [8 May 2004], p. 21; Christopher Dewdney, *Acquainted with the Night: Excursions in the World After Dark* (London, 2004), p. 250; Philippa Gander, *Sleep in the 24-Hour Society* (Lower Hutt, 2003), pp. 59, 133. As Gander reports (p. 58), the New Zealand population is 'small enough to take a random sample of the entire adult population at reasonable cost'. Getting 'real cross-section information' is more difficult in larger countries.

8 James A. Horne, 'Is There a Sleep Debt?', *Sleep*, XXVII/6 (2007), pp. 1053–4; 'Epidemic of Daytime Sleepiness'.

9 Benca, 'Insomnia', p. 36; Shneerson, *Sleep Medicine*, pp. 161–2; Michael Wang, 'The Psychological Treatment of Insomnia', chapter in Jacob Empson, *Sleep and Dreaming*, 3rd edn (Basingstoke, 2002), p. 197.

10 Barry C. Lynn, *End of the Line: The Rise and Coming Fall of the Global Corporation* (New York, 2005), p. 3.

11 John D. Palmer, *The Living Clock: The Orchestrator of Biological Rhythms* (New York, 2002), p. 46; Murray Moore-Ede, *The Twenty Four Hour Society: Understanding Human Limits in a World that Never Stops* (Reading, MA, 1993), pp. 25, 30–31; also Palmer, *The Living Clock*, p. 65, emphasis added; Gander, *Sleep in the 24-Hour Society*, cited in Bone, 'Too Wired', p. 21; Dewdney, *Acquainted with the Night*, pp. 138–9; Gander, *Sleep in the 24-Hour Society*, p. 28.

12 Moore-Ede, *The Twenty Four Hour Society*, pp. 64, 151–9; Gander, *Sleep in the 24-Hour Society*, pp. 107–19; Dewdney, *Acquainted with the Night*, p. 108; Melbin, *Night as Frontier*, pp. 109–10; 194, note.

13 Paul Tam, 'Sleepless in Loughborough: Sleep Deprivation and Cognitive Function', 1998:

www.lboro.ac.uk/departments/hu/groups/sleep/ wellcome.htm; Yvonne Harrison and James A. Horne, 'The Impact of Sleep Loss on Decision Making: A Review', *Journal of Experimental Psychology: Applied*, VI (2000), pp. 236–49: gateway.ut.ovid.com. ezproxy.auckland.ac.nz/gw1/ovidweb.cgi

14 Harrison and Horne, 'The Impact of Sleep Loss'; Tam, 'Sleepless in Loughborough'.

15 Karin Widerberg, 'Embodying Modern Times: Investigating Tiredness', *Time and Society*, XV/1 (2006), pp. 108, 114; Walter W. Powell, 'The Capitalist Firm in the Twenty-First Century', in Amy S. Wharton, ed., *Working in America: Continuity, Conflict and Change*, 3rd edn (Boston, MA, 2006), p. 81.

16 Widerberg, 'Embodying Modern Times', pp. 114–15; also Diane Perrons et al., 'Work, Life and Time in the New Economy: An Introduction', *Time and Society*, XIV/1 (2005), pp. 56–7.

17 Thomas L. Friedman, *The World Is Flat: A Brief History of the Twenty-First Century* (New York, 2005); Julia Brannen, 'Time and the Negotiation of Work – Family Boundaries: Autonomy or Illusion?', *Time and Society*, XIV/1 (2005), p. 113; Widerberg, 'Embodying Modern Times', p. 115.

18 Widerberg, 'Embodying Modern Times', p. 109.

19 Ibid., p. 114.

20 RETORT (Iain Boal, T. J. Clark, Joseph Matthews and Michael Watts), *Afflicted Powers: Capital and Spectacle in a New Age of War* (London, 2005), pp. 181–2.

21 Wayne Hope, 'Global Capitalism and the Critique of Real Time', *Time and Society*, XV/2–3 (2006), pp. 276, 279; Karin Knorr Cetina and Urs Bruegger, 'Traders' Engagements with Markets: A Postsocial Relationship', *Theory, Culture and Society*, IX/2–3 (2000), p. 179, quoted in Hope, 'Global Capitalism', p. 279; Zygmunt Bauman, 'Time and Space Reunited', *Time and Society*, IX/2–3 (2000), p. 179, quoted in Hope, 'Global Capitalism', p. 283.

22 Gander, *Sleep in the 24-Hour Society*, p. 83; James Gleick, *Faster: The Acceleration of Just About Everything* (New York, 1999), p. 122; D. G. McNeil, Jr, 'Drug Makers and the Third World: A Case Study in Neglect', *New York Times* [21 May 2000], p. 1, cited in Marcia Angell, 'The Pharmaceutical Industry: To Whom Is It Accountable?', in Patricia Illingworth and Wendy E. Parmet, eds, *Ethical Health Care* (Upper Saddle River, NJ, 2006), p. 375.

23 Ray Moynihan and Alan Cassels, *Selling Sickness: How the World's Biggest Pharmaceutical Companies Are Turning Us All into Patients* (New York, 2005); Jacky Law, *Big Pharma: How the World's Biggest Drug Companies Control Illness* (London, 2006); Leonard J. Weber, *Profits before People? Ethical Standards and the Marketing of Prescription Drugs* (Bloomington, IN, 2006), pp. 93–105; Benca, 'Insomnia', pp. 37–42.

24 Wendy Parkins and Geoffrey Craig, *Slow Living* (Oxford, 2006), p. 41; Peter Meiksins and Peter Whalley, *Putting Work in Its Place: A Quiet Revolution* (New York, 2002), pp. 5–34; Hope, 'Global Capitalism', p. 284; International Dark Sky Association: www.darksky.org/; Dewdney, *Acquainted with the Night*, pp. 105–6.

25 Moore-Ede, *The Twenty Four Hour Society*, p. 27; Brigitte Steger, 'Sleeping through Class to Success: Japanese Notions of Time and Diligence', *Time and Society*, XV/2–3 (2006), pp. 197–214; Li Yi, 'Discourse of Mid-Day Napping: A Political Windsock in Contemporary China', in Brigitte Steger and Lodewijk Brunt, eds, *Night-time and Sleep in Asia and the West: Exploring the Dark Side of Life* (London, 2003), pp. 45, 197. China has its own historical contradictions in the attitude to daytime napping, with Taoism regarding it as a salutary example of yielding control while Confucians have seen it as a lapse of moral as well as physical exertion. Communist China nonetheless inherited a daytime napping culture that was, in the 1970s, regarded by Westerners as a sign of socialist complacency. Li Yi, 'Discourse of Mid-Day Napping', pp. 46–7.

26 Steger, 'Sleeping through Class to Success', pp. 197, 204–6, 208–9.

27 Gander, *Sleep in the 24-Hour Society*, p. 140; Camille W. Anthony and William A. Anthony, *The Art of Napping at Work* (London, 2001); Vern Baxter and Steve Kroll-Smith, 'Normalizing the Workplace Nap: Blurring the Boundaries between Public and Private Time', *Current Sociology*, LIII/1 (2005), pp. 33–55, both cited in Simon J. Williams, 'The Social Etiquette of Sleep: Some Sociological Reflections and Observations', *Sociology*,

XLI/2 (2007), pp. 320–21.

28 Maurice Blanchot, *The Space of Literature* [1955], trans. Ann Smock (Lincoln, NE, and London, 1982), p. 265.

29 Stephen King, *Insomnia* [1994] (London, 1995), p. 23. Unless otherwise stated, quotations and citations are from this edition.

30 William Dement and Christopher Vaughan, *The Promise of Sleep* (New York, 1999).

31 Stephen Minta, *Gabriel García Márquez: Writer of Colombia* (London, 1987), p. 144; Gabriel García Márquez, *One Hundred Years of Solitude* [1967], trans. Gregory Rabassa (London, 1972), p. 45. Unless otherwise stated, quotations and citations are from this edition.

32 Elizabeth A. Spiller, '"Searching for the Route of Inventions": Retracing the Renaissance Discovery Narrative in Gabriel García Márquez', in Harold Bloom, ed., *Gabriel García Márquez's* One Hundred Years of Solitude (Philadelphia, 2003), p. 57; Minta, *Gabriel García Márquez*, pp. 163–4, 179.

33 Minta, *Gabriel García Márquez*, pp. 164, 168–72; Edwin Williamson, 'Magical Realism and the Theme of Incest in *One Hundred Years of Solitude*', in Bernard McGuirk and Richard Cardwell, eds, *Gabriel Garcia Marquez: New Readings* (Cambridge, 1987), p. 61.

34 Karl Polanyi, *The Great Transformation: The Political and Economic Origins of Our Time* [1944] (Boston, MA, 1957), p. 73, quoted in RETORT, *Afflicted Powers*, p. 194.

35 Hope, 'Global Capitalism', p. 298; Ludwig Siegele, 'How About Now? A Survey of the Real Time Economy', *Economist* (2–8 February 2002), pp. 3–5, cited in Hope, 'Global Capitalism', p. 287; Gleick, *Faster*, pp. 66–8.

Bibliography

Akinari, Ueda, *Ugetsu Monogatari: Tales of Moonlight and Rain: A Complete English Version of the Eighteenth-Century Japanese Collection of Tales of the Supernatural* [1776], trans. and ed. Leon M. Zolbrod (Vancouver, 1974)

Ariosto, Ludovico, *Orlando Furioso (The Frenzy of Orlando)* [1516], trans. Barbara Reynolds, 2 vols (Harmondsworth, 1975)

Aveni, Anthony F., *Empires of Time: Calendars, Clocks and Cultures* (New York, 1989)

Beard, George Miller, *American Nervousness: Its Causes and Consequences* (New York, 1881)

Bellamy, Edward, *Looking Backward, 2000–1887* [1888], ed. John L. Thomas (Cambridge, MA, 1967)

Ben-Ari, Eyal, 'Sleep and Night-time Combat in Contemporary Armed Forces: Technology, Knowledge and the Enhancement of the Soldier's Body', in Brigitte Steger and Lodewijk Brunt, eds, *Night-time and Sleep in Asia and the West: Exploring the Dark Side of Life* (London, 2003), pp. 108–25.

Benca, Ruth M., 'Insomnia', in Alon Y. Avidan and Phyllis C. Zee, eds, *Handbook of Sleep Medicine* (Philadelphia, 2006), pp. 36–69

Blanchot, Maurice, *The Space of Literature* [1955], trans. Ann Smock (Lincoln, NE, and London, 1982)

Bone, Alistair, 'Too Wired, Too Tired', *New Zealand Listener* (8 May 2004), pp. 16–21

Bouwsma, William J., 'Anxiety and the Formation of Early Modern Culture', in Barbara C. Malament, ed., *After the Reformation: Essays in Honor of J. H. Hexter* (Philadelphia, 1980), pp. 215–46

Braun, Stephen, *Buzz: The Science and Lore of Alcohol and Caffeine* (New York, 1996)

Brunt, Lodewijk, 'Between Day and Night: Urban Time Schedules in Bombay and Other Cities', in Brigitte Steger and Lodewijk Brunt, eds, *Night-Time and Sleep in Asia and the West: Exploring the Dark Side of Life* (London, 2003), pp. 171–90

Burke, Thomas, *English Night-Life from Norman Curfew to Present Blackout* (London, 1941)

Cashford, Jules, *The Moon: Myth and Image* (London, 2003)

Chandler, Simon B., 'Shakespeare and Sleep', *Bulletin of the History of Medicine*, XXIX (1955), pp. 255–60

Chekhov, Anton, 'A Case History', in *The Kiss and Other Stories*, trans. Ronald Wilks (Harmondsworth, 1982), pp. 154–64

Christopher, Nicholas, *Somewhere in the Night: Film Noir and the American City* (New York, 1997)

Coleridge, Samuel Taylor, 'The Pains of Sleep', in *Coleridge: Poems and Prose*, selected by Kathleen Raine (Harmondsworth, 1985), pp. 99–100

Collier, Mary, 'The Woman's Labour: An Epistle to Mr Stephen Duck', in E. P. Thompson and Marian Sugden, eds, *'The Thresher's Labour' by Stephen Duck and 'The Woman's Labour' by Mary Collier: Two Eighteenth-Century Poems* (London, 1989), pp. 13–24

Coyne, Kevin, *A Day in the Night of America* (New York, 1992)

Dalley, Stephanie, ed., *Myths from Mesopotamia: Creation, the Flood, Gilgamesh and Others* (Oxford, 2000)

Dannenfeldt, Karl H., 'Sleep: Theory and Practice in the Late Renaissance', *Journal of the History of Medicine and the Allied Sciences*, XLI/4 (1986), pp. 415–41

Davenport-Hines, Richard, *Gothic: 400 Years of Excess, Horror, Evil and Ruin* (London, 1998)

Davis, William C., '"The Pains of Sleep": Philosophy, Poetry, Melancholy', *Prisms: Essays in Romanticism*, IX (2001), pp. 51–63

Deagon, Andrea, 'The Twelve Double-Hours of Night: Insomnia and Transformation in *Gilgamesh*', *Soundings*, LXXXI/3–4 (1998), pp. 461–89

Deguchi, Midori, 'One Hundred Demons and One Hundred Supernatural Tales', in Stephen Addiss, ed., *Japanese Ghosts and Demons* (New York, 1985), pp. 15–23

Dement, William C., 'What All Undergraduates Should Know about How Their Sleeping Lives Affect Their Waking Lives', in *Sleepless at Stanford* (1997): www.stanford.edu/ %7Edement/sleepless.html

—, and Christopher Vaughan, *The Promise of Sleep* (New York, 1999)

Dewdney, Christopher, *Acquainted with the Night: Excursions in the World after Dark* (London, 2004)

Dickens, Charles, 'Lying Awake', *Household Words*, VI/136 (1852), pp. 145–8

—, 'Night Walks' [1860], in Michael Slater and John Drew, eds, *Dickens' Journalism, Vol. IV: The Uncommercial Traveller and Other Papers, 1859–70* (London, 2000), pp. 148–57

Dohrn-Van Rossum, Gerhard, *History of the Hour: Clocks and Modern Temporal Orders* [1992], trans. Thomas Dunlap (Chicago, 1996)

Ekirch, Roger A., *At Day's Close: A History of Nighttime* (London, 2005)

Ellis, Markman, *The Coffee-House: A Cultural History* (London, 2004)

Fontana, Ernest L., 'Literary Insomnia', *New Orleans Review*, XVII/2 (1990), pp. 38–42

Gander, Philippa, *Sleep in the 24-Hour Society* (Lower Hutt, 2003)

Gardner, John, and John Maier, trans., *Gilgamesh* (New York, 1984)

Gilman, Charlotte Perkins, *The Yellow Wallpaper* [1892], ed. Dale M. Bauer (Boston, 1998)

Goltzius, Hendrik, *The Complete Engravings and Woodcuts*, ed. Walter L. Strauss (New York, 1977)

Hadfield, Phil, *Bar Wars: Contesting the Night in Contemporary British Cities* (Oxford, 2006)

Hammond, William A., 'Insomnia and Recent Hypnotics', *North American Review*, CLVI (1893), pp. 18–26

Harrison, Yvonne, and James A. Horne, 'The Impact of Sleep Loss on Decision Making: A Review', *Journal of Experimental Psychology: Applied*, VI (2000), pp. 236–49: gateway.ut.ovid.com.ezproxy.auckland.ac.nz/gw1/ovidweb.cgi

Head, Franklin H., *Shakespeare's Insomnia, and the Causes Thereof* (Boston, MA, 1886)

Hinton, David, ed. and trans., *Mountain Home: The Wilderness Poetry of Ancient China* (Washington, DC, 2002)

Hirsch, Edward, 'Sleeplessness', in *How Poets Use Dreams*, ed. Rod Townley (Pittsburgh, 1998), pp. 58–63

Hogle, Herrold E., 'The Gothic in Western Culture', Introduction to Jerrold E. Hogle, ed., *The Cambridge Companion to Gothic Fiction* (Cambridge, 2002)

Homer, *The Iliad*, trans. Robert Fagles (New York, 1990)

—, *The Odyssey*, trans. Robert Fagles (New York, 1996)

Hope, Wayne, 'Global Capitalism and the Critique of Real Time', *Time and Society*, XV/2–3 (2006), pp. 275–302

Horne, James A., 'Is There a Sleep Debt?', *Sleep*, XXVII/6 (2007), pp. 1053–4

Howard, Donald R., 'Renaissance World-Alienation', in Robert S. Kinsman, ed., *The Darker Vision of the Renaissance: Beyond the Fields of Reason* (Berkeley, CA, 1974), pp. 47–76

Ingalls, Daniel H. H., ed. and trans., *An Anthology of Sanskrit Court Poetry: Vidyakara's 'Subhasitaratnakosa'* (Cambridge, MA, 1965)

James, Jack E., *Understanding Caffeine: A Biobehavioral Analysis* (London, 1997)

Jayadeva, *Gitagovinda: Love Song of the Dark Lord*, ed. and trans. Barbara Stoler Miller (Delhi, 1977)

Johnson, Samuel, *Selected Writings*, ed. Patrick Cruttwell (Harmondsworth, 1982)

Keshavadasa, *The Rasikapriya of Keshavadasa*, ed. and trans. K. P. Bahadur (Delhi, 1972)

King, Stephen, *Insomnia* [1994] (London, 1995)

Kiser, Lisa J., 'Sleep, Dreams, and Poetry in Chaucer's *Book of the Duchess*', *Papers on Language and Literature*, XIX/1 (1983), pp. 3–12

Kyoka, Izumi, 'The Holy Man of Mount Koya' [1900], in Charles S. Inouye, trans., *Japanese Gothic Tales* (Honolulu, 1996), pp. 21–72

Landes, David S., *Revolution in Time: Clocks and the Making of the Modern World* (Cambridge, MA, 1983)

Law, Jacky, *Big Pharma: How the World's Biggest Drug Companies Control Illness* (London, 2006)

Lyman, Henry M., AM, MD, *Insomnia and Other Disorders of Sleep* (Chicago, 1885)

McAlpine, Thomas H., *Sleep, Divine and Human, in the Old Testament* (Sheffield, 1987)

Macfarlane, A. W., MD, *Insomnia and Its Therapeutics* (London, 1890)

Macey, Samuel L., *Clocks and the Cosmos: Time in Western Life and Thought* (Hamden, CT, 1980)

—, 'Hogarth and the Iconography of Time', in *Studies in Eighteenth-Century Culture*, vol. V, ed. Ronald C. Rosbottom (Madison, 1976), pp. 41–53

Márquez, Gabriel García, *One Hundred Years of Solitude* [1967], trans. Gregory Rabassa (London, 1972)

Marx, Karl, *Capital: A Critical Analysis of Capitalist Production* [1889], trans. Samuel Moore and Edward Aveling, ed. Frederick Engels, vol. I (London, 1943)

—, 'The German Ideology: Part One' [1845], trans. Roy Pascal, in Robert C. Tucker, ed., *The Marx-Engels Reader*, 2nd edn (New York, 1978)

Melbin, Murray, *Night as Frontier: Colonizing the World After Dark* (New York, 1987)

Moorcroft, William H., *Understanding Sleep and Dreaming* (New York, 2003)

Moore-Ede, Murray, *The Twenty Four Hour Society: Understanding Human Limits in a World that Never Stops* (Reading, MA, 1993)

Muchembled, Robert, *A History of the Devil: From the Middle Ages to the Present* [2000], trans. Jean Burrell (Cambridge, 2003)

National Sleep Foundation, 'Epidemic of Daytime Sleepiness Linked to Increased Feelings of Anger, Stress, and Pessimism': www.sleepfoundation.org/site/c.huIXKjMOIXF/b.2417359/k.3028/Epidemic_of_Daytime_Sleepiness_Linked_to_Increased_Feelings_of_Anger_Stress_and_Pessimism.htm

—, 'National Sleep Foundation: Tackling American's Sleep Debt': www.sleepfoundation.org/site/c.huIXKjMOIXF/b.2428019/k.F850/National_Sleep_Foundation_Tackling_Americas_Sleep_Debt.htm

—, 'National Sleep Foundation 2002 *Sleep in America* Poll Results Relating to September 11': www.sleepfoundation.org/site/apps/nl/content2.asp?c=huIXKjMOIXF&b=2428021&ct=3454757

O'Malley, Michael, *Keeping Watch: A History of American Time* (Washington, DC, 1990)

Padel, Ruth, *In and Out of the Mind: Greek Images of the Tragic Self* (Princeton, 1992)

—, *Whom Gods Destroy: Elements of Greek and Tragic Madness* (Princeton, 1995)

Palmer, Bryan D., *Cultures of Darkness: Night Travels in the History of Transgression* (New York, 2000)

Palmer, John D., *The Living Clock: The Orchestrator of Biological Rhythms* (New York, 2002)

Poe, Edgar Allan, 'The Man of the Crowd' [1840], in G. R. Thompson, ed., *The Selected Writings of Edgar Allan Poe* (New York, 2004), pp. 232–9

Pope, Alexander, *The Rape of the Lock*, ed. Cynthia Wall (Boston, MA, 1998)

—, 'Satire I: To Mr Fortescue', in *The Poems, Epistles and Satires of Alexander Pope* (London, n.d.)

Rabinbach, Anson, *The Human Motor: Energy, Fatigue and the Origins of Modernity* (Berkeley, CA, 1990)

—, 'Neurasthenia and Modernity', in Jonathan Crary and Sanford Kwinter, eds, *Incorporations* (New York, 1992), pp. 178–89

Radcliffe, Ann, *The Mysteries of Udolpho: A Romance*, ed. Bonamy Dobrée (London, 1966)

Richter, Antje, 'Sleeping Time in Early Chinese Literature', in Brigitte Steger and Lodewijk Brunt, eds, *Night-time and Sleep in Asia and the West* (London, 2003), pp. 24–44

Rolfs, Daniel, 'Sleep, Dreams and Insomnia in the *Orlando Furioso*', *Italica*, LIII/4 (1976), pp. 453–74

Schama, Simon, *The Embarrassment of Riches: An Interpretation of Dutch Culture in the Golden Age* (New York, 1987)

—, 'The Unruly Realm: Appetite and Restraint in Seventeenth-Century Holland', *Daedalus*, CVIII/3 (1979), pp. 103–23

Schelling, F.W.J., *The Unconditional in Human Knowledge: Four Early Essays, 1794–1796* [1795], trans. Fritz Martin (Lewisburg, 1980)

Schiller, Francis, 'Semantics of Sleep', *Bulletin of the History of Medicine*, LVI/3 (1982), pp. 377–97

Schivelbusch, Wolfgang, *Disenchanted Night: The Industrialisation of Light in the Nineteenth Century* [1983], trans. Angela Davies (Oxford, 1988)

Schlör, Joachim, *Nights in the Big City* [1991], trans. Pierre Gottfried Imhof and Dafydd Rees Roberts (London, 1998)

Schmidt, Roger, 'Caffeine and the Coming of the Enlightenment', *Raritan*, XXIII/1 (2003), pp. 129–49

Shakespeare, William, *Julius Caesar*, ed. David Daniell (Walton-on-Thames, 1998)

—, *Macbeth: Texts and Contexts*, ed. William C. Carroll (Boston, MA, and New York, 1999)

Shneerson, John, *Sleep Medicine: A Guide to Sleep and its Disorders* (Malden, MA, 2005)

Steger, Brigitte, 'Negotiating Sleep Patterns in Japan', in Brigitte Steger and Lodewijk Brunt, eds, *Night-Time and Sleep in Asia and the West: Exploring the Dark Side of Life* (London, 2003), pp. 69–86

—, 'Sleeping through Class to Success: Japanese Notions of Time and Diligence', *Time and Society*, XV/2–3 (2006), pp. 197–214

Stephens, Carlene E., *On Time: How America Learned to Live by the Clock* (Boston, MA, 2002)

Stevenson, John, *Yoshitoshi's One Hundred Aspects of the Moon* (Leiden, 2001)

Summers-Bremner, Eluned, 'Watching and Learning', *Parallax (Pupils of the University Issue)*, XII/3 (2006), pp. 17–26

Tam, Paul, 'Sleepless in Loughborough: Sleep Deprivation and Cognitive Function', 1998: www.lboro.ac.uk/departments/hu/groups/sleep/wellcome.htm

Thompson, E. P., 'Time, Work-Discipline and Industrial Capitalism', in *Customs in Common* (London, 1991), pp. 352–403

Thomson, James, 'The City of Dreadful Night' [1874], in *Victorian Poetry: 'The City of Dreadful Night' and Other Poems*, ed. N. P. Messenger and J. R. Watson (London, 1974), pp. 136–65

Verdon, Jean, *Night in the Middle Ages* [1994], trans. George Holoch (Notre Dame, IN, 2002)

Virgil, *The Aeneid*, trans. C. Day Lewis (London, 1954)

Wang, Michael, 'The Psychological Treatment of Insomnia', in Jacob Empson, *Sleep and Dreaming*, 3rd edn (Basingstoke, 2002), pp. 196–208

Weber, Max, *The Protestant Ethic and the Spirit of Capitalism* [1904–5], trans. Stephen Kalberg, 3rd edn (Los Angeles, 2002)

Wenzel, Siegfried, *The Sin of Sloth: Acedia in Medieval Thought and Literature* [1960] (Chapel Hill, 1967)

Widerberg, Karin, 'Embodying Modern Times: Investigating Tiredness', *Time and Society*, XV/1 (2006), pp. 105–20

Williams, Simon J., 'The Social Etiquette of Sleep: Some Sociological Reflections and Observations', *Sociology*, XLI/2 (2007), pp. 313–28

Wordsworth, Dorothy, *The Journals of Dorothy Wordsworth*, vol. II, ed. Ernest de Selincourt (New York, 1941)

Wordsworth, William, *The Prelude: A Parallel Text*, ed. J. C. Maxwell (Harmondsworth, 1984)

—, 'To Sleep', in *The Poems, Vol. 1*, ed. John O. Hayden (Harmondsworth, 1977), pp. 562–3

Wright, Lawrence, *Warm and Snug: The History of the Bed* (London, 1962)

Yi, Li, 'Discourse of Mid-Day Napping: A Political Windsock in Contemporary China', in Brigitte Steger and Lodewijk Brunt, eds, *Night-time and Sleep in Asia and the West: Exploring the Dark Side of Life* (London, 2003), pp. 45–64

Young, Edward, *The Complaint, and the Consolation; or, Night Thoughts* (London, 1796)

—, *Night Thoughts* [1742], ed. Stephen Cornford (Cambridge, 1989)

Acknowledgements

Many people assisted with the completion of this book. I am fortunate to be working in an English department at Auckland with many first-rate scholars and a spirit of good will and kindness. For useful questions and for alerting me to insomniacs past and present, thanks to Tracy Adams, Graham Allen, Mark Amsler, Bill Barnes, Brian Boyd, Elisabeth Bronfen, Paul Gough, Rebecca Hayward, Stephanie Hollis, Ken Larsen, Rose Lovell-Smith, Selina Tusitala Marsh, John Morrow, Nieves Pascual, Roger Schmidt, Peter Simpson, Jeremy Tambling, Rosie Tooby, Stephen Turner and Lee Wallace. Audiences for early versions of insomnia material were inquisitive and enthusiastic. Thanks to Andrew Douglas for arranging an audience at Goldsmiths College London, attendees of the 'Alternative Persuasion' panel in Ghent and the Beckett Symposium in Sydney, and to my students in English at Auckland, who let me talk about Gilgamesh and Homer in contemporary contexts with impunity. For friendship, helpful thoughts and interest, thanks to Patricia Allmer, Wok Bremner, Jan Cronin, Bob Eaglestone, Lucy Holmes, Tracey Kerr, Sarah McMillan, Valda and Murray Mehrtens, Dany Nobus, Dianna West and Janet Wilson. Thanks to my bright stars Liv Macassey, Eu Jin Chua and Andrew, for the same, and to Soong Phoon and Simon Zhou for being so clever and creative. Thanks to Ramiro and Sandra Silva for the fabulous apartments that are my second homes in London, and John Wrighton for making London times more fun. Without Dave Hoek this book would not have found its home, and without Kathy McKay I couldn't call myself a recovering insomniac – thanks to both of you. Also thanks to Joan Copjec for her razor-sharp logic, and Mel Anderson, whose writing improved my own. This book could not have been completed without generous financial help from the University of Auckland, which enabled a substantial period of research and study leave in the UK, along with shorter trips supported by its Staff Research Funds. Staff in the interloans department at the University of Auckland General Library, especially Sarah Giffney, have been most helpful, as have staff in London at the British Library, the University of London Library at Senate House, and the wonderful Warburg Institute. Most of the research for *Insomnia* was completed while

I was a Research Fellow at the Institute of English Studies in the School of Advanced Study, University of London. I am grateful to Warwick Gould and the Institute for their welcoming spirit and support. Lastly, thanks are due to my commissioning editor at Reaktion, Vivian Constantinopoulos, for all her help with the project, to Steve Connor, for being himself and thus the best of mentors, and to Possum, for helps too many and longstanding to list. May Stephanie and Daniel allow better sleep soon.

Photo Acknowledgements

The author and publishers wish to express their thanks to the following sources of illustrative material and/or permission to reproduce it. Locations, etc., of some items are also given below.

Australian War Memorial, Canberra: p. 108; photos Bridgeman Art Library: pp. 51 (ALI 142975), 106 (CHT163238); British Museum, London: p. 96; Gemäldegalerie Neue Meister, Dresden: p. 87; Imperial War Museum, London: p. 107 (IWM ART 2242); photo Library of Congress, Washington, DC: p. 122 (LC-USZ62-5367); Österreichische Nationalbibliothek, Vienna: p. 51 (*Codex Vindobonensis*, fol. 101r); photo Rex Features/Sutton-Hibbert: p. 141 (555898C); photo Roger-Viollet/Rex Features: p. 105 (689364A); photo Jeff Wall Studio: p. 127.